SO-AEP-629

Economic behavior within organizations

STEPHEN A. HOENACK

University of Minnesota

CAMBRIDGE UNIVERSITY PRESS

Cambridge
London   New York   New Rochelle
Melbourne   Sydney

Published by the Press Syndicate of the University of Cambridge
The Pitt Building, Trumpington Street, Cambridge CB2 1RP
32 East 57th Street, New York, NY 10022, USA
296 Beaconsfield Parade, Middle Park, Melbourne 3206, Australia

© Cambridge University Press 1983

First published 1983

Printed in the United States of America

Library of Congress Cataloging in Publication Data
Hoenack, Stephen A., 1941–
Economic behavior within organizations.
Bibliography: p.
1. Organization – Economic aspects.
I. Title.
HD38.H63   338.5   82-1330
ISBN 0 521 23993 1   AACR2

MUHLENBERG COLLEGE LIBRARY
ALLENTOWN, PA. 18104

Economic behavior within organizations

to MEG

Contents

vii

Preface

This book is an attempt to extend economic theory to the resource allocation choices that are made within a firm or other organization. A number of criteria guided my work. One was that an economic theory of organizations should not depend on restrictive assumptions that employees desire to maximize particular variables such as sales or budgets. Another criterion was that an organization's supplies of its outputs should be derivable from the supply behavior of its individual employees. I also wanted the theory to take account of the investments that employees make in their jobs and to yield implications from this behavior for the organization's internal structure and growth.

My main purpose, however, was to see whether economic theory could provide a wide-ranging set of hypotheses about issues of interest to economists and organization theorists. For example, could economic theory provide hypotheses about the implicit prices that employees attach to resources, employees' supplies of their contributions to outputs, and their demands for information about production possibilities? Could it provide hypotheses about the formal and informal mechanisms by which employees coordinate their activities? Although this book's analysis is only a beginning, I am convinced that economics is a useful tool for analyzing both types of issues. I have also concluded that when economic analysis and organization theory deal with the same issues, their results do not generally conflict. Although economic analysis has a different role in focusing on employees' choices in allocating resources, it does not emerge as a competing approach to organizations, and the many quotations in this book from the literature on organizations suggest that it is often complementary. I predict that further advances in our understanding of organizations will require economists to make use of insights provided by organization theorists and vice versa.

Many conclusions about economic activity within an organization can be derived from the cost advantages that particular employees have about production possibilities and about quantities, characteristics, and uses of inputs and outputs. These information cost advantages are derived from the production functions for an organization's outputs in Chapter 2, where they are shown to lead employers to delegate discretion over resource allocation to employees. Employees can take advantage of this discretion to pursue their own objectives at their employers' expense. Chapter 3 analyzes how employers impose constraints on employees to limit their costs of employees' contributions to output. Once these constraints are in place, the organization's resource allocation can be analyzed in short- and long-run periods. Chapters 4 through 6 present the analysis of the short run; Chapters 7 through 9, the analysis of the long run.

In the analysis of the short run, I first consider in Chapter 4 the economic behavior of individual employees under the artificial assumption that there are no technological spillovers among different employees' productive activities. This assumption is then relaxed, and the implications of such spillovers are explored. Subsequently in Chapter 5, I derive hypotheses about the short-run supply behavior of private corporations and private nonprofit organizations from the supply behavior of their individual employees. After presenting an analysis of the economic behavior of individual legislators and of legislatures as organizations, Chapter 6 analyzes the short-run supply behavior of public organizations.

In the long run, employees' investments to increase their well-being within the organization come to fruition. For example, employees establish means of coordinating their activities in order to reduce the effectiveness of the constraints imposed on them. Chapter 7 explores these investments and analyzes their effects on employees' supply behavior. This chapter provides an analysis of employers' choices in using and delegating authority and contrasts cases where authority and voluntary arrangements are used to coordinate employees' actions. Chapters 8 and 9 analyze the effects of employees' investments on long-run resource allocation in two separate contexts. In Chapter 8, I assume that the organization continues to produce the same outputs and cannot change its status from being, for example, a private corporation, to being a public organization. In Chapter 9 it is assumed that an organization can produce different outputs and might be able to change its status, and the roles of employees in making these changes are analyzed. For example, employees' roles in mergers and acquisitions of private corporations and in a legislature's establishment of public organizations are considered.

Chapter 1 presents an overview of the main concepts of the theory, and Chapter 10 summarizes some of the hypotheses presented. Separate summaries of hypotheses are presented after most of the major sections within Chapters 4 through 9. Definitions of core terms are presented in Chapter 1. These terms are again described with their first use in the subsequent chapters and are also defined in a glossary at the end of the book.

The following individuals made valuable comments on an early draft of the manuscript: David J. Berg, Edward M. Foster, T. Paul Schultz, Donald S. Watson, and William C. Weiler. Leonid Hurwicz's comments on the manuscript were especially helpful, and his enthusiasm about the project was very encouraging in the early stages when the work seemed most difficult. Douglas C. Dacy and Vernon W. Ruttan also provided invaluable criticism and encouragement. Robert T. Kudrle's insightful reviews of two separate drafts of the manuscript resulted in many important improvements in the theory. Thomas P. Chester made substantial contributions to Chapter 6 and a section of Chapter 3 by pointing out several errors. An anonymous reviewer's extremely helpful suggestions became a blueprint for one major revision of the manuscript.

Colleen T. Davidson and Faith E. Jaycox ostensibly aided me with the writing, but in fact most often helped me with the thinking. In particular, Faith Jaycox urged me to develop several of the key points in the arguments of Chapters 2, 3, and 4. Colleen Davidson gave me advice on almost every part of the book and was instrumental in the selection of the illustrative examples.

I gratefully acknowledge the generous support of the University of Minnesota Administration. This assistance greatly sped up the completion of the manuscript.

Jean Twite typed a seemingly endless number of drafts of each chapter and also helped me with editing. I greatly appreciate all of her work. Virginia M. Dahm also helped out a great deal with the typing and editing.

I especially thank Colin L. Day, American Branch Editorial Director of Cambridge University Press, for his encouragement, persistent belief, and excellent advice at many stages of my work on the manuscript. This book's becoming a reality is in no small part due to him. I would also like to thank Edith Feinstein of Cambridge University Press for all of her help during the production of the book.

My wife, Margaret Dougherty Hoenack, to whom this book is dedicated, convinced me that an economic analysis of organizations could lend insight into a number of issues that have largely concerned organization theorists. But, most important, our life together has given me a state of mind in which projects like this seem more achievable.

S.A.H.

Minneapolis
June, 1982

CHAPTER 1

Introduction

Much of society's resource allocation takes place within organizations. With some important exceptions such as agriculture, organizations are the prevailing structure where there is profit-oriented productive activity, both in free market economies and in economies that are controlled in varying degrees; in most industries it has become unusual for individual producers to deal autonomously with markets. Virtually all of every economy's governmental and private nonprofit enterprises take place within organizations. Consequently, when economic analysis of exchanges among organizations is not concerned with economic behavior within organizations, it overlooks a large part of society's resource allocation.

If employees competed on the basis of the external market forces of demands for the organization's outputs and supplies of its inputs, neglect of resource allocation within organizations could be unimportant. However, if economic forces that act independently of these external forces are generated within the organization, neglect of economic behavior within organizations could result in incomplete and perhaps incorrect conclusions about resource allocation.

This book presents a positive economic theory of resource allocation within organizations. Based on recent developments in the economic theory of information, the theory extends to individuals within an organization the received theory of firm and industry supply. In the theory presented here, information costs lead employers to delegate discretion over an organization's resource allocation to employees. Employees take advantage of this discretion by pursuing their own objectives at the expense of their employers' objectives. Employers can limit the costs of this behavior by imposing constraints on employees. The nature of these constraints depends on the costs of imposing them and how much they reduce employers' costs of employees' contributions to the organization's outputs. Although it may in some cases be feasible to prevent entirely employees from pursuing their own objectives at their employers' expense, employers' optimal setting of constraints ordinarily limits their costs of this behavior to some determinate amount.

1

When employees use the organization's resources to achieve their own objectives, they establish demands for resources independent of those external to the organization. These create an economy within the organization that is responsive to employees' own goals as well as to clients' and owners' goals. Employees' uses of their discretion affect the scope of activities occurring within the organization and raise by a determinant amount what must be paid for the organization's outputs.

A systematic analysis of the choices employees make within the imposed constraints provides the basis for a set of positive hypotheses about an organization's resource allocation and its efficiency. Although much work remains, enough hypotheses about resource allocation within organizations are derived to show that the range of these hypotheses is roughly comparable to the range of existing hypotheses about resource allocation among organizations. The derived hypotheses pertain to an organization's supply of its final and intermediate outputs for short-run and long-run periods, the implicit or explicit prices that guide employees' uses of resources, and the organization's demands for inputs. Hypotheses also pertain to employees' investing resources to enhance their prospects of pursuing their own goals and to the effects of these investments on the organization's resource allocation in the long run.

Other hypotheses concern the total incomes (including noncash incomes) of an organization's employees; the influences of employees on an organization's internal structure and on its growth and transition; and the allocation of resources to employees' acquisition of information. Most of the derived hypotheses apply to behavior in any type of organization; some, however, apply specifically to private corporations, private nonprofit organizations, or public organizations. None of the hypotheses depends on particular variables, such as levels of sales or budgets in employees' utility functions, none require aggregating employees' goals, and none depends on the active role of an owner-entrepreneur in the organization's management.

A   Overview of the theory and core definitions

In order to extend economic theory to the constrained choices of an organization's employees, it is necessary to resolve the following questions. What kind of information costs lead employers to delegate discretion over resource allocation to employees? How can this discretion be defined in economic terms? What are the constraints applicable to employees and how do information costs influence employers' choices among them? How can employees alter these information costs and thereby reduce the effectiveness of constraints facing them? Who outside the organization might impose constraints on employees and, should no one deliberately impose constraints, what would limit employees' using the resources delegated to them to pursue their own goals? The following overview outlines how the theory deals with these issues and presents the core definitions used in the description of the theory.

The analyses of information costs, employees' information cost advantages, and their discretion over resource allocation are based on the production functions for the organization's intermediate and final outputs. A number of economies result from multiple final and intermediate outputs being produced by a single organization. These include reduced costs of coordinating input applications when two or more outputs share the same production function. For example, the production of one output may confer technological spillovers on the production of another that can be dealt with more economically if both are produced in the same organization. There can be economies from a single organization coordinating uses of an indivisible input to produce multiple outputs instead of separate organizations for each output having to deal with another organization that coordinates uses of this resource. It can be more costly to establish and enforce contracts for the external supply of inputs having unique characteristics than to produce them internally. An informed owner-entrepreneur ensures that the organization produces a combination of final and intermediate outputs that maximizes his net return after his costs of coordination. In contrast, when there is no owner-entrepreneur actively involved in the organization's management, the opportunity costs of production in separate organizations represent limits on the costs of production in a single organization. There are often smaller limits on these costs, however.

Given the outputs produced by an organization and the production functions encompassed by it, an important issue is what is known about these functions and by whom. In addition to determining productivities of inputs, production functions help determine employees' and employers' relative costs of information about possible resource substitutions. Those employees directly involved in applying inputs may face lower costs than do others of obtaining information about production possibilities. The absence of similar production elsewhere or high costs of comparing such production, combined with employees' information about production possibilities being a by-product of their productive activities, contribute to these cost advantages. Spatial dispersion of production and intangible characteristics of inputs or outputs can contribute to costs of comparing production and can also give employees information cost advantages regarding the amounts or characteristics of the inputs they use or the outputs they produce.

Information cost advantages lead to the delegation to an organization's employees of discretion over resource allocation within production functions. Those delegating discretion to an employee may actually possess only sketchy information about the relevant possibilities for input or output substitutions. An employee's *production domain* is the subset of the organization's production functions over which he holds discretion to apply inputs within some range of their possible values. [To avoid awkward wording, the masculine pronoun is often used in the generic sense to mean "he or she".] There are varying incentives for others within the organization to obtain information about some of the possible input substitutions within an employee's production domain. There also are differing incentives for others to measure and attach values to the inputs used within an employee's production domain and to the resulting outputs or contributions to outputs.

Information cost advantages and the resulting discretion granted to employees make it possible for employees to derive rents from their employment. Employees' uses of these gains lead them to allocate part of the organization's resources to their own ends and in long-run periods to alter to their benefit the organization's stocks of tangible and intangible capital. Thus, employees' use of their discretion over input applications to pursue their ends not only transfers welfare to them but influences the organization's supplies of its outputs and demands for its inputs and affects the efficiency of its resource allocation.

Employees' pursuit of their own ends brings them into conflict with those who delegate discretion to them. An organization's *funding authority* is the individual or group holding ultimate control over the availability of revenues to the organization's employees. Thus, the funding authority of a private corporation is its stockholders, that of a private nonprofit organization is its donors, and a public organization's funding authority is its legislature. When information cost advantages create an incentive for a funding authority to delegate discretion over resource substitutions to employees, often these employees have the incentive further to delegate discretion to other employees. The cash-equivalent costs to an employer of his employees' uses of resources in ways other than those that would maximize his welfare are referred to as *resource diversions* (or diversions, for short).

Resource responsibility and the *funding limit* are two separate constraints that can act separately or simultaneously to restrain employees' resource diversions. Resource responsibility (or responsibility, for short) is a costly constraint that is deliberately placed on an employee by the funding authority or by another employee who has been delegated the necessary authority. The same resource responsibility constraint can affect a single employee or multiple employees. In contrast, the funding limit is not deliberately established and is applicable to all employees in the organization. This constraint reduces the amount of resources available to the organization's employees when the funding authority faces increases in the costs of disposing the organization's outputs according to his interests. Neither of these constraints necessarily applies in any particular situation. It may not be economically worthwhile to impose resource responsibility on an employee, and the resource diversions allowed by the responsibility facing an organization's employees may not be large enough in a particular situation for the organization's funding limit to be binding.

Imposing resource responsibility constraints requires authority, derived from that of the funding authority, to extract or augment employees' rents from working in the organization. There are alternative types of responsibility constraints, all of which have in common that they connect employees' actions or results of their actions with the monetary or nonmonetary incomes they receive from working in the organization. The choice to impose responsibility is voluntary for the funding authority, but employees have no choice to avoid the responsibility constraints facing them, or any changes in them, so long as they continue to associate with and derive rents from the organization. If an employee were under a completely specified contract, resource responsibility would constrain the degree to which he could avoid performing some of his contractual obligations. However, employers usually do not find such contracts economical, and resource responsibility also limits employers' costs of employees' outputs when employment contracts are incomplete. The responsibility imposed on an employee ordinarily changes many times during his tenure with a particular organization.

The effectiveness of responsibility depends on the amount spent on information by the one imposing it. Thus, information costs, not the option to avoid responsibility constraints, enable employees to retain rents from their employment. If employees can increase employers' information costs they can augment their rents.

The funding authority delegates his right to augment or extract employees' rents to those employees, referred to as *managing employees*, who impose responsibility constraints on other employees. The term *managing employee* is used here instead of the frequently used term *manager* to emphasize that a managing employee is both a manager and an employee, and the analysis of constrained employee resource diversion behavior always applies to him. Depending on the authority granted to him by the funding authority or the managing employees above him, a managing employee places resource responsibility constraints on his employees. However, since managing employees maximize their own personal welfare subject to the constraints that they face, they do not necessarily impose the same responsibility constraints as would the funding authority. Either the funding authority or a managing employee can be an "employer." This term is used when the analysis applies to the behavior of either.

There are three types of resource responsibility constraints. One of these, *complete pricing overall responsibility* (CPOR), involves a set of prices on each of the employee's resources and a tax on his income, which lead the employee to maximize the achievement of his employer's objectives. It is so costly in practice to establish this type of responsibility that we can in most cases expect that one of the other two types, *overall value responsibility* (OVR) or *specific responsibility* (SR), will be imposed. The former of these holds the employee accountable for the estimated value of his output or contribution to output in relation to the estimated value of the inputs delegated to him; if the value of this contribution falls below a critical value, the employer obtains the contribution via another source, makes the necessary adjustments to do without the contribution, or switches to specific responsibility. Variants of overall value responsibility include whether or not cash prices are attached to inputs and outputs and an accounting profit is attributed to the employee's production domain.

Specific responsibility directly influences some of the employee's particular uses of individual resources and does not hold him accountable for the value of his output or contribution to output in relation to the value of the inputs delegated to him. The many alternative means for an employer to influence uses of resources can be direct or indirect: Among the former are penalties or rewards, whereas the latter include such measures as enforcing regular work hours to reduce alternative uses of the employee's time. The employer selects among these according to cost effectiveness in particular situations and often finds it preferable not to influence or only minimally affect many of the employee's uses of the resources delegated to him.

The costs of identifying and attaching values to the employee's inputs and outputs or contributions to outputs play a role in an employer's choice between overall value and specific responsibility; the higher these costs the more likely specific responsibility is imposed. Also affecting the choice are the cost effectiveness of the feasible variants of specific responsibility in the particular situation and the availability of alternative means of obtaining the employee's contributions to output or of substitutes for these contributions.

The second constraint on resource diversions, the *funding limit*, can reduce the combined resource diversions of an organization's employees below the sum of those allowed by the responsibility individually placed on them. In a private corporation, increased resource diversions reduce the return on invested capital and can thereby decrease the supply of investment funds. This responsiveness of investments to resource diversions constitutes the private corporation's funding limit. Employees' long-run gains from the organization can depend upon these investments; the degree of dependence is related to the nature of the industry and whether Schumpeterian competition or rapid technological change is present. When employees are willing to reduce resource diversions at the margin to encourage further investments, the funding limit is binding. In private nonprofit organizations and public organizations the funding limit is determined, respectively, by the responses of funding by donors and by the legislature to quantities of the organization's outputs that are disposed of according to the interests of these funders. When the funding limit is binding, it leads employees to develop means of coordinating their actions to reduce their combined resource diversions below those allowed by the responsibility placed on them individually.

Given an organization's production functions along with the information cost advantages that they impart, the discretion over inputs and outputs that is delegated to employees, and the responsibility imposed on employees, the organization's resource allocation can be analyzed in the short run and the long run. The short run is defined in the Marshallian sense as a time period over which the effects of investments, including those of employees, may be held constant. In the short run, positive refutable hypotheses can be derived about an employee's rate of output, given his budget; the response of the employee's budget to demand for his output; the implicit prices that guide his uses of resources, and the efficiency of the related resource allocation; and the behavior of employees in relation to technological spillovers among their production domains. These hypotheses differ substantially depending on the type of resource responsibility imposed. Following Leonid Hurwicz's concept of analyzing effects of alternative resource allocation mechanisms on the information held by those possessing and not possessing information cost advantages, it is possible to analyze specifically how the type of responsibility placed on an employee affects both his and others' demands for information about his production domain and about the preferences of interested parties.

Employees' benefits from resource diversions can be currently consumed or invested for the purpose of increasing future benefits. Aside from devoting resources to coordinating themselves in their mutual interests, employees' investments include a variety of individual and coordinated actions that lead employers to change boundaries of production domains and the responsibility imposed. Employees' investments are also directed to increasing the internal and external demands for their outputs, and to altering the returns that employers expect from their own investments.

The type of resource responsibility imposed on an employee influences investment behavior in two ways. First, it plays an important part in determining the net returns to his own investments and affects his influence over returns to the investments of others. Second, by determining the amount of his allowable resource diversions and the present and prospective uses to which he can place resources, the type of responsibility affects the employee's potential supply of resources to investments. Other factors affecting net returns to employees' investments are the costs of coordinating the actions of different employees with respect to mutually beneficial investments and whether the organization operates in an environment where new products are frequently introduced by competitors or in which there is rapid technological change.

The endogenous investment behavior leads to the organization's equilibrium in the long run, which is analyzed in two contexts. In the *first long run* we hold constant the organization's status as a private corporation, private nonprofit organization, or a public organization, as well as the nature of its final outputs. In this time period employees' investments can raise resource diversions allowed by responsibility up to the funding limit or as close to the funding limit as they can reach. The first long-run behavior of employees in increasing rents from their jobs provides a reason independent of owner's entrepreneurship for rising marginal costs in the long run. The *second long run* encompasses the effects of employees' investments on the numbers, sizes, and types of organizations. In this time context, additional constraints on employees become operative that are not necessarily controlled by funding authorities or managing employees. These include legal and governing institutions as well as costs of alternative institutional arrangements for supply of an organization's outputs. In the second long run, employees can affect an organization's choices of final outputs as well as the returns to mergers with or acquisitions of other organizations. With a given demand for final outputs, the funding limit on resource diversions is larger in public organizations than in private corporations. Thus, under some conditions unrealized potential for resource diversions can call forth employees' investments that lead to a corporation's outputs being produced instead by a public organization. However, the introduction of Schumpeterian competition or technological change creates offsetting incentives for employees to attract capital from private markets.

An analysis of economic behavior within a legislature makes it possible to derive a legislature's demands as a function of price for the outputs of other organizations. Legislative demands represent most of the demands for the outputs of public organizations and are often important parts of the demands for outputs of private corporations and private nonprofit organizations. An evaluation of the economic efficiency of an organization's resource allocation must take account of the degree to which a legislature's demand for its output reflects the welfare that citizens actually derive from it.

The analysis of legislative behavior depends on the same assumption that underlies Stigler's (1971) analysis of regulation. The citizens who would oppose a governmental action, if informed about it and if opposition were costless, often do not stand to lose enough individually to make them willing to bear the actual costs of deciding and registering their opposition. The winner of an election between an incumbent legislator and his opponent may dispense economic benefits to constituents. Candidates' platforms of commitments of these benefits are hypothesized to be responsive to marginal voters within informed interest groups, not the median voter in candidates' districts. Each legislator's share of the total economic benefits distributed by the legislature is determined by the value of his vote within the legislature plus whatever resource diversions are allowed to him due to any roles that he plays as a specialized legislator. By delegating the tasks of arranging vote trades to specialized legislators (i.e., committees) all members of a legislature benefit from economies in information and time. Given each legislator's share of legislative spending and his commitments of economic benefits to constituents, we can straightforwardly derive legislative demand as a function of price and analyze the forces (e.g., information costs to constituents manipulatable by an organization's employees) that shift this demand.

The problem faced by legislators of economizing on the information needed for vote trading is an example of the general problem employees confront in any organization of economizing on the information needed to coordinate their actions for their mutual benefit. To deal with this problem, an organization's employees delegate to specialized employees the task of arranging the coordination. Specialized employees qualify by the possession of information cost advantages or particular coordinating capabilities. Depending on whether these employees also hold authority over the coordinated employees, they effect the coordination either through voluntary mechanisms that employees establish for this purpose or through use of authority that is often intended for other purposes. Each employee's benefit from voluntary coordination is based on his opportunity cost of participating in it, whereas his benefit from coordination via authority is based on his allowable resource diversions under the responsibility placed on him.

B   Three analytical points and progress in connection with them

The presentation of the theory in the following chapters describes many respects in which it is related to and indebted to the large body of existing analyses of behavior within organizations or in relation to them. There are, however, important differences between this and other behavioral theories of organizations. The following discussion considers three analytical points that suggest limitations of many well-known theories and shows how some recent work provides a foundation for dealing effectively with them.

One point is that it is usually necessary to analyze separately individual employees' constrained optimizations, given the resource responsibility imposed, in order to introduce resource diversions and costs of imposing responsibility into the costs of employees' outputs that decision makers face. Without such analysis, it is not possible to account properly for the influences of these costs on employers' choices about rates of their employees' outputs or contributions to outputs. The second point is that unnecessary complexity is introduced by aggregating the goals of different employees. Finally, much generality is lost when a behavioral theory relies on highly restrictive assumptions about the particular objectives pursued by an organization's employees, that is, about the importance of particular variables such as sales or budgets in their utility functions.

In regard to the first point, the seminal work of Simon (1961) does not, for example, explicitly account for the determination of allowable resource diversions or the effects of diversions on the organization's behavior. Simon's work provides a positive theory of how managers deal with limited capacity to acquire and assimilate information. The result is "bounded rationality," where a manager's capability to exercise control over resource allocation to achieve goals is limited by the information available to him, its costs, and his personal capacity to evaluate it. This work makes possible a much improved understanding of the decision-making process and elucidates decision makers' rational choices in obtaining incomplete information. With respect to our more limited concern with deriving hypotheses about resource allocation choices in the organization, decision makers' limited capacity to deal with information helps explain why their employees are delegated discretion over specific parts of the organization's productive activity. However, one must also consider the degree to which these employees take advantage of this discretion to pursue their own ends. That is, there should be a separate determination of the allowable resource diversions that enter into the costs faced by those making decisions. If the influences of these costs on decision makers' choices are not directly incorporated into the analysis, the derivation of refutable hypotheses under bounded rationality about the resources made available to different employees and their expected contributions to outputs depends upon the particular specifications of employees' goals and the weights assigned to them in the process of decision making. Thus the underlying derivation of the supply behavior of an organization's employees is made very complex. Shortcuts that do not provide for the separate optimizations of employers and their employees subject to constraints of production functions and the costs of achieving employees' compliance (i.e. imposing responsibility) are likely to be analytically incorrect.

The issue of avoidable complexity is evident in the work of Cyert and March (1963), which was influenced by Simon's analysis of bounded rationality. Cyert and March argue that goals are aggregated through a political process within the organization where employees' cooperation or compliance may be achieved by incorporating their goals into the organization's goals. Thus, while the derivation of an organization's supply response to demand depends on these goals, the aggregation of individual goals is determined as part of the supply response. Alternatively, taking account of employers' costs of employees' outputs, including allowable resource diversions, makes it possible to avoid the complexity and possibly incorrect solutions involved in aggregating goals. By achieving their own goals, that is, by increasing resource diversions within constraints, employees raise costs faced by their employers. Similarly, an organization's "top" managing employees pass on these costs plus the costs of their own resource diversions to the funding authority. At each level, decisions are based on the costs faced at that level in relation to demand. Consequently, the effects on resource allocation of the pursuit by employees of their own goals may be analyzed without explicit consideration or aggregation of employees' goals.[1]

Regarding restrictive assumptions about the important variables entering employees' utility functions, a number of authors, most notably Baumol (1959) and Niskanen (1971),[2] postulate particular objectives of employees. By implicitly assuming limits on resource diversions that permit a given degree of achievement of these goals at the expense of the funding authority, refutable hypotheses about the organization's supply behavior can be derived. Baumol posits that the top executives of a firm seek to maximize sales subject to the constraint of achieving a minimum return on the firm's capital. Niskanen posits that employees of a public organization maximize the organization's budget subject to legislative demand for the organization's outputs. These theories have made major contributions to subsequent attempts to analyze effects of employees' discretion on the behavior of organizations. In regard to the analytical point at hand, these theories do not incorporate employees' resource diversions and the costs of imposing resource responsibility on employees into the costs faced by the organization's top managing employees or its funding authority when selecting desired rates of the organization's outputs. When these costs are incorporated, a theory's predictions can be made independent of the particular ways in which employees choose to benefit from resource diversions allowed by the constraints facing them.

In the 1970s, a number of scholars made considerable progress in connection with these three analytical points. A theory presented by Alchian and Demsetz (1972) is an important step in the direction of refutable hypotheses about employees' supply behavior that do not require that the theorist posit individual employees' objectives or aggregate them. Alchian and Demsetz analyze the firm as a "policing device" in which employees voluntarily associate, without authority, because of jointness, that is, employees working together produce more than they would separately. The authors argue that it may be more costly to "meter" each employee's productivity and appropriately reward it than would be worthwhile to do so; the required costs of observation may exceed the benefits of eliminating employees' "shirking." Regardless of the particular goals of employees, productivity will be lower and costs higher as a result, and labor market competition cannot be counted upon to eliminate the resulting misallocation.

In fact, one of the strengths of the Alchian and Demsetz theory is that it can hold under perfect competition. However, jointness is only one reason why employees are placed in a situation in which resource diversions can occur, and metering and rewarding an employee's productivity is only one among many possible means of imposing responsibility on him. In general, those who delegate discretion over resource allocation retain authority[3] to place responsibility on employees and choose the type and variant of responsibility that yields the most benefits in terms of reduced resource diversions in relation to its costs. Responsibility constraints create incentives on employees that affect how they allocate resources within an organization, and the incentives of specific and overall value responsibility affect resource uses in very different ways.

Further, there is the funding limit on resource diversions. The owners of a private firm have alternative uses of the capital resources engaged with the jointly productive employees; the stockholders' option to employ their capital elsewhere can give employees an incentive to reduce the costs of their outputs. For example, employees may allocate resources to coordinate themselves in order to maintain productivity at a level high enough to avoid owners' withdrawing their capital. The funding limit has comparable effects in other types of organizations.

Recent work on the theory of agency analyzes the design of optimal contracts when there is uncertainty about the level of output that results from a given set of inputs. (See Ross, 1973; Harris and Raviv, 1978; Holmström, 1979; and Shavell, 1979.) Given the attitudes toward risk on the parts of the "principal" and the "agent," the appropriate weights that should be given to outputs in Pareto optimal contract specifications can be determined, where social welfare is that of the principal and agent together. This valuable work is relevant to an employer's choices in imposing resource responsibility. However, I shall emphasize the roles of measurement costs, employers' alternative supply sources for employees' outputs or substitutes for them, and the cost-effectiveness of available applications of specific responsibility as determinants of whether and how measures of employees' outputs are included in the constraints facing them. These factors tend to dominate employers' choices in imposing responsibility to the extent that risks faced by an organization are not attributed to the performance of individual employees or their employers. For example, risks such as those related to market demands, technological changes outside the organization, and the state of nature, are often diversified by being absorbed over broad categories of employees or even at the level of the entire organization. We shall usually be concerned with social welfare effects of responsibility that are broader than those of an employee and his employer. For example, the effect of responsibility on the welfare created vis-à-vis the final demands for the organization's outputs will often be analyzed.

A number of researchers have analyzed the possibility that resource allocation within organizations can reduce or avoid problems of resource allocation in the market. This work includes the important contributions of Radner (1961, 1972), Arrow (1975), and Williamson (1975) on potential economies in uses of information that are achievable by bringing resource allocation into organizations. Williamson argues that resource allocation within organizations can improve the allocation of risk and save on contracting costs, and then points out many important implications of employees' opportunistic behavior. (See also Williamson et al., 1975.) Williamson's more recent study (1979) analyzes the implications of what he refers to as "idiosyncracies" of resources for choices whether to specify contracts with external suppliers or to rely on internal supply. Klein, Crawford, and Alchian (1978) analyze the equilibrium expected rent[1] received by an investor in such a resource having characteristics costly to specify in detail in a contract that is enforced under each possible contingency. A situation frequently develops in which the investor's behavior is similar to that of an employee under overall value responsibility. The work of Klein et al. and that of Williamson not only give a crucial reason why organizations can achieve economies but also provide a foundation for analysis of resource allocation within organizations. The analysis of this book is very much in the spirit of these contributions.

Major research contributions that are more generally applicable than to organizations have been directed to normative rules for the pricing of resources. This includes the well known scheme of Dantzig and Wolfe (1960) for the pricing of resources shared by multiple decision-making units. (See also Dantzig, 1963, chap. 23; Baumol and Fabian, 1964.) The related work of Davis and Whinston (1962, 1966) deals with the appropriate pricing of technological externalities among such units. Hirshleifer (1956, 1957) has derived conditions for interdivisional charges within an organization.[5] However, it is important to keep in mind that explicit pricing, like monitoring and rewarding employees' productivity, is only one among several ways of imposing responsibility. Also, when explicit pricing is used the allowable rates of resource diversions and the corresponding effects of diversions on costs must be taken into account, as in the case of any type of responsibility placed on employees. Alternative types and variants of responsibility have different costs and benefits (in terms of reduced resource diversions), depending on the context. Therefore, normative pricing proposals should be accompanied by positive analysis of the relative desirability of implementing them.

For an economic theorist, perhaps the most challenging research relevant to economic behavior within organizations is that of Leibenstein (1966). Leibenstein concluded that traditional economic analysis cannot explain the very large measured improvements in productivity that are often attendant upon the introduction of incentive systems or new managerial techniques. Coining the phrase "X-efficiency," Leibenstein argued that perhaps factors related to inspiration and attitudes toward work and constraints can explain the improvements. He subsequently developed this hypothesis in a book titled *Beyond Economic Man* (1976). One of the purposes of the present book is to show how a straightforward extension of traditional price theory can explain economic behavior within organizations, including the data on productivity.

CHAPTER 2

Definitions and determinants of employees' discretion over an organization's resources and production

The discretion that employees hold over an organization's productive activity and the incentives that they face determine the ways resources are allocated within an organization. This chapter examines the nature and range of employees' discretion by considering the influence delegated to them over the applications of inputs and choices of outputs within the organization's production functions. We first examine these production functions and define an employee's "production domain." Considered next are the relative costs to an employee and other interested parties of information about his production domain and the concepts of externally and internally designed production domains. Finally, we explore the conditions under which production domains are externally and internally designed.

A   An organization's production functions, its production domains, and its employees' discretion over resource substitutions

In order to analyze the motivation for delegating discretion to employees over an organization's resource allocation, it is necessary first to consider the nature of the production functions that an organization encompasses. We can then specify an employee's discretion in terms of his influence over possible resource substitutions within these production functions.

Production functions

Organizations usually produce many intermediate and final outputs. The rate of production of each of these outputs can typically be achieved in different ways, that is, with alternative rates of application of the various inputs which can contribute to each output. A production function expresses the set of known technologically feasible ways of transforming inputs into one or more outputs.[1] Two or more outputs share a single production function when the same application of an input contributing to one output affects the rate of production of another output. Such an input may contribute to a second output directly or do so indirectly by altering the contribution of other inputs to this output. Many discussions of production functions implicitly assume that information about the various alternative means of transforming inputs into outputs is costless. However, in organizations this information is usually costly, and these information costs have important implications for the organization's resource allocation.

Much of the economic behavior within an organization involves choices about applications of inputs in production functions, and an organization's internal suborganization can be characterized in terms of the discretion over choices of inputs and outputs that is delegated among its employees. It is thus useful to know about the production functions that an organization encompasses. This combination of production functions is determined by the organization's choices of intermediate and final outputs.[2] In the following discussion, the nature of the intermediate outputs that are typically produced within an organization is first examined. Subsequently, we consider the behavioral issue of how the final and intermediate outputs to be produced in the same organization are determined.

An organization's intermediate outputs. It is useful to consider intermediate outputs and their production functions in two categories. In the first category are those outputs other than information produced in the organization that contribute to the production of the organization's other intermediate outputs or its final outputs. There are a number of well-known possibilities for such intermediate outputs. Inputs used to produce a final or intermediate output may of course be produced within the organization. A final or intermediate output may be made up of "component" parts or services, some of which are produced within the organization, whose assembly represents one of the organization's intermediate outputs. Separate productive activity within the organization can be devoted to altering inputs before they are used in production or to altering outputs before they are delivered as final outputs. There are many managerial intermediate outputs, such as placing resource responsibility on employees, coordinating employees' activities, deciding how to conform to laws and regulations, initiating or adapting to technological change, and choosing long-term strategies about final outputs and clientele served.

The second category of intermediate output is information that is economically valuable in making choices about inputs and outputs and in producing the managerial outputs just mentioned. This information can deal with such internal phenomena as production possibilities within production functions and employees' activities in applying inputs and delivering outputs. For example, when input or output prices change, it may become worthwhile to invest in information about the desirable resource substitutions and the preferred means of enforcing them. Also, organizations often produce information about external phenomena, such as its clientele's demands, competitors' activities, and governmental enforcement activities.

Such information can be produced jointly with the organization's other intermediate and final outputs; in other cases it must be separately produced. Joint production of information occurs when those involved in producing other outputs learn about internal phenomena or gain capability to use data about external phenomena as they produce the organization's other outputs. When produced separately, information is a planned outcome that has one or more separate production functions. The popular term *knowledge worker* usually seems to apply to those employees who find themselves largely involved with such production functions.

Studies of production functions for outputs produced by organizations often do not take explicit account of the production of intermediate outputs. To express an organization's final outputs as functions of only those inputs procured from outside the organization implicitly inserts the parameters of production functions for intermediate outputs into any other production functions where these outputs appear as independent variables so that only those inputs produced outside the organization remain as independent variables. The resulting composite production function aggregates production trade-offs; the constrained choices in producing the organization's various outputs, including both categories of its intermediate outputs, cannot be analyzed separately. For example, it is not possible to analyze the production of information that is used within the organization.

Determination of the intermediate and final outputs to be produced within the same organization. Producing multiple final outputs or producing inputs instead of purchasing them from independent suppliers can possibly give the funding authority the following economies. First, when multiple outputs share a production function, costs of coordination can be lower if they are produced in the same organization. For example, if the rate of production of an intermediate or final output directly affects another output or alters the productivity of inputs producing the other output, it could be less costly to coordinate activities via resource responsibility in a single organization than to coordinate activities in separate organizations.

The second source of cost savings can occur when the smallest unit of an input that contributes to the production of multiple intermediate or final outputs is larger than the amount of this input that would be economical in producing the demanded quantity of any single output. If there is a separate organization for each output, the supplier of the indivisible input would coordinate multiple organizations' usage of it. It may be more economical for a single organization producing multiple outputs to coordinate usage of the indivisible input for each output. Examples of such indivisible inputs are research and development resources and managerial and technical expertise.[3]

The third source of cost savings applies only to an organization's production of its intermediate outputs. There can be economies from producing, rather than purchasing, an input that has one or more characteristics different from inputs demanded by any other organization or individual. Sources of an organization's demand for unique inputs, discussed later in this chapter, include unique characteristics of final outputs, the production of unique combinations of nonunique outputs, and unique skills of employees resulting from experiences in production that are different from those occurring elsewhere. The costs of obtaining such a unique resource from an independent supplier, including the costs both of obtaining and transmitting the requisite information about it and preparing and enforcing a contract, might exceed the costs of production within an organization. Klein, Crawford, and Alchian (1978) and Williamson (1979) have most notably analyzed these comparative costs.

In Williamson's analysis, the costs of specifying contracts depend on the nature of the good or service contracted and its productive role within the organization employing it. He shows that the more an input possesses unique ("idiosyncratic" is the term Williamson uses) characteristics, the more costly it is to make and enforce contracts with an independent supplier and the stronger the incentive for production within an organization.

We shall see that when imposing resource responsibility on an employee, an employer can communicate much less precise information about his desired characteristics of the employee's output than is ordinarily required for a contract with someone in another organization. However, Klein et al. suggest that the costs of making and enforcing a detailed contract with an independent supplier could be avoided by ensuring enough reciprocal business to make him willing to take the risk of investing in a specialized asset (alternatively, there could be an advance payment to compensate this risk) and consenting to pay subsequently a long-term premium that offsets any expected short-term gain to him from failing to comply with an agreement. An interruption of supply or an alteration in important characteristics could, of course, be costly to the buyer of the services of a specialized resource that are not immediately available from other suppliers. Although detailed enforceable contracts potentially avoid such costs, "They entail costs of specifying possible contingencies and the policing and litigation costs of detecting violations and enforcing the contract in the courts" (Klein et al., 1978, p. 303). It can be costly to compensate the risk of independent ownership of a unique resource. Long-term premiums to independent suppliers can also represent substantial costs if there is a potentially large increase in competing demands for use of such a resource. Bringing the specialized resource into the organization avoids the costs of either of the alternatives of specifying and enforcing detailed contracts or of compensating risks and paying the long-term premiums analyzed by Klein et al. These savings, however, tend to be offset by the costs of imposing resource responsibility and any costs associated with employees' independent behavior.

Most economic analyses of the size and composition of organizations have been confined to private firms whose owners are involved in management and are informed about the details of the firm's production functions and its employees' activities. In these analyses the firm's outputs are determined by the informed owner-entrepreneur's costs and benefits of coordinating activities within the organization versus making the necessary contracts in the external market. Coase (1937) has, for example, argued that "a firm . . . consists of the system of relationships which comes into existence when the direction of resources is dependent on an entrepreneur" (p. 393).

An owner-entrepreneur might personally balance the costs and benefits of producing versus purchasing inputs and of adding final outputs. If so, he would take account of spillovers within the organization, his costs of employees' independent behavior, and his outlays for imposing responsibility, plus the cash equivalent of his direct personal costs. His choice whether to produce an input would depend on whether these costs are less than the necessary outlays and direct personal costs for arranging and procuring independent supply. Similarly, he adds outputs when all of these costs for the added outputs are less than the increase in revenues.[4] The entrepreneur's direct personal costs include his own efforts in obtaining information, in coordinating employees and in imposing resource responsibility on them, and in assuming risks.

However, an organization's funding authority, representing the owners of a private corporation or donors or a legislature in the case of private nonprofit and public organizations, need not be actively involved in management. In most cases the funding authority has only sketchy information or no information at all about the organization's production functions or the activities of its employees and the organization's employees are granted discretion over most or all of the resource allocation occurring within the organization.

Additional forces come into play in the determination of production to occur within the organization when the funding authority is not actively involved in management. The cost savings from producing versus purchasing inputs are those faced by employees, given the resource responsibility placed on them and the funding limit. Thus, while employees also are motivated to coordinate activities to economize on information costs, external contracting costs, and premiums to ensure supplies, they are motivated by those particular cost savings that either directly benefit them or which they are motivated to achieve by the responsibility they face and the funding limit. Within these constraints, employees' investments can enhance their influences over the productive activities that occur within an organization. Such investments (analyzed in Chapter 7–9) include the addition of intermediate or final outputs that yield employees higher benefits from resource diversions. For example, employees' information cost advantages may enable them to obtain authorization to produce an output that raises the funding limit on resource diversions, renders less effective the resource responsibility imposed on them, or diversifies risks unimportant to the funding authority.

Whether or not an owner-entrepreneur is actively involved in management, the costs and benefits of alternative resource responsibility on employees affect the outputs produced within an organization. For example, large economies in placing responsibility on multiple employees can make the organization produce more outputs than otherwise.

*Production domains and employees' discretion over
input substitutions within them*

This section defines the discretion held by employees over an organization's resource allocation. An employee may be granted discretion
to make choices about the application of particular inputs in the
organization's production functions within some range of their possible values. These choices can affect current outputs and can also
influence the allocation of the organization's resources over time.
Employees are granted such discretion when it is not economical for
their employers to make the relevant input substitutions themselves,
even when employees take advantage of the discretion to pursue
their own goals.

When multiple employees hold discretion over the same input
substitution, the singular term *employee* is used wherever it is possible
to do so unambiguously. There can be situations where one employee alone has discretion over some resource substitutions and
others are at the joint discretion of him and one or more other
employees (perhaps including managing employees). For example,
Blauner (1964) suggests that "the most characteristic feature of auto-
mation is its transfer of focus from an individual job to the process
of production. The perspective of the worker is shifted from his own
individual tasks to a broader series of operations that includes the
work of other employees" (pp. 172–3). It is possible to aggregate
multiple employees' responses to incentives when each individual's
response to the variables considered is determinate. The responsibility imposed on each individual employee can produce this result.
When multiple employees delegate the task of coordinating their
actions to a specialized employee, this result also occurs. (See
Chapter 7.)

An employee's discretion can be characterized in relation to the
organization's production functions. An employee's *production domain* is the part of these production functions over which he holds
discretion to apply inputs within some ranges of their possible values. In familiar terms, an employee's production domain might be
characterized by his discretion over resource allocation related to
his assigned "tasks" or "functions" or his discretion over the resource allocation occurring within his "unit," "department," "section," or "work station." In the simplest case, an employee's production domain is identical to a production function. In this case
the employee has discretion over the applications of all inputs producing a final or intermediate output, although usually within a

restricted range of variation of these inputs. Within this range the rate of application of each input and the rate of production of the output are determined by the employee's maximization of his own welfare subject to his constraints, including the responsibility placed on him.

However, the employee's production domain is not necessarily identical to a production function. Typically, an employee's production domain encompasses the application of less than all of the inputs that enter into one or more production functions. Thus when other employees hold discretion over remaining inputs, the employee's decisions may only in small part determine the rate of production of an intermediate or final output. In such cases, an employee's own output is taken to be his contribution to any one of these outputs, that is, the appropriate cumulated marginal products of inputs he applies in his production domain.

Inexact alignment between production domains and production functions is not necessarily undesirable for the funding authority or for economic efficiency for three reasons. First, the costs of information may be lower for someone to make choices for only some of the inputs in a production function. Second, economies from the spatial dispersion of production or from uses of specialized capabilities of particular employees may make it uneconomical or even infeasible for a single individual to control more than a small fraction of the inputs in a production function. The same spatial dispersion may create an indivisibility of an individual and his skills, creating economies for him to apply inputs in parts of multiple production functions. Third, it might be more economical to impose responsibility on an employee delegated discretion over only a part of a production function. However, particular divisions of production functions into production domains can unnecessarily raise costs by inappropriately utilizing employees and raising costs of coordinating and imposing responsibility on them. Chapter 7 analyzes how employees can increase benefits from resource diversions by influencing the division of an organization's production functions into production domains.

An employee's discretion over resource allocation decisions within his production domain is usually not closely related to the degree to which his tasks are specialized. Highly specialized tasks, such as those in an assembly line and many other machine-paced settings, may involve little discretion over how these tasks are performed. Conversely, an employee's discretion can include possible decisions about broad categories of resource allocation within an organization, as in the case of a top managing employee's production domain.

The popular concept of a managing employee's span of control is closely related to that of his production domain. The placing of responsibility on employees and the coordination of their activities constitute intermediate outputs, and the managing employee has some degree of discretion over their production. The span of control concept can be interpreted to encompass the application of managerial inputs within the managing employee's production domain. For example, Williamson (1970) states that "increasing the span of control means that while each supervisor has more productive capability responsive to him he has less time to devote to the supervision of each . . ." (p. 33). The concept of a managing employee's production domain focuses attention on his discretion over alternative means by which he might carry out activities such as imposing responsibility on his employees and how he might use this discretion to pursue his own ends.[5]

B   Information about production domains

The production functions for an organization's outputs consist of all knowledge that exists inside or outside the organization about how to produce these outputs. Economic gains can result from increased amounts of such knowledge being held by those within the organization who can make productive use of it. However, this information is costly because it results either from communication with individuals now holding it or from devoting resources to creating it, for example, experimenting with production possibilities. Creating knowledge about production possibilities does not necessarily imply that the same information does not exist elsewhere; it may simply be more economical to create it in particular cases than to elicit the cooperation of individuals holding the knowledge and communicating with them.

From the perspective of a particular organization's employees, technological change can be regarded as any newly existing knowledge held by anyone, including those outside the organization, about more technologically efficient production possibilities (whether or not there also are newly existing inputs). Technological change implies that there is a new production function because there is at least some knowledge of production possibilities that did not exist previously. However, as just suggested, increased information within an organization about production possibilities can have economic value regardless of whether these possibilities are known elsewhere.

The following discussion focuses on the relative amounts of information that employers and employees obtain about the production functions for an organization's outputs. A discussion of externally and internally designed production domains is followed by an analysis of reasons for internal design.

Externally and internally designed production domains

Production domains can be distinguished according to how information is obtained about them. A production domain is *internally designed* if the information about it held within the organization is originated by the employee having discretion over it. A production domain is *externally designed* if the organization's information about it originates with someone else. Of course, a production domain could be partly internally and partly externally designed. When an employee originates a substantial amount of the information held within the organization about his own production domain, it is referred to as internally designed rather than "partly" or "largely" internally designed when no ambiguity results.

An employee's possession of an information cost advantage does not necessarily imply that his production domain will be internally designed. His and his employer's information demands in relation to their respective information costs determine the knowledge each chooses to obtain about production possibilities. The incentives within the responsibility placed on an employee determine his gain from alternative information he might obtain and thus help establish his demands for information. An employer's information demands are also influenced by his optimal choices in imposing responsibility.

A production domain is externally designed under either of two sets of circumstances. The funding authority or managing employee may decide to hire someone other than the employee holding discretion to obtain information about his production domain. For example, engineers might be hired for this purpose, and employees' knowledge about their production domains would be obtained via the instructions that accompany their assigned tasks. In her major study of English firms, Woodward (1965) commented that "standardized production and all that it implied had taken the perceptual and conceptual elements of skill out of the main production task, although much of the work still required a fair degree of motor skill and manual dexterity. In most of the large batch and mass production firms studied, the patterns of behavior were no longer determined by the skilled men" (pp. 62–63). Lawrence, Barnes, and

Lorsch (1976) pointed out that "when the task is highly certain and predictable (e.g., an assembly line, turning out a standard product), the subsystem, if it is effective, will tend to have a highly formalized organization. Subsystems with more uncertain tasks (and again effective outputs) tend to have less formalized organizational inputs" (p. 212).[6] The relative effectiveness of experience working with a production domain and of independent technical expertise can influence how information about a production domain is obtained. An employer has an additional incentive to use specialists for external design if the cost effectiveness of responsibility placed on employees would thus increase.

Similar production domains in other organizations and relatively low costs of comparison by employers can also contribute to external design. Even when there are variations in some inputs' productivities, "rules of thumb" of acceptable accuracy about a production domain may be made available via the existence of other production domains. Aspects of production domains that contribute to external design via comparison are similarity (i.e., comparison will be more exact when production domains have fewer unique characteristics) and low costs of the information necessary for comparison. The presence of competition for employees working with similar production domains makes external design more likely.

In order for an employee's production domain to be internally designed, both possibilities for external design must be uneconomical for his employer. For example, if the employer does not hire others than the responsible employee to obtain information about his production domain but does so via comparisons with other production domains, the employee's production domain will be externally designed.

When an employee has an internally designed production domain, he can, but will not necessarily, obtain complete information about production possibilities within it. The amount of such information he obtains depends on his costs of experimenting with alternative resource substitutions and his gains from doing so. (These are analyzed in later chapters.) To maintain the employer's costs of imposing resource responsibility, an employee often will find it in his interest not to disclose information about his production domain. For example, Lawrence et al. (1976) described a discussion between a programmer and his employer. In response to the employer's request for a progress report on a computer program, "[the programmer's] reply was to the effect that none of the work was in such a form that it would mean anything ..." Notes in his file and "some finalized operations . . . would be valueless . . . and were more than likely subject to change in any event" (p. 287).

In contrast, when an employee's production domain is externally designed, his information about feasible resource substitutions within it cannot contribute to his discretion. However, the employer's costs of measuring input applications and of measuring and attaching values to employees' outputs may, nonetheless, contribute to such discretion. Therefore, the hypotheses in later chapters about employees' uses of resources to their own advantages within determinate limits can apply when production domains are externally as well as internally designed.

The means by which information about an employee's production domain is obtained, combined with the incentives determined by the responsibility imposed on him and the demands for his outputs, largely determine his control over his work environment. Thus, internal versus external design is relevant to the issue of employees' feelings of personal involvement with and influence over their jobs. In his study of worker alienation, Blauner (1964) states that "it is my contention that control over the conditions of employment and control over the immediate work process are most salient for manual workers, who are most likely to value control over those matters which affect their immediate jobs and work tasks and least likely to be concerned with the more general and abstract aspects of powerlessness" (pp. 16–17).

*Conditions that contribute to the internal
design of production domains*

This section can be omitted by the reader who accepts the proposition that internally designed production domains are widespread. Although one cannot predict whether a production domain is internally designed without taking account of the responsibility placed on its employee and his employer, a number of conditions strongly influence the likelihood of internal design. Because the dispersion of information about production domains can have important effects on an organization's resource allocation, it is worthwhile to explore these conditions. We first consider how differentiation of outputs can contribute to uniqueness of production functions. Next we consider how employees can have cost advantages in obtaining information about unique parts of production functions. We then turn to conditions that can make it possible for the production domains of employees that produce identical outputs in different organizations to be internally designed.

The production of differentiated outputs as a reason for lack of comparable production domains in other organizations. Private corporations that are monopolies, differentiated oligopolies, or monopolistically competitive by definition produce outputs that are differentiated in at least some characteristics. In addition, public organizations and private nonprofit organizations typically produce outputs that have unique characteristics. Given that a final output is differentiated from any output of another organization, how different is its production function from those for similar outputs of other organizations and to what extent do these differences make external design based on comparisons a less likely outcome? This question can be answered by considering the production functions involved and their separability relative to any inputs entering them that have unique effects.

Unique production possibilities implied by uniqueness of outputs can range from relatively unimportant production trade-offs or the unique combination of nonunique outputs to largely unique production functions requiring many unique inputs. At an extreme, if the differentiated feature of a unique output is an added-on style difference, that output may have a production function closely comparable to other production functions; most of the feasible technological trade-offs would be the same as in other organizations that produce outputs different in style only. Comparison costs could be raised by a suborganization with a differentiated division of the production function into production domains. However, the production functions themselves do not differ substantially.

When a unique output is produced by combining nonunique components in a unique way, the differentiation of production functions can be more substantive than a style difference. An example of such a situation is tailoring characteristics of an output to the particular preferences of individual clients. The productive activity involved in combining the components, including the interpretation of preferences and relating technical information about the production of each characteristic to these preferences, can involve a large part of all the resources producing the output. Another way in which a substantive difference can occur is if variation in inputs producing one component affects the relative productivities of inputs producing other components, reducing the usefulness of comparisons with the production elsewhere of components not produced together.

A unique output might have a production function that is largely different from any other. The uniqueness of a production function need not consist only of inputs having unique productive effects. There can also be inputs to a production function that do not enter the most technically comparable production function elsewhere. If variation in either category of these inputs should affect productivity of other inputs in the production function, comparisons would be even less useful.

The costs of measuring input applications and rates of employees' outputs (including any variations in input or output characteristics) influence employers' costs of comparing production possibilities, even when the compared production functions are identical. Costs of accurately measuring input applications and employees' outputs can be especially high when these resources have intangible characteristics, where access for observation is difficult, and when interpretative information about an employee's production domain or the specialized demands of his internal or external clients is needed.

Employees' cost advantages in obtaining information about production domains. If comparisons do not contribute to external design, the costs of performing two tasks help determine whether there is external design nonetheless because someone other than the responsible employee (such as an engineer) is hired to establish the organization's information about production possibilities.

One task is that of mapping out all desired actions of the employee in response to each possible demand, that is, every request made of him weighted by its probability of occurrence and its importance to the employer. These requests include any subtle variations in responses that could be costly or infeasible to communicate. If only a few readily defined actions are demanded and if the alternative productive responses to demand are few, it may be economical for someone other than the responsible employee to obtain information about his production domain. Another consideration is that the particular types of expertise highly productive in planning the desirable actions of one employee could be applicable to others and might be unnecessarily duplicated if held by every one of these employees.

Conversely, there may be many dimensions of demand and the most economically valuable responses can require interpretations of preferences underlying demand or judgments about appropriate actions to take that vary with each situation. In such cases, it may be essential for the employee himself to have substantial knowledge about his production domain in order to respond to demand; someone else mapping out the employee's desirable actions in response to demand would duplicate the employee's necessary expertise. The more costly the skills and the less applicable they are to other production domains, the more costly the duplication. However, the cost of duplication of even modest skills can prevent external design. For example, in relatively unskilled work such as driving small lift trucks, "slight variations in the ordering of the flow can cause major differences in the time requirements on such jobs as stacking and unstacking. These ambiguities provide a fruitful field for . . . the group to improve job conditions" (Sayles, 1958, p. 23).

The second task is that of measuring an employee's input applications and outputs and of attributing inputs to outputs. If characteristics of inputs and outputs are intangible or specifically tailored to particular situations, it may be necessary for someone other than the employee to be present on a continuing basis, although perhaps via sampling, to make the interpretations of the employee's resource uses that are necessary to learn about his production possibilities.

Such ongoing observations and interpretations may also be necessary to determine whether a production domain believed to be externally designed is in fact internally designed. An employee might improve on design while superficially conforming to the external design. For example, he might create an opportunity to use resources to his own ends by covertly streamlining a job. In reference to a workshop, Berg (1963) states that "ingenious jigs are developed—carefully hidden from methods experts . . . Welders will make bench tools . . . that can be adapted to different types and sizes of steel frames—tools that will disappear when an assistant department superintendent makes his rounds" (p. 38). The continuing costs of determining whether the employee's actions correspond to what is prescribed for each variation in demand could initially discourage the choice to use external design.

The production domains of those who produce economically valuable information within the organization are internally designed when the information is unique and there is no standard procedure for obtaining it. For example, interpreting the applicability to the organization of laws and regulations or determining production possibilities involving spillovers among production domains frequently represent productive activities that are specific to the organization. The production domains of those employees who provide information leading to the external design of other production domains are often internally designed. Drucker (1974) has suggested that "knowledge cannot be productive unless the knowledge worker finds out . . . how he works best. There can be no divorce of planning from doing in knowledge work. On the contrary, the knowledge worker must be able to plan himself" (p. 33).

It is interesting to consider the potential managerial uses of data bases centrally provided within organizations when production domains are internally designed. Even when many characteristics of inputs and outputs are intangible, a large volume of data about an organization's productive activity can usually be obtained economically. For example, crude measures of inputs and outputs not capturing variations in their characteristics as well as data on employees' activities are typically readily accessible from an organization's accounting records on budgets, payrolls, shipments, purchases, schedules, workloads, and so on. However, without information about employees' production domains, these data have very limited usefulness for guiding decisions leading to more efficient production. Blau (1963, chap. 3) found that if an employer collects measures of relatively unimportant aspects of his employees' activities, the measures can nonetheless serve as implicit prices on these activities having behavioral effects inconsistent with the employer's interests.

On the possibility of differences among organizations in what is known about production functions for identical outputs. I now consider how the production of information as an intermediate output might create differences among organizations in what is known about production functions.[7] The context of this discussion is when identical outputs are produced by multiple organizations. For example, the cases of perfect competition and homogeneous oligopoly immediately come to mind. An implication of the discussion is that when production domains are internally designed, there can be differences in what is known about production functions and resulting differences in costs of production in otherwise competitive firms. The discussion can also be applied to organizations with differentiated outputs when production functions have components identical to those for outputs of other organizations.

Consider the following assumptions that are consistent with the perfect competition model: (1) there is a known single best (in terms of costs of the firm's outputs) method of dividing a firm's production functions into production domains; (2) information about this best method is costless for prospective (firm) entrants;[8] (3) information about employees' production possibilities in each production domain is costless for employees and owners alike; and (4) employees can be costlessly transferred among production domains and organizations. Under these assumptions, each firm is forced to use the single best division of production functions into production domains. Also, in the long run no employee would be able to allocate resources in a manner inconsistent with profit maximization.

Alternative assumptions can allow for unique information held by employees about an organization's production domains. These include, first, that existing and prospective employees and owners must bear costs of obtaining information about production functions and the most desirable divisions of them into production domains. Second, employees' costs of information about production possibilities in their own production domains are lower than for owners or other employees, and this cost advantage, given employers' and employees' information demands, results in production domains being internally designed. Third, during a time period more lengthy than required for entry or for investment in an organization, the longer employees' time on the job (i.e., their "experience"), the greater their information cost advantages.

If relatively experienced employees' skills were equally valuable in and costlessly transferred to other firms, wages would be bid up to the value of the cost savings that experience can achieve. However, an employee's own information costs can lead to the outcome that his experience is more valuable in his own organization than in others. Essentially the same point has been made by other economists. For example, Prescott and Visscher (1980) point out that "the information set that makes a person productive in one organization may not make that person as productive in another organization even if both firms produce identical output" (p. 458). When employees face costs of acquiring information about their production domains, they will ordinarily take different sequences of actions in exploring alternative production possibilities within them. Such differences would derive from differences among individuals in attitudes toward risk and in perceptions of the outcomes of different experimental choices as well as from random chance. For each alternative initial action, different information about payoffs to further actions can result. If different employees have diverse preferences and the benefits they reap from their information cost advantages must be taken in kind, there will be even more diverse sequences of experimental choices of resource substitutions within production domains. The resulting diversity reduces the productivity of experience in other firms below what it is in the firm in which it was gained and thus makes specific the skills resulting from experience. Because of the idiosyncracies introduced by costs of information in otherwise competitive firms, prospective entrepreneurs might be interested in the cost experiences of typical firms, such as the Marshallian "representative" firm, in deciding whether to enter an industry.

Information cost advantages not only can prevent external design of employees' production domains and competition by inexperienced employees, but they can also prevent newly entering firms from forcing (via competition) all firms to have more nearly identical suborganizations, that is, divisions of production functions into production domains. It is of interest which of two constraints is binding on employees. If owners intervene to impose responsibility before competition from prospective employees or other firms limits employees' discretion, the firm's internal organization is more likely to result from intentional planning. If competition by new employees or new firms forms the effective constraint on employees, market competition takes a role in the internal organization of firms, and both employees and owners have less discretion over the division of production functions into production domains. Woodward's (1965) analysis of whether conscious planning tended to be associated with success in firms having different production technologies suggested that "conscious planning produces better results in some kinds of industry than in others" (p. 77). Successful firms with unit and small batch and with continuous flow production tended not to employ conscious planning, whereas successful firms with large batch production did. This result might be explained in part by the fact that unit and small batch firms are often in relatively competitive industries. However, it seems reasonable to expect that technology alone would largely explain why conscious planning about suborganization is unimportant to the success of continuous process firms.

Experienced employees with skills that are less valuable in other firms may nonetheless be able to obtain rents from their employments. For example, they might be able to make their employers' costs of their outputs as high as they would be with less experienced employees. The exact costs that employers would have to pay depend on the cost effectiveness in the particular situation of the resource responsibility available to place on employees.

CHAPTER 3

Employees' resource diversions and employers' imposition of resource responsibility

We have seen why the employer finds it in his interest to delegate to an employee discretion over a subset of the organization's productive activity. This chapter explores the ways the employee can use this discretion to increase his own welfare at the employer's expense and how the employer imposes constraints that limit his costs of this behavior. By connecting an employee's actions or results of his actions with the rent he derives from his employment, these constraints establish the incentives on the employee that the employer controls. Given the employee's discretion over resource allocation and these constraints, the employee's equilibrium resource allocation behavior can be analyzed in the short and long run.

Employees' resource diversions are introduced and the information required for an employer to make inferences about diversions is described. The alternative types of resource responsibility available to employers to limit resource diversions are then considered. After discussing the possible influence of employees' benefits from their resource diversions on the organization's labor supply, we consider how employees' cash salaries are established. Finally, the employer's selection of a type of responsibility to impose on an employee is analyzed.

A   Employees' resource diversions

This section defines employees' resource diversions and considers the costs and productivity of information that an employer can use to make inferences about diversions.

Behavior of the employee in relation to the employer's welfare and employees' resource diversions

When an employee's utility function does not contain a variable for his employer's welfare, the employee has the motivation to use his

34

discretion over resources delegated to him to increase his utility at the employer's expense. More generally, even if the employer's welfare does enter an employee's utility function, the employee's adherence to the employer's welfare could be tempered by other variables in his utility function. The analysis of employees' resource diversion behavior is not always applicable, however, because an employee could be motivated by a completely overriding commitment to his employer's welfare.[1]

Lacking such an overriding commitment, an employee nonetheless uses delegated resources in such a way as to maximize his employer's welfare when he is under a particular constraint. We are not concerned at this point with whether it would be feasible for the employer to impose this constraint and, if feasible, whether the employer's costs of the necessary information would be justified. Suppose that the employee is charged a cash price for every individually variable characteristic of each input delegated to him that equals the employer's marginal cash equivalent value of his best alternative use of it, whether in another production domain, personal use, or exchange. For example, the employee's alternative applications of his different efforts and skills are thus priced when they have alternative uses to the employer outside the employee's production domain. Let the employee be paid the employer's cash equivalent marginal value of each output characteristic and also be paid or assessed the employer's cash equivalent marginal value of the effects of his activities on the outputs of other employees. Assume that the employee is fully informed about alternative production possibilities within his production domain and that he selects characteristics of his inputs and outputs and rates of application of each input and production of each output that maximize his cash net income. (This net income could be negative.) Subsequently, the employer taxes (or supplements) this amount so that the employee's remaining cash income equals the minimum amount necessary for him to continue his employment. The remaining after-employer-taxed net income is referred to as the employee's *compensated opportunity cost.*[2] By assumption, every time there is a change in the employee's non-cash benefits from his job, the employer readjusts his cash income to his compensated opportunity cost. Thus, for example, the employee may exchange cash income for resources withdrawn for personal use at the prices established. His choices between cash income and personal uses of inputs that have no value to the employer outside his production domain are based on these resources' marginal contributions to priced outputs.

The amount of the employee's tax (which can be negative) is referred to as the employer's *net income attributable to the employee*. When this amount is maximized subject to the requirement that the employee continues in his current job, three aspects of the employee's behavior are noteworthy. First, all of the employee's uses of resources, including his applications of his own skills and knowledge, are guided by the employer's marginal values of them and of the outputs they produce. Second, his own personal benefits – whatever combination of cash income and personal uses of resources – are the minimum cash equivalent cost for the employer to maintain his employment. Third, his relative supplies of his skills and efforts are influenced at the margin by the utilities or disutilities he derives from applying them. Similarly, the employee's mix of outputs and output characteristics is influenced by his utility function.

Let us now assume that this constraint is not imposed and consider an employee's usage of one or more resources that reduces his employer's net income attributable to him below the maximum described. The amount by which this cash equivalent net income decreases from the maximum constitutes the employee's *resource diversions* (or *diversions*, for short). The expression "diversion of a resource" refers to an employer's cash equivalent loss of income owing to his employee's usage of that resource. If the prices faced by an employee are not those specified above, if there are restrictions on his uses of resources that prevent the required profit maximizing uses, or if his personal income is not appropriately adjusted, some of his uses of resources result in diversions. In turn, the constraints actually imposed on employees can be evaluated according to the resource diversions they allow. Any action of an employee that increases his employer's cash-equivalent net income attributable to him is characterized as being in the employer's interest. Thus a diversion of a resource is contrary to the employer's interest.

The term *diversion* as it is used here is consistent with the definition "the turning aside (of anything) from its due or ordinary course or direction" (*Oxford English Dictionary*). Although the diversion of a resource over which an employee has discretion is a cash equivalent income loss for the employer, it involves any uses different from those his employer would prefer.[3] Other definitions of the word *diversion*, such as "deviation from a course" or "pastime," are not implied by the term as used here; although the diversion of resources can involve roundabout means of production or provide amusement to employees, it does not necessarily do so and perhaps, as suggested in the following examples, ordinarily does not do so. Diversions are not usually explicitly accounted for in agreements among employers and employees. But they are determined by the constraints that employers place on employees and continue indefinitely until employees' constraints change. Employees' resource diversions can involve high as well as low rates of employees' activity.

Resource diversions are not always worth preventing and do not necessarily provide personal monetary or nonmonetary income to employees. Specifically, it can be infeasible or too costly for the employer to establish the constraint that maximizes his cash-equivalent net income attributable to an employee. Employers typically find it economical to establish constraints that limit but do not eliminate resource diversions. Such constraints can contain incentives leading to efficient resource allocation within an employee's production domain, but, if so, the employee is not required to pass on all the benefits to the employer. Alternatively there can be incentives leading to inefficient resource allocation, and diversions may thus fail to increase an employee's welfare. However, an employee seeks resource diversions that do increase his monetary or nonmonetary income from his job to the extent that his constraints allow him to do so. We are largely concerned with the motivating effect of these resource diversions on employees' behavior.

There may be variation in the utility an employee derives from a given decrease in his employer's net income. For example, at one extreme a diversion may result from the personal use of a resource, such as power, that is unavailable in the market and from which an employee derives more utility than he does from a cash benefit equal to the value of the resource involved to the employer. However, the employee's utility from personal use of resources is typically less than that from this cash amount, and diversions often yield the employee no utility at all.

Perhaps the most obvious example of resource usage resulting in diversions is "leisure on the job." Other obvious examples are given in a list of offenses that one company posted for its employees: "Defective work, tardiness, absence, disobedience, carelessness, intoxication, laxness in safety, gambling on Company time, possession of intoxicating liquor, other" (Gouldner, 1954, p. 67). Uses of resources leading to diversions can be less obvious than these examples and can involve very energetic and highly productive behavior on the part of personnel who are producing outputs other than those that the employer would select. As we shall see, however, what appears to result in a diversion does not necessarily (although it usually does); employees might, for example, take exchanges of cash for in-kind income that are advantageous to employers as well as to themselves.

In general, resource diversions can result from an employee's producing outputs that are not demanded by his employer or from his failure to deliver demanded outputs, as well as from not applying inputs efficiently within his production domain. For example, an employee in an applied research laboratory may produce basic research for the purpose of furthering his personal professional reputation. Other employees may acquire general skills or make their personal accomplishments known to colleagues and potential employers at their employer's expense. An employee might pursue what he believes to be the true interests of the organization's funding authority – or the public – over his employer's opposition or despite his indifference. An employee might supply an output to a client that his employer would prefer to go to another client. Employees may actually be able to exchange outputs for their direct personal benefit. For example, some Russian factories apparently busily produce outputs for sale in private markets as well as outputs delivered to the state (Simis, 1981). In all these instances, resource diversions can result from an employee's directing highly productive activity to ends other than those most valued by his employer. An employee's thoughts, efforts, or creativity may often be the most significant resources that he uses to produce outputs aside from those demanded by employers. Downs (1967) provides an imaginative discussion of employees' energetic uses of their discretion to pursue their own ends.

Resource diversions can yield an employee present or future utility, or both. Those yielding present utility include the consumption of inputs such as an employee's own time and potential effort or creativity. Outputs can be consumed, too. However, an employee may be able to use his own time and other resources to increase his future welfare. Such investments include both those that enhance earning power in the labor market and those that increase rents from working in the same organization.

The cash equivalent reduction in the employer's net income that resource diversions represent differs if we alternatively take as an employee's employer (1) the managing employee directly above him, (2) a "higher" managing employee, or (3) the funding authority. Because of his own resource diversions, the constraints that a managing employee places on his employees usually differ from those the funding authority would impose. Thus, for example, an employee not diverting resources vis-à-vis his managing employee could be diverting resources vis-à-vis the funding authority.

The costs and productivity of information in making inferences about resource diversions

An employer can make inferences about resource diversions by comparing productivity with expected performance or by directly observing the employee's uses of resources, but these inferences will be accurate only if he possesses the right information.

A production domain's overall value productivity and more specific measures. If an employee's production domain coincides with one or more production functions, his *overall value productivity* is the difference between his employer's cash equivalent marginal valuations of his outputs and of the inputs delegated to him. In this case, measurement of overall value productivity can be accomplished by measuring and valuing the employee's inputs and outputs. When the employee does not produce one or more separate intermediate or final outputs or when his activities create spillovers affecting productivity in other employees' production domains, measuring overall value productivity requires additional information about marginal products. The measurement costs can be reduced by sacrificing accuracy. Inputs and outputs can be measured or valued imprecisely, and applications of inputs and their marginal productivities can also be less accurately assessed.

The costs of measuring overall value productivity may lead the employer to limit himself to measuring only an employee's specific uses of some of his inputs or outputs. If so, there may be a combination of his production domain with those of other employees for which it is economical for his employer to measure the overall value productivity of the employees taken together.

Uses of information about productivity to make inferences about resource diversions. A measure of an employee's overall value productivity is not sufficient to determine his resource diversions. In addition his potential overall value productivity must be measured so that it can be compared with actual productivity. To obtain an accurate measure of an employee's potential overall value productivity in the absence of competitive bids from alternative suppliers, the employer requires information both about production possibilities within the employee's production domain and about his preferences regarding alternative uses of his skills and efforts and other inputs (to determine the employee's compensated opportunity cost). The employer might economize on information by using "norms" for the employee's application of skills and efforts or crude measures of production possibilities within his production domain. For example, assembly jobs are often "timed." However, such approximations can be very inaccurate.

Alternatively, the employer might attempt to make inferences about resource diversions by observing the employee's specific uses of each resource delegated to him. Observation can be very costly or infeasible, particularly in regard to the employee's application of skills, effort, and creativity. However, even with accurate measures of the employee's uses of inputs, the employer cannot discern whether the chosen input combinations are the most advantageous to him if he lacks information about the employee's preferences and the production possibilities within his production domain.

In conclusion, when an employer lacks information about an employee's preferences, about production possibilities within his production domain, or about his uses of inputs and outputs, he does not accurately infer the employee's resource diversions. We shall see, however, that the employer nonetheless does measure either an employee's overall value productivity or some of his specific uses of resources when he finds it economical to impose constraints to limit resource diversions; the manner and accuracy of measurement of an employee's productivity depend on the employer's optimal choice of resource responsibility.

B   Types of resource responsibility

Employers place constraints on employees, referred to as *resource responsibility*, or responsibility, for short, to limit their costs of employees' outputs. In unusual cases where employment contracts are complete, resource responsibility constrains the degree to which employees can avoid their contractual obligations. When employment contracts are incomplete, resource responsibility additionally leads employees to take noncontractual actions that reduce employers' costs of their outputs. Responsibility is the employer's exercise of authority, derived from the funding authority if the employer is a managing employee, to extract or augment the rents that employees derive from their jobs.[4] In particular, responsibility connects employees' actions or results of their actions with these rents and thereby creates incentives for them to further employers' interests.

Authority over an employee is limited not only by the funding authority, higher managing employees, and by law, but also by the fact that given the employee's cash remuneration, he must derive a certain amount of satisfaction from his job if he is to continue his employment. Further, the employer's exercise of authority requires costly information; he thus influences the employee's actions only when his resulting benefits exceed these costs. Lacking reciprocal authority, the employee nonetheless affects the employer's optimal choices in imposing resource responsibility by exerting influence over the employer's information costs.

There are three types of resource responsibility by which an employer can reduce resource diversions. They are termed *complete pricing overall responsibility* (CPOR), *overall value responsibility* (OVR), and *specific responsibility* (SR). Each produces different incentives for the employee to use delegated resources in the employer's interest; thus each limits diversions in different ways. The employer chooses among them according to his costs of imposing each and his benefits of reduced cost of the employee's output.

The first two types of responsibility hold the employee accountable for the total value of his output in relation to the total value of the inputs delegated to him. They differ in whether resource diversions are prevented altogether or whether they are restricted to a determinate level. Explicit prices and a tax on the employee's cash net income are sufficiently precise when CPOR is imposed that the employee does not divert resources. When overall value responsibility is imposed, resource diversions are limited by the employer's costs of obtaining the employee's overall value productivity from another source or by imposing specific responsibility instead. There are two categories of overall value responsibility, namely, *incomplete pricing overall responsibility* (IPOR), and *nonpricing overall responsibility* (NPOR), which differ according to whether an accounting profit is explicitly attributed to the employee's production domain. When imposing specific responsibility an employer influences some of his employee's uses of individual resources in ways depending on cost effectiveness in the particular situation; the employee is not held accountable for his overall value productivity.

In the following description of each type of responsibility, the "employer" may be a managing employee or the funding authority. An employer can economize on information by delegating authority to impose responsibility, for example, when another employee has a relevant information cost advantage. The delegating employer's costs of employees' outputs can be lower as a result, and equilibrium output rates higher (see Chapter 7). However, as noted before, a managing employee's interests often conflict with his employer's, and he imposes responsibility in his employer's interest and yields the resulting benefits to his employer only insofar as he is required to by the responsibility placed on him. We now separately consider each of the three types of responsibility.

Complete pricing overall responsibility

Complete pricing overall responsibility (CPOR) is the already described set of prices and tax on (or supplement to) the employee's cash net income that in turn maximizes the component of the employer's net income that is attributable to the employee. Although this type of responsibility eliminates resource diversions entirely, it requires the employer to bear such high information costs that it is rarely, if ever, imposed. The following detailed discussion of the information requirements of this type of responsibility can be skipped by the reader who is mainly interested in the types of responsibility that are hypothesized to be actually in widespread use in organizations.

An understanding of CPOR and its information requirements illuminates the sources and some of the economic effects of resource diversions. An employer imposing CPOR must measure and attach a price to every individually variable characteristic of an employee's inputs and outputs having marginal value to him outside the employee's production domain that equals his cash equivalent of this marginal value. For example, each alternative application of the employee's skills and efforts that has such an external marginal value is measured and priced. The employer must also make sure that the employee maximizes his net income, after which the employer must tax any excess over or make up any deficit under his compensated opportunity cost, that is, the amount necessary to induce the employee to continue in his job.[5]

The employee leaves his job if there is a deficit of his net income below his compensated opportunity cost. If the employer does not tax any excesses of the employee's income from the organization to this opportunity cost or if he fails to attach the described price to each economically important characteristic of any input or output and correctly measure these resources, there are resource diversions. This can be seen as follows. The employer's net income decreases by the amount of any excess of the employee's income over his compensated opportunity cost. Any lack of measurement of a resource or absence of a price leads the employee to place it in uses according to the utility he derives from them. For example, if the employee lacks personal uses of an unpriced input (or input characteristic) that the employer in fact values and if the employee derives utility at the margin from applying it in production, it will be overutilized in the employer's interest (at his expense) so that its marginal value product is less than its marginal cost to the employer. But if the employee derives utility from personal uses of the input or does not derive utility at the margin from applying it in production, it will be underutilized in the employer's interest and its marginal value product will exceed its marginal cost to the employer.

What information about preferences and production domains must the employer hold to establish prices reflecting his best alternative uses of each input and output, to measure quantities of each input and output, and to adjust the employee's pretax net income to his compensated opportunity cost? We consider each of these categories of information separately.

Information required for the establishment of prices. The present discussion of pricing for CPOR deals with the case where variation in an employee's applications of inputs in his production domain does not affect the productivity of inputs or directly affect outputs in other employees' production domains. The more complex case where there are technological spillovers among production domains is analyzed in Chapter 4.[6]

Consider the following two categories of inputs. In the first category are inputs immediately available at a constant external market price plus any costs of purchasing, storage, inventory risk, and the like. Inputs in the second category are either fixed in quantity to the employer or are available to him at rising marginal cost whether from an external or internal supplier. We are concerned with the pricing of those second category inputs that could be used productively in multiple employees' production domains.

Pricing the first type of resource requires no information other than about variable bookkeeping and inventory costs and market prices. Correct prices for inputs in the second category that could contribute to multiple employees' outputs depend on their productivities in production domains. Let the marginal productivities of these second category resources be constant so as to make linear the constraint for each of these resources in which the sum of the amounts needed in the production of different employees' outputs is equated to the total amount of the resource at hand in the organization. Assume that the employer assigns a unit profit for every output and requires each employee to propose amounts of the outputs that he will produce. The employer then calculates the costs to other employees of each employee's production of his own outputs (resulting from his uses of inputs in the second category that they could use) and on the basis of this calculation revises the unit profit figure. If each employee maximizes his pretax net income at each step and the employer taxes this quantity to the employee's compensated opportunity cost, the decomposition method (Dantzig and Wolfe, 1960; see also Dantzig, 1963, chap. 23; Baumol and Fabian, 1964) would enable the employer in a finite number of steps to establish a set of prices that corresponds to a maximum of his total net income from all of his employees. Since the employer continually adjusts the employee's cash income to his compensated opportunity cost, any trade at the established prices of reduced cash income for reduced output produced by the employee is equivalent or profitable for the employer, and thus personal resource uses do not result in diversions.[7]

Although this procedure requires the employer to have information about the employee's preferences to adjust his income to his compensated opportunity cost, it might seem that use of the decomposition method at least enables the employer to avoid obtaining information about productivities in employees' production domains of inputs in the first category and of those inputs in the second category that are not productive in other employees' production domains. (He would need information about the assumed constant marginal productivities of inputs in the second category that are productive in multiple employees' production domains.) Note, however, the implications of the seemingly innocuous assumption that the employee maximizes his pretax net income. Whenever it is costly for an employee to obtain information about more efficient input substitutions in his production domain, he lacks incentive to obtain it when he knows that using it will result in his income being taxed back to his compensated opportunity cost. Thus, the employer must generally obtain information about the employee's production domain to ensure that the employee's pretax net income is maximized. It may be possible to reduce these information costs by allowing the employee to retain temporarily a fraction of the excesses of his net income over his compensated opportunity cost. Aside from the employer's foregoing these quantities and his costs of delay, he must obtain sufficient information about production domains to control the employee's in-kind benefits from resource diversions when his income is not taxed to his compensated opportunity cost.

When the employee directly faces internal or external demands for his outputs or supplies of his inputs, the employer must know about the alternative transactions the employee can make so he can price them according to the degree to which they serve his interest.[8] When there are multiple sources of demand for the employee's outputs or supplies of his inputs, the employer must learn about each. It may be necessary for the employer to observe each transaction to determine which alternative the employee has chosen.

In order for CPOR to maximize the funding authority's welfare, it must be imposed on all of an organization's employees. Also, there can be no monopoly pricing within the organization: intermediate outputs with downward sloping internal demands must be priced at demand, not marginal revenue. That is, the pretax profit maximization of each employee supplying an intermediate output is based on this rule being enforced.

Information required to measure an employee's quantity uses of inputs and outputs. An employer's costs of measuring the amounts of inputs that an employee uses and his delivery of outputs depends on their accessibility to measurement and the resources' intrinsic characteristics, such as their tangibility and size. The employee's skills and efforts are examples of resources that are difficult or infeasible for the employer to observe. Measuring the employee's uses of such inputs may also require information about his production domain.

In the case analyzed by Alchian and Demsetz (1972) where an employee's output is a contribution to a jointly produced output of multiple employees, it is ordinarily costly to observe each employee's contribution. Also, when multiple inputs are applied by an employee, it can be costly to observe his application of each input. When an employee directly delivers his output to a third party inside or outside the organization and he and the client negotiate intangible characteristics, the employer may have to undergo the expense of interviewing the client in order to measure the output.

Information required to determine an employee's compensated opportunity cost. An experimental, or trial-and-error, method of determining an employee's compensated opportunity cost is to raise the tax on (or reduce supplements to) an employee's net income until he gives notice, then reduce the tax slightly. The employee's net income would have to be readjusted whenever his nonpecuniary benefits from his job vary, as can occur, for example, when he responds to varying demands for his outputs. The desirability of such an experimental procedure is further diminished by the possibility of making a mistake and having to replace an employee who has committed himself to another job before giving notice. The cost of replacing an employee can be substantial when his production domain is internally designed. In an environment where incomes are mistakenly reduced below employees' compensated opportunity costs, employees would face uncertainty and undergo job searches, the costs of which would add to their compensated opportunity costs.

Alternatively, an employer might base income adjustments on information about preferences obtained from frequent conversations with employees about applying their skills and efforts. Such a procedure would be costly, and when employees realized the purpose of the conversations it would become infeasible.

In conclusion, it is costly to increase an employee's cash income to compensate exactly for distasteful applications of skills and efforts and to decrease it by just the right amount when these applications are pleasant. Basing an employee's cash income on external market characteristics – marketable skills and experience – is much less costly but inevitably leads employees' incomes to differ from their compensated opportunity costs.

An apparent shortcut to CPOR is to assign ownership interest so that an employee has, to some extent, the interests of an owner. If some capital resources applied within the employee's production domain could be sold or assigned to the employee, it would no longer be necessary to price the long-run effects of his skills and efforts on these resources' returns. However, the fundamental source of conflict of interests – the level of the employee's pecuniary and non-pecuniary income – would remain intact. Assigning ownership interest in the organization might be considered a possibility. However, the cost of transferring to an employee more than a small fractional ownership would usually considerably exceed the present value of his resource diversions; yet with only a small fraction of ownership, an increase in an employee's diversions has an insignificant effect on his returns to his ownership.[9]

Conclusions. Imposing CPOR ordinarily requires the employer to have information about the employee's production domain and preferences and often requires him to have information about clients' and suppliers' preferences. Thus, taking each production domain as a separate unit, resource allocation under CPOR is not informationally decentralized according to the concepts proposed by Hurwicz (1960b, 1969, 1972). We shall see that resource allocation is not informationally decentralized under the other types of responsibility either, although the employer chooses them because they give him much lower information costs. These lower costs, however, are reflected in employees' resource diversions. Interestingly, we shall see that when employees can divert resources they obtain information about other employees' preferences and production domains in order to pursue their own ends.

In the analyses of price and output determination of later chapters, resource allocation under other types of responsibility is often contrasted with that occurring when CPOR is imposed on all employees and demand prices are attached to intermediate outputs.

Overall value responsibility: Incomplete pricing overall
responsibility and nonpricing overall responsibility

The high costs of CPOR lead the employer to choose a less costly type of responsibility that limits employees' resource diversions to a positive, determinate level. These types include overall value responsibility and specific responsibility. Under these types of responsibility, the employee has a salary (and sometimes other cash income) which combined with his cash equivalent value of non-pecuniary benefits from his job, often exceeds his compensated opportunity cost. The determination of the employee's salary under overall value and specific responsibility is analyzed in Section C of this chapter.

The distinguishing feature of overall value responsibility is the employer's concern with the overall value productivity of the employee's production domain; he does not influence the employee's specific uses of particular resources. While higher resource diversions usually increase an employee's cash or in-kind income from his job, they reduce overall value productivity and increase the employer's cost of the employee's output. In response, the employer can take the following actions to limit these cost increases: (1) replace the employee; (2) change his policy and exercise influence over how the employee uses individual resources, that is, impose specific responsibility; and (3) find an alternative supply of the employee's output or make do without it such as by using a substitute. The alternative supply or substitute can be from outside the organization, from an existing supplier inside the organization, or via a different delegation of discretion over the parts of production functions represented by the employee's production domain, that is, a "reorganization."

The first action requires the employer to bear transition costs.

Assume that a new employee would derive personal gain from re-source diversions at the margin. Unless he wants to impress the employer to achieve a larger future gain (for example, a promotion), it would not be in this new employee's interest – once installed in the job – to make the employer's cost of his output any lower than those another employee was able to maintain. Thus, the employer impos-ing overall value responsibility generally succeeds in limiting his costs to those that result from taking the second or third possible action. Which of these two is preferable depends on the relative costs of imposing specific responsibility and using an alternative supply source. When the second action is preferred, the employer imposes overall value responsibility up to some critical value of his cost that will trigger him to impose specific responsibility. If the employee is better off under overall value responsibility, he controls his resource diversions to keep the employer's cost below this critical level. (Of course, if the employee is worse off under overall value responsibil-ity, he raises the employer's cost of his output until specific responsi-bility is placed on him.)

Alternatively, the employer may find it more economical to take the third action, which ordinarily would substantially reduce the employee's total income from the organization. The employer's cost of the employee's output on which he bases the decision whether to take this action is referred to as the employee's *output replacement cost*. This is the cost of the employer's best alternative to having an output provided via the employee's production domain. It includes the ex-pense of obtaining an identical output with an alternative supply arrangement, or the compensating amount that makes the employer equally well off without the employee's output. With respect to this compensating amount, the example emphasized in the analysis of Chapter 4 is the employer's minimum combined cost both of obtain-ing a quantity of an imperfect substitute and of making the neces-sary adjustments of resource uses so that his welfare remains the same as if he were using the employee's output. However, in another example, the employer's best alternative to using his employee's out-put as an input is to produce another output himself. Here the compensating amount is that which makes the employer equally well off producing the other output.

An employee's output replacement cost is distinguished from his *personal replacement cost*, the cost of replacing the employee with another in the same production domain.[10] Output replacement cost (like personal replacement cost) has transitional and longer-term components. Transitional components of output replacement cost are imposed by disruption of production, temporary use of less cost effective substitutes, recruiting new personnel and establishing new supplier relationships, and any resulting obsolescence or required acquisition of equipment. The continuing components of output replacement cost are continuing differences in costs of obtaining the same output or of obtaining a substitute and adjusting resource uses so as to be equally well off with it. There are variable and fixed amounts within the continuing component of an employee's output replacement cost that respectively do and do not depend on the rate of his output. In assessing an employee's output replacement cost, the employer need not assume that the continuing component of this cost will remain the same in the future; he may, for example, assume that costs will grow at a rate based on his past experience with other employees and alternative suppliers. Competition can trigger and influence the employer's estimate. Marris (1964) and others have mentioned the threat of takeovers in limiting the discretion of corporate managers, and Alchian and Demsetz (1972) formulate the more general hypothesis that "Incumbent [jointly productive] members will be constrained by threats of replacement by outsiders . . . ." (p. 781). Competitive offers are not necessarily made, however; and if they are, the employer cannot necessarily enforce them. (See Section C of this chapter.)

The *allowable limit* on the resource diversions of an employee under overall value responsibility is the lesser of his output replacement cost and the level of the employer's cost at which specific responsibility is imposed, minus what would be the employee's cost under CPOR of the output delivered to his employer.

Output replacement costs and critical cost values at which the employer switches to specific responsibility create incentives for employers and employees to allocate resources to obtaining information. An employer's estimates of these costs will ordinarily vary with the technical information he has at hand plus his knowledge about alternative supply opportunities. In turn, this information depends on his own experiences and interests, as well as any contacts he has with potential suppliers. If indications are that these alternative costs exceed his current cost of an employee's output, the employer will not devote resources to estimating them carefully and he may have only a vague idea of their magnitudes. However, if he perceives that one of these alternative costs no longer exceeds his current cost, the employer has an incentive to obtain a more precise estimate. If the employee has a cost advantage in estimating the costs of the employer's alternatives, he will communicate information about these costs when it appears that the employer's estimate is lower than the actual magnitudes. When an employee lacking an estimate of the employer's alternative cost of his output observes his employer devoting resources to obtaining an accurate estimate of this cost or actually taking first steps to select the alternative, he has a warning to reduce the employer's current cost of his output.

A managing employee's recognition that employees are approaching critical values and his resulting decision to switch from placing overall value to specific responsibility on them are described in a case provided by Lawrence et al. (1976, pp. 124–5). In this example, the employees who worked a packaging machine usually produced at somewhat less than capacity in order to draw overtime pay. When a new foreman took over and reprimanded them for the slowdown, the crew retaliated with a further reduction in their rate of output and fed the wrapping machine improperly. The foreman's supervisor noticed the decrease in output and, in the foreman's words, gave

orders to weigh each roll of paper before we started wrapping each night and to weigh it again when we finished. I was to record the weights on tabulation control sheets kept in his office. That night, before starting work, I told the crew what had happened and what [was] said to me . . . I had no more incidents of this sort, and the crew continued to meet the output schedule as they had previously.

The crew thus accepted the warning to reduce the employer's cost of output. If instead the supervisor (or his superiors) had taken steps to have an outside contractor take care of packaging or had arranged for packaging to be performed as a by-product of manufacturing, the example would have illustrated employees' raising employers' costs above output replacement costs.

The preceding example also illustrates how an employee working under overall value responsibility has a reserve of excess capacity in the sense that he does not have to supply his employer the quantity of output that he could. One can find varied work situations where employees use such a reserve to increase their welfare. For example, an employee working on a quota system may be able to reserve output and avoid delivering more than required. A claims adjustor noted that

some claims are harder to handle than others, but as far as the quota is concerned they all count the same. So I always try to keep a few easy cases aside to handle at the end of the month if it looks like I won't be able to meet the quota without them. I try not to turn in too many cases in any month or they'll always expect me to work that hard (Sayles and Strauss, 1966, p. 382).

Employees will often conceal productivity improvements that they create within their production domains in order to avoid employers' reducing critical costs at which they would switch to specific responsibility or replace their outputs via reorganization. In one case where a new tool was developed that increased productivity by 50 percent, the inventor (Dufresne) and designer-draftsman (Latour)

decided not to submit the idea as a suggestion but to keep it as the property of their group . . . [They] also felt that there were definite hazards to the group if their secret were disclosed. They feared that once the tool became company property, its efficiency might lead to layoff of some members in their group, or at least make work less tolerable by leading to an increased quota at a lower price per unit . . . Through informal agreement with their fellow workers, Latour and Dufresne "pegged production" at an efficiency rate that in their opinion would not arouse management's suspicion or lead to a restudy of the job, with possible cutting of the rate. This enabled them to earn an extra 10% incentive earnings (Lawrence et al., 1976, pp. 140–1).

The remaining productivity increase was used in ways that directly increased the employees' utility.

The capability of employees to deliver more output than required has been documented in the Soviet economy. According to Berliner (1957, pp. 82–3):

Finding ways of keeping the plan targets low is apparently no great problem. Mention may be made of such practices as concealing some output and of not overfulfilling the plan beyond a certain point in order to maintain a reserve for the next planning period. Another technique is underreporting actual production capacity. This can be done in a variety of ways, the particular choice depending upon the nature of the productive process . . . New elements of slack are added as production techniques are improved and the full potential of these improvements is not reported . . . In the absence of changes, the ministry gradually increases its knowledge of the actual situation in its enterprises and it is more difficult for the enterprise to conceal resources. But when changes occur, the ministry is more dependent upon the information which the enterprises submit to it . . . Within the enterprise each official seeks to maintain a little factor of safety unknown to his immediate superior. The consequence is a cumulative discrepancy between actual capacity and plan targets. The senior management, which negotiates with the officials of the ministry over the final plan, often does not know how large a safety factor actually exists in the enterprise as a whole.

Employees under overall value responsibility can usually raise their benefits from resource diversions by increasing efficiency within their production domains. (See Chapter 4.) When benefits from resource diversions may be taken in cash, the employee chooses in-kind benefits only when he values them more than cash equal to their cost to his employer. However, a third party's (e.g., stockholders') information costs about resource diversions are often higher when benefits from them must be taken in kind. Another reason for this restriction is that it often enables employers to exchange increases in employees' cash incomes for net decreases in their resource diversions.

We now separately consider the two types of overall value responsibility: incomplete pricing overall responsibility (IPOR) and nonpricing overall responsibility (NPOR).

Incomplete pricing overall responsibility. Under IPOR cash prices are attached to some but not all of an employee's inputs and outputs, and the employer treats the employee as a profit center by attributing a cash net income to him and his production domain. Some inputs and outputs (and their characteristics) are not given cash prices by the employer in order to make it more costly for third parties to make inferences about them or simply because it is more costly than worthwhile to establish explicit prices. When such resources have differing external market prices or divergent explicit prices in other parts of the organization, the employer's implicit prices guide their usage. (The employer's motivations for implicit prices are discussed in more detail later in the discussion of NPOR.) The reason is that the employer holds the employee accountable for those unexplicitly priced resources for which he individually or in combination has a conscious marginal valuation, and the employee thus has an incentive to infer these implicit values. However, often some inputs or outputs will neither be priced explicitly nor have implicit values at the margin because of the cost of attributing them to particular employees. Cash benefits from resource diversions can be restricted by holding the employee's cash income to a market-determined salary. Alternatively, higher salaries can be paid, and the employee can be given a bonus or a share of his production domain's attributed net income.

IPOR has two basic variants depending on whether (1) the outputs produced by the employee or (2) the financial return that is attributed to his production domain, are the outputs of primary importance to the employer. In the latter case – when the financial return is what is most important to the employer – output replacement consists of the employer's alternative opportunities for receiving a return on the resources he delegates to the employee, whether by deploying these resources elsewhere or by seeing to it that they are managed differently. Lacking a need to learn about alternative sources of supply, the employer's information costs for imposing this variant of IPOR are ordinarily much lower than when the employee's produced outputs are what is important to the employer (variant 1). Often in practice, however, both variants of IPOR are applied to the same employee because the employer has a demand for some of the employee's outputs while others are sold to third parties.

IPOR can be imposed in many different situations and can be tailored to particular circumstances. Alternative restrictions can be placed on inputs the employee may purchase. For example, varying degrees of justification of each purchase can be required. Also, the employee can be given different restrictions on the contracts he may make that obligate his employer or the organization. An employee can be given restrictions on the prices he can establish for his outputs, or these prices can be set for him. The cash net income attributed to him and his production domain may be taxed in various ways, but not below the lesser of output replacement cost or the critical value of the employer's cost at which he imposes specific responsibility, given the employer's desired rate of the employee's output. IPOR can be placed on employees producing either intermediate or final outputs, and alternate returns on resources are especially likely to constitute output replacement cost in the latter case. Vancil's study (1979) is a rich source on the variety of ways in which IPOR is imposed in large corporations.

Because the employer does not explicitly price all resources, an inexperienced employee might mistakenly fail to give weight to the employer's implicit prices, which fully compete with explicit prices. Vancil's concept of "organizational climate," which is interpreted here to constitute the various means by which restrictions are placed on the autonomy of corporate divisional managers under IPOR, is relevant. Divisional managers were found by Vancil to rely heavily on "personal interactions" with their superiors in determining the rates of their outputs and their uses of inputs. Vancil (1979, p. 127) provides this illustration:

The reason managers travel great distances to have face-to-face contact is that written or spoken words cannot convey the entire message – body language and other forms of nonverbal behavior still play a critical role in building and maintaining effective interpersonal relationships: "When I told the boss what I'd done, all he said was 'that's OK,' but he frowned a little and squirmed around in his chair."

Bower (1970, p. 55) provides another example of the importance of implicit prices:

The accounting system treated depreciation as a corporate expense thereby putting a premium on new facilities when return on investment criteria were used . . . Thus while the manual of Capital Appropriations Procedure explained that an important objective of the company was the maximization of return on stockholders' equity, there were other stronger influences on the decisions of subordinate managers.

Because there is a cash net income attributed to the employee's production domain under IPOR, this type of responsibility superficially resembles CPOR. However, IPOR differs from CPOR in the major respect that the employer does not tax the employee's cash income to his compensated opportunity cost. Also, some inputs or outputs (or characteristics) are only implicitly priced and others not priced at all. The employer's failure to price resources implicitly, if not explicitly, and to tax the employee's income to his compensated opportunity cost results from no lack of desire to do so but from the high costs of doing so.[11]

Klein et al. (1978) analyze a case where an independent suppliers' output is purchased under conditions that can become similar to IPOR based on output replacement cost being imposed on an employee. In this case it would be very costly for the buyer to specify fully in a contract the characteristics he would want the supplier's output to have under every possible contingency, and see to it that the contract is enforced. Instead of going to this expense, the buyer pays a price over an extended period that is high enough to offset some level of expected short-term gain that the seller might achieve by interrupting supply or reducing its quality. To minimize his cost of full compliance, the seller has the incentive to obtain detailed information about the buyer's demand. Given the size of the premium and the expected short-term gain to the supplier from reneging, the "parties to a contract know exactly when and how much a contract will be broken" (p. 305). If it subsequently becomes clear that competitive demands on the external supplier will not arise during the contract period, his expected rent effectively gives the buyer authority over him. However, the buyer would not have a free hand in renegotiating the premium or requiring a larger rate of output than had been agreed upon. Assuming that there are no effects of other business between the parties on this transaction, the independent supplier can charge the buyer an amount equal to his output replacement cost.[12] This cost can be large if there are no available close substitutes for the supplier's output or if substitutes can be obtained only at premium prices.

This analysis raises the following question: How does the organization select between internal and external suppliers in such cases? The choice is partly determined by whether there would be favorable or unfavorable technological spillovers with other production domains if the external supplier were within the organization, as well as by any resulting possibilities for more intensive use of indivisible inputs. Aside from these considerations, the costs and benefits of placing resource responsibility on an internal supplier provide the answer. If, given the expected competing demands on an external supplier, it would be more economical to obtain the output via responsibility imposed on an internal supplier, the option of obtaining supply internally would be chosen.

Nonpricing overall responsibility. Under NPOR the employer does not explicitly account for his cash net income attributable to the employee and his production domain, and typically none of the employee's outputs is explicitly measured and priced by the employer. Yet the employee must deliver a combination of outputs and output characteristics having the same value as the employer can obtain with the employee's budget from an alternative source within or outside the organization or by imposing specific responsibility. Within his discretion over his outputs and their characteristics, the employee selects among the feasible ones that are equally valuable to the employer the combination that is least costly for him to produce. As under IPOR, the employee has an incentive to concern himself with the productivity of each input applied within his production domain because his benefits from resource diversions are a residual that accrues to him.

There are two reasons for the employer not to apply separate measures and prices to each characteristic of every output. First, the costs of establishing and communicating explicit prices can be high. By being vague about his intensity of demand for each output and characteristic variation he makes the employee bear the costs of determining his (the employer's) implicit valuations. The second reason is that third parties' information costs about prices are considerably higher when they are implicit. Specifically, an employee's output might represent a resource diversion of his employer. For example, an employer may not want his actual quality standards to be known. One employee quoted by Lawrence et al.

(1976) stated: "The other day [a foreman] had a meeting with the workers to talk about quality. After that an employee brought to his attention a defect in some products. He answered, 'Send it out anyway.' And they had just finished talking to us about quality" (p. 408).

NPOR is especially likely to be imposed on an employee whose outputs are identifiable but intangible and have many possible characteristics. Employees who supply managerial services in governmental and private nonprofit organizations are frequently under NPOR, as are employees who manage parts of corporations that are not profit centers. NPOR is often imposed on those providing professional and specialized technical services. Employers are usually either continually concerned with such employees' overall value productivity or become actively concerned when this productivity decreases to "unacceptable" levels.

When the choice of NPOR is motivated by raising information costs for third parties, the restriction of largely in-kind benefits from resource diversions is especially likely.

Specific responsibility

An employer imposing specific responsibility does not hold the employee accountable for the value of his outputs in relation to the value of the inputs delegated to him. Instead, he places incentives on the employee to make uses of resources that are in his interest and to avoid other resource uses that are not in his interest. These incentives result from rewarding or penalizing some uses of resources, controlling the conditions under which particular resources may be used, and providing complements for desired activities and substitutes for those to be discouraged. Examples are required hours on the job, monitoring an employee's activities, spot checking inventories or rates of production of selected outputs, attaching prestige to certain tasks, and providing some employees with convenient recreation facilities. Resource diversions result when it is more costly to the employer than worthwhile to exercise complete control in his interest over all of the employee's uses of resources.

When imposing specific responsibility the employer faces a number of options regarding each resource under an employee's discretion. Should he control any of the employee's uses of it? If so, which should he select among numerous alternative means of directly or indirectly influencing these uses? These are referred to as the alternative *applications of specific responsibility* available to the employer. Each application can vary in thoroughness, for instance, in detail of monitoring, and the employer must decide the most cost effective application in each case. The employer's optimal imposition of specific responsibility is shown in Chapter 4 to depend on (1) the employer's estimated marginal benefits or costs resulting from the employee's alternative uses of each resource; (2) the alternative applications of specific responsibility that are feasible for influencing these uses; and (3) the behavioral effects and costs of each.

The optimal imposition of specific responsibility is highly sensitive to the particular circumstances. When production domains are externally designed, the employer's costs of controlling uses of resources are usually lower than with internal design because it is easier to interpret the employee's uses of resources. Similarly, it is less costly to control uses of tangible resources than of intangible ones. It is especially difficult for an employer to elicit thought and creativity in his interest with specific responsibility. The less costly to influence the use of a resource and the more valuable to the employer the use, the stronger the incentive he places on the use.

With specific responsibility, the employer devotes more attention to the nature of inputs he allows the employee to use than with overall value responsibility. For example, it may be uneconomical to delegate a potentially productive input because without prohibitively costly monitoring it would not be used in the employer's interest. In turn, the employer's concern with the nature of allowed inputs affects how outputs are produced.

Even when employees have information cost advantages that would lead to internal design under overall value responsibility, specific responsibility brings incentives for employers to obtain some information about employees' production domains. Employees have weaker incentives to learn about their own production domains than under overall value responsibility.

An employee under specific responsibility is frequently influenced by the imposition of overall value responsibility at a level that includes his output along with those of other employees. Thus, multiple employees under specific responsibility often face incentives to concern themselves with their combined resource diversions. Their coordination of their activities for this and other purposes is analyzed in Chapter 7.

*A note on determinants of cash and in-kind components
of an employee's budget*

An employee's budget is defined to include any cash designated for
him to purchase inputs plus the employer's cash-equivalent marginal
value of those resources delegated in kind that he attributes to the
employee. An employee's budget need not include all the resources
he uses because some resources can be more costly to attribute than
is worthwhile. For example, corporations often do not attribute to
divisions their uses of corporate support staff, and universities infre-
quently attribute library usage to departments. Because he compares
the employee's budget, as defined, with his value of the employee's
output, an employer imposing overall value responsibility is more
generally concerned with attributing inputs to employees than is an
employer imposing specific responsibility.

The same factors that influence whether employees' outputs are
not explicitly priced also influence whether some or all resources
within their budgets are delegated in kind. By delegating inputs in
kind a managing employee can avoid costs of establishing and communicating explicit prices and raise third parties' information costs.
For the latter reason, a managing employee's own employer might
require him to establish cash budgets for his employee's inputs. In
such cases, however, differing implicit prices, not the cash prices,
govern uses of these resources. An employer imposing specific responsibility often finds that it is more economical to influence employees' uses of some inputs than others. His resulting incentive to
exercise control over the particular inputs employees may use thus
reduces or eliminates the cash component of budgets under this
type of responsibility. An employee under overall value responsibility must bear the costs of inferring his employer's implicit values of
resources attributed to him that are delegated in kind or whose
cash prices differ from their implicit values. It is helpful to keep in
mind that even under IPOR part of an employee's budget can be
in kind. There is a wide variety of alternative and often arbitrary
means of attributing an employee's uses of resources that are
shared with other employees, as has been shown for example by
Vancil (1979).

An employee's own skills, energies, and abilities are important
inputs that can be used in separately variable quantities. The separate flows of these economically important resources must be measured and priced under CPOR when for the employer they would
have value at the margin in production domains other than the

employee's. In actual practice usually only an employee's salary is attributed to him.

C The determination of cash salaries under overall value and specific responsibility and the supply of labor to the organization

Many skills are specific to employees' own production domains and thus are not marketable. In comparison with the potential numbers of these specific skills, there are usually many fewer characteristics of an organization's employees that are in demand in the external market. An employee's marketable labor characteristics are usually limited to his education, general skills, and measures of experience that are common to many production domains other than his own. Such measures might, for example, include numbers of employees supervised, types of equipment used, overall performance ratings, the nonunique characteristics of his outputs (e.g., accounting, sales, or inspection), and the nonunique characteristics of outputs to which his own outputs contribute as inputs.

I assume that (except when imposing CPOR) employers economize on information by specifying initial qualifications for tasks within the organization's production domains largely in terms of these externally marketable characteristics.[13] When the organization's market labor demands are thus based on these characteristics, salary schedules are usually much less diverse than employees' actual economically important skills.

A cohort of employees initially hired by an organization can receive randomly different assignments to production domains and thereby acquire differing experiences leading to diverse specific skills, all the while receiving identical salaries. However, because of differences in their production domains and in employers' related optimal imposition of responsibility, the employees' total incomes including personal benefits from resource diversions can differ substantially. In time, differences in cash salaries can also emerge because diverse general skills are mastered by employees as a result of working in different production domains. Employees can also have different opportunities through collective bargaining or other forms of coordination to exchange reduced in-kind benefits from resource diversions for higher cash incomes.

We now consider the relationship between employees' benefits from resource diversions and the supply of labor to the organization. This issue is important because if employees accept lower wages in the expectation of benefiting from resource diversions, the lower wages themselves reduce diversions. Although diversions would not be eliminated without the other elements of CPOR, they could perhaps become small in many cases.

Three separate issues determine the extent to which benefits from resource diversions affect wages. First, how do resource diversions motivate potential employees' labor supply? Second, what are the employer's costs of replacing incumbent employees? Finally, would a new employee have fewer resource diversions allowed by the responsibility facing him than the previous employee after establishing himself in his new job?

When benefits from resource diversions can be and are taken in cash, and cash incomes are publicized, potential employees face relatively low costs of information about incumbent employees' total incomes. However, when diversion benefits are not or cannot be taken in cash, it can be costly to obtain information about employees' total incomes. Such benefits as chauffered limousines, lodges, or monumental buildings are, of course, relatively observable. However, it can be very difficult for prospective employees to discern such benefits as leisure on the job, the exercise of power, and the production of undemanded outputs unless employees derive utility from displaying their personal satisfactions from them. It is relatively economical for managing employees to prevent the most obvious in-kind diversion benefits; they have the incentive to do so whenever such benefits would reflect negatively on their own performances.

It seems reasonable to assume, nonetheless, that prospective employees make rough estimates of in-kind personal benefits from resource diversions. What motivating effect might such estimates have on their labor supply? Since a prospective employee may have little basis for estimating his particular pattern of job assignments, he will probably realize that his estimate most likely does not reflect the positions within the organization that he would actually experience. Further, there may be a considerable time delay from the date of initial employment in the organization before an employee can achieve his highest benefits from resource diversions. When prospective employees have positive discount rates and are averse to risk, the motivational effect of their estimates of benefits from resource diversions can be small. Another consideration is that when in-kind benefits from resource diversions yield less utility than their cash value to employers, they have a reduced motivating effect on labor supply. An offsetting factor is that, as many observers have noted, individuals most attracted to the particular types of in-kind income from an organization will be heavily represented among those supplying labor to it.

Consider now the possibility that a prospective employee with the same compensated opportunity cost as an incumbent's either offers to work at the same wage with the promise to reduce the employer's cost, or offers to accept a lower wage. In deciding whether to accept the offer, the employer must take account of both the costs of replacing the incumbent employee and whether his total cost including the resource diversions of a new employee would actually turn out to be smaller. Personal replacement cost prevents him from taking the offer lightly; the offer is acceptable only if the prospective employee's resource diversions would be lower enough to offset this cost. A prospective employee receiving the same wage would be willing to create the impression or explicitly promise smaller resource diversions than the incumbent. In fact, if feasible, he would make a binding commitment. However, once the incumbent has been replaced, the new employee would usually be going against his own self-interest to reduce his own resource diversions below those allowed by responsibility. (An exception occurs when an employee perceives that reducing his diversions below this amount will increase his promotion opportunities.)

If the same overall value responsibility imposed on the original employee were to be imposed on the new employee, or if these employees were to have allowable resource diversions up to the same large enough personal replacement cost under specific responsibility (see Chapter 4), the employer's benefit from a lower salary for the new employee would be offset by the increased amount of other diversions allowable to him. In contrast, labor market competition can reduce the resource diversions of employees under specific responsibility whose personal replacement costs are low.

D   Issues affecting the employer's optimal choices in imposing resource responsibility constraints

The following discussion first considers a number of influences on the employer's optimal choice of responsibility and subsequently focuses on the effects of costly information on this choice.

Influences on the employer's optimal choice

Each type of responsibility requires the employer to bear some costs that are fixed and others that vary with the employee's output. For

CPOR these include fixed costs of establishing those prices that do not vary with output and the variable costs of measuring resources used and outputs delivered, recalculating compensated opportunity cost as it varies with output, and adjusting those prices that also vary with output. Determining rates of overall value productivity at which to replace an employee's output or to impose specific responsibility on him can be a fixed cost of overall value responsibility. The variable costs of this type of responsibility include attributing inputs to the employee and assessing his outputs. Specific responsibility requires fixed costs of choosing and establishing the particular applications used, each of which has variable costs of continuing operation.

In a given situation, the costs of imposing alternative types and variants of responsibility, in relation to the effectiveness of each in reducing his costs of employees' outputs, determine an employer's choice among them. Relative costs and effectiveness of the alternatives vary importantly with characteristics of the employee's production domain and of his inputs and outputs; these characteristics establish the employer's cost of estimating overall value productivity, and determine the cost effectiveness of each alternative application of specific responsibility. The lower the costs of measuring overall value productivity, that is, of identifying an employee's outputs and attributing to him the inputs he uses, the more cost effective it is to impose overall value responsibility. The need to elicit creative efforts from employees, and employees' possession of large information cost advantages about their production domains also favors this type of responsibility. When overall value responsibility is imposed, it is more likely to be based on output replacement rather than the threat of imposing specific responsibility when there are cost-effective alternative means of producing the employee's output, competitive bids from potential suppliers, or a ready supply of reasonably close substitutes for this output.

Uncertainty about changes in demands for outputs or supplies of inputs or about the future flow of new production techniques usually weighs in favor of overall value responsibility because of its superior incentives for the employee to adjust favorably (with respect to the employer's net income) to the changes.[14] (See Chapter 7.) Uncertainty can have offsetting effects, however. For example, when there are shifts in demand, any necessary recalculations of output replacement cost or costs at which to impose specific responsibility can be more costly than the required readjustments in applications of specific responsibility.

The employer's optimal imposition of responsibility is interrelated with his optimal choices of suborganization[15] and inputs and outputs allowed. An employer also takes account of expected future resource diversions. For example, he may devote more resources to limit employees' investments that raise future diversions (analyzed in Chapter 7) at the cost of spending less to limit those that occur in the present.

A managing employee's employer can find it in his interest to influence how he imposes responsibility. When an employer imposes specific responsibility, he is more affected by how his employee would in turn impose responsibility than if this employee were under overall value responsibility. When variations in the resource diversions of the employees of a managing employee under overall value responsibility do not affect the critical cost at which his output would be replaced or he would be placed under specific responsibility, they do not affect net income of the managing employee's employer except in cases where spillovers affecting other managing employees are important. An employer can often economically evaluate a managing employee's imposition of specific responsibility by a modest extension of the specific responsibility already in place.

The costs of information to third parties, say, the funding authority and regulators, about the incidences of costs and benefits among an organization's employees, suppliers, and clientele are usually lower under overall value responsibility and when IPOR instead of NPOR is chosen.

Effects of costly information about returns to alternative types of responsibility on the employer's choice[16]

This discussion argues that under particular assumptions an employer's choice between specific and overall value responsibility is biased in favor of the former. It can be passed over by the reader with no loss of continuity.

In order to make an informed choice, an employer must obtain costly information about returns to alternative types of responsibility. However, he faces uncertainty as to the usefulness of particular expenditures on information in estimating returns. In the following paragraphs we shall consider how costly information of uncertain usefulness affects the employer's choices among alternative types of responsibility. I take the simplest case where the employer's net income attributable to his employees is in cash and his utility function with respect to money is strictly concave; that is, from any given amount of money, he derives less utility from an additional quantity of money than he loses from the sacrifice of an equal amount. Corresponding to every feasible variant of each type of responsibility, there is an estimated density function of his cash net income. These distributions vary with the amount of relevant information that he holds. How does he select the type of responsibility that has the most favorable estimated density function of cash net income?

Two offsetting forces affect the employer's expenditures on information. These expenditures directly reduce his utility while additional relevant information increases his expected utility via improved estimates of returns. The concept of stochastic dominance[17] enables us to determine the employer's optimal expenditures by analyzing the expected monetary outcomes that result from more information.

Consider two density functions of the employer's cash net income for alternative types of responsibility that are described by their means and variances. It is well known that if both have the same mean, the one with the lower variance is preferred under the assumption we have made about the employer's utility function. Similarly, a density function with a higher mean is preferred among two with the same variance. The concept of stochastic dominance makes it possible to make more general statements because it establishes preference orderings among density functions that do not depend on the employer's particular weighting of means and variances so long as his utility function is strictly concave. That is, it permits us to rank alternative situations without direct reference to a specific utility function. For example, we can use stochastic dominance to evaluate choices between density functions where one has both a lower mean and variance than another or where these functions cannot be described by mean and variance alone. Stochastic dominance does, however, require us to analyze differences in cumulative density functions.

As already implied, stochastic dominance is defined in terms of the areas under density functions of the employer's estimated cash net income. These areas can most conveniently be considered in terms of each distribution's cumulative density function (CDF), which expresses the employer's estimated probability that his cash net income will be less than or equal to specified values. Consider CDFs plotted with the employer's cash net income on the x axis and probability on the y axis. If one CDF is lower than another for some possible values of cash benefits and nowhere above the other, the theorems of stochastic dominance prove that this lower CDF is preferred by the employer if his utility function is strictly concave.[18] Intuitively this outcome is plausible, since it implies that an employer prefers those types of responsibility that reduce the likelihood of low returns.

We assume that the employer seeks to select a type of responsibility whose CDF is partly below and nowhere above the CDFs for alternatives, that is, he seeks to reduce the probability of small net income attributable to the employee. Such a selection requires him to make choices as to whether and how to acquire costly information that shifts his estimated CDFs. When he spends on information about a type of responsibility, the new CDF, for example, may or may not turn out to be below the previous one. If it is below this CDF, it may not be lower enough to justify the cost of the information.

Because specific responsibility has many separate applications – like monitoring or enforcing work hours, and variants on each – any feasible application ordinarily involves a modest cost in relation to the total cost of specific responsibility. I assume, therefore, that the employer expects small successive expenditures on information about specific responsibility will reliably yield modest downward shifts of the CDF for this type of responsibility. However, except when IPOR is imposed with a rate-of-return criterion for replacement or the employer receives enforceable competitive offers from alternative suppliers of the employee's input, overall value responsibility requires making an estimate of output replacement cost or the critical cost at which it is more economical to impose specific responsibility. This can be a sizable undertaking. To determine the latter cost, the employer must estimate his net income from all of the applications of specific responsibility that he would find worthwhile. If he has not actually imposed specific responsibility on the employee, small expenditures on information about individual applications may not improve these estimates appreciably; a large expenditure on multiple applications of specific responsibility would then be needed to shift the CDF for overall value responsibility. The employer may not have an expectation whether the initial CDF would shift up or down as a result of this expenditure.

Regarding output replacement cost, there are multiple means of obtaining an employee's output or a substitute. For example, the means of supply might be combining all or part of the employee's production domain with others, relying on other production domains elsewhere in the organization or external sources. A substantial expenditure to learn about one means of output replacement can yield a very different CDF than the same expenditure on another means. However, small expenditures may not yield prior information about the relative positions of these CDFs. If so, the employer faces a large gamble in selecting the order in which to evaluate alternative means of output replacement. For example, evaluation of one means might shift up the CDF, whereas evaluation of another shifts the CDF down.

Under the conditions described, the employer not yet imposing responsibility spends more on evaluating specific than overall value responsibility when their initial CDF's are identical. Due to his strictly concave utility function, he first devotes resources to evaluating specific responsibility. If these initial expenditures on information shift the CDF for specific responsibility downward, he must then expect correspondingly larger returns to overall value responsibility. Because of the relatively large and risky expenditures on information about this type of responsibility, he may not evaluate it at all. If his initial expenditures turn out to shift up the CDF for specific responsibility, he is more likely to evaluate overall value responsibility. However, the strict concavity of his utility function makes him willing to make the relatively large and risky expenditures on information to evaluate this method equally only when he expects that there will be a larger downward shift of its CDF.

In conclusion, information costs and strictly concave utility functions combine to produce a bias for the selection of specific responsibility rather than overall value responsibility.

Cases where overall value responsibility and specific responsibility are imposed together

An employee can be under both specific and overall value responsibility, and depending on how thoroughly one type of responsibility supplements the other, the resulting incentives can be largely characteristic of either.

The employee's producing two different outputs[19] (or output characteristics) with variable relative rates of production can result in his being under both types of responsibility. Incentives of both types of responsibility influence the production of each output when they are jointly produced.

An employer might impose both types of responsibility because, although he prefers overall value responsibility, resource diversions involving particular uses of resources are highly visible to third parties. For example, he may appear to his superiors to be improperly placing responsibility on his employees if certain benefits from resource diversions are highly visible. He may thus bear extra costs of specific responsibility vis-à-vis the relevant resource uses. The extra incentives have little effect when they involve uses of resources that are relatively unimportant in production.

Another example is the case where the employer intends to switch to specific responsibility at some level of his cost of the employee's output. Such an employer might find it worthwhile to experiment with applications of specific responsibility in order to refine his estimate of the critical value of this cost.

When the same types of resources are used both by employees on whom specific responsibility is placed and by those on whom overall value responsibility is placed, it may be less costly to impose specific responsibility on all employees' uses of such resources.

The employer's costs of attributing inputs to particular employees and their production domains can also lead to both types of responsibility being imposed. For example, it may be more costly than worthwhile to attribute to employees their uses of indivisible resources shared with other employees, or of intangible resources such as the skills of other employees. The employer imposing overall value responsibility vis-à-vis the attributed inputs may supplementally impose specific responsibility to uses of the other inputs. The employee will have incentives of both types of responsibility.[20]

Finally, as already noted, overall value responsibility based on output replacement alternatives is frequently imposed on a combination of employees under specific responsibility who together produce a readily measurable output. The output replacement limit can be less than the sum of resource diversions allowed by specific responsibility, and if so, the employees are affected by the incentives of both types of responsibility.

CHAPTER 4

Short-run resource allocation under fixed budgets

This and the next two chapters analyze the resource allocation behavior of individual employees and of their organizations in the "short run." The short run is a time period within which current investment behavior does not affect resource allocation. Two types of past investments determine the capital stock underlying the organization's short-run productive activity. The first and more obvious includes the organization's plant and equipment and its employees' skills. The second consists of those investments analyzed in Chapter 7 that determine the division of the organization's production functions into production domains, the information held by employees about production domains, the placing of resource responsibility on employees, and the means by which employees voluntarily coordinate themselves. In the short run all the results of both types of past investments are given and fixed.

This chapter first analyzes resource allocation under overall value and specific responsibility, making the simplifying assumption that there are no technological spillovers among employees' production domains. For each of these two types of responsibility a separate section explains how the equilibrium quantities of an employee's outputs are determined, derives the employee's and his employer's costs of these outputs, determines the employee's uses of each input and output, and derives the implicit prices that he attaches to these resources. The employee's and his employer's demands for information about production domains and preferences are also explained. Resource allocation under these two types of responsibility is contrasted with that occurring under CPOR. A subsequent section relaxes the assumption that there are no technological spillovers among production domains and analyzes the incentives under each type of responsibility for employers and employees to coordinate their actions in relation to these spillovers. The last section summarizes employees' incentives to obtain and interpret information about production domains and preferences, and describes the resulting implications for the dispersion of information in an organization.

68

A   Resource allocation with a fixed budget and no
     spillovers under overall value responsibility

A simple model with only one output and two inputs is initially used
to analyze much of the resource allocation occurring within the production domain of an employee under overall value responsibility.
In this model the employee's cost of producing his output is assumed to be lower than his employer's cost of using an alternative
source of the same output or an equivalent substitute output. I also
assume that the employer possesses the authority to select one of
these alternatives or to switch to imposing specific responsibility on
his employee. The employee's budget can be cash restricted to the
purchase of a defined set of resources, or an allocation of quantities
of particular resources that his employer attributes to him, or a
combination of both.

*Analysis of economic behavior under
overall value responsibility*

Consider an employee who produces (or makes a determinate contribution to) a single intermediate or final output Q with two inputs
X_1 and X_2 delegated to him by his employer. The employer's cash
equivalent marginal valuations of X_1 and X_2, P_1 and P_2, are determined by their best uses other than in the employee's production
domain. The values P_1 and P_2 need not be expressed in cash or even
be explicitly communicated, but the employer does use these prices
in determining the total cash equivalent value of inputs, $P_1X_1 +$
P_2X_2, for which he holds the employee accountable. The employer is
concerned with this total value (in comparison to his total value of
the employee's output), not with the employee's relative uses of X_1
and X_2 within the total. In the following discussion, it becomes clear
that the employee has the wherewithal and incentive to estimate
those of the employer's prices that are not explicitly communicated.
The term *budget* is used as defined in Chapter 3 to include the
employer's cash-equivalent value of all inputs he attributes to the
employee, whether or not he does so explicitly.

We have seen that when overall value responsibility is imposed on
an employee his resource diversions are limited either by the employer's option to impose specific responsibility instead or by the
employee's output replacement cost, that is, the cost of the employer's best alternative means of obtaining the employee's output or
the costs of doing without it such as by obtaining and making adjust-

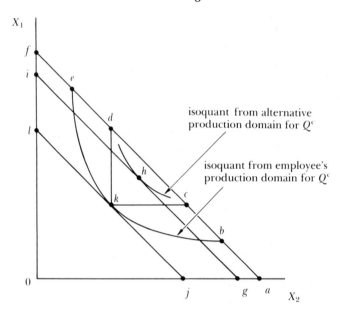

Figure 4.1. An employee's production domain and his employer's next-best alternative.

ments to an imperfect substitute. In Figure 4.1, the higher isoquant illustrates the possibility that the employer's best alternative means of obtaining an amount of Q, Q^c, is with the use of the same inputs X_1 and X_2 that the employee uses. This isoquant is tangent at point h to the budget line gi that represents a higher cost than the employee's minimum cost of producing Q^c. The employee's minimum cost is represented by the budget line jl, which is tangent to the employee's own lower isoquant for Q^c. It could instead be that the employer would find it the most economical to use inputs other than X_1 or X_2 that cost him the amount represented by budget line gi. Another possibility is that the employer's best alternative is to pay this amount to use the output of another employee or another organization. If the employer's best alternative is to make do without the employee's output, the budget line gi represents the compensating amount that would make him equally well off without this output. The example we shall use is where gi includes the employer's minimum combined cost of obtaining a quantity of a substitute and of making any continuing adjustments in resource uses so that he is equally well off as with Q^c. If his best alternative is to switch to specific responsibility, the budget line gi represents the employer's cost of obtaining the employee's output using this type of responsibility.

Although obtaining a replacement for an employee's output or switching to imposing specific responsibility on him is accomplished over the long run, I assume that the employer bases his decision to make one of these changes on the employee's short-run performance; that is, he extrapolates into the future his current costs of obtaining the output from the employee and of his best alternative. Also, he amortizes any transition costs to a constant per period cost premium, his present value of which equals these costs. Therefore, when output replacement cost limits the employee's resource diversions, the budget line gi represents the employer's expected minimum, continuing, per period cost of obtaining Q^c (or a quantity of a substitute after making any continuing adjustments of resource uses so he is equally well off with it) from an alternative source, given that the transition has been made. The line af adds to these costs the per period amortized value of the one-time transition costs: severance and other costs of dismissing or transferring employees, capital costs minus the value of the next best use of any equipment and other fixed resources no longer used to produce the output; disruption costs of lost production in the interim; and any fixed costs associated with the new means of obtaining the output such as those incurred in reorganization, acquiring and placing equipment, construction, training, and contracting.

When the limit on the employee's resource diversions is the employer's cost of the employee's output at which he would switch to specific responsibility, the amount represented by gi is the employer's estimated continuing per period cost of obtaining Q^c via this type of responsibility and af additionally includes amortized transition and other one-time costs of making the switch. The possibility of being under specific responsibility can limit the employee's resource diversions only when he prefers to remain under overall value responsibility.

Thus, the rate of output Q^c is a critical rate that the employee must maintain when his budget is af (and is expected to remain at this amount) to prevent the employer from deciding to replace his output – that is, obtain it from another source or use a substitute – or to impose specific responsibility. In the rhetoric accompanying budgetary and other negotiations between employer and employee, the employer's stated output requirement may differ from the actual output rate below which he will take one of these actions.

Output replacement or a change to specific responsibility does not necessarily imply that the employee will be fired or that he will no longer contribute in any capacity to the production of the output. However, he will ordinarily be worse off because he will no longer possess the cost advantage depicted in Figure 4.1 and any personal benefits he can derive from it. If the employee's budget is the amount represented by af, he will deliver at least Q^c to the employer to maintain his total income; with the receipt of Q^c in return for this amount, the employer is indifferent as to whether to select his best supply alternative. If the employee's budget is reduced or increased, he will supply an amount less or more than Q^c such that the employer continues to be indifferent or slightly disinclined to replace his output or impose specific responsibility. In general, the employee's supply of Q in response to varying budgets depends on the critical quantities at which the employer will either replace the employee's output or impose specific responsibility. If the employer is prone to give little warning when output falls short of the critical value, a risk-averse employee will maintain his rate of output somewhat above his imperfect estimate of the critical value.

Assuming for the moment that the employee's marginal utility from personal uses of Q equals zero, he will select an input combination on his own isoquant for Q^c when his budget is the amount represented by af. If his marginal utilities from personal uses of X_1 and X_2 remain positive, and the isoquant is strictly convex from below, he selects the input combination k on the isoquant. If instead he employed one of the combinations e or b, he would use all of his budget in the production of Q. As the employee substitutes X_2 for X_1 between e and k, increasing amounts of his budget can be used for purposes other than the production of Q^c; thus, substituting X_2 for X_1 makes more of X_1 as well as X_2 available for him to put to uses that benefit him. Analogously, he would substitute X_1 for X_2 along kb. If he operates at point k, the maximum value of X_1 and X_2 is available for personal benefit. Thus, the employee minimizes the cost of producing Q^c (represented by the line jl) and in doing so is guided in his uses of X_1 and X_2 by the employer's marginal values of these resources in uses outside the employee's production domain.

If all the employee's benefits from resource diversions must be taken in kind (i.e., personal uses of X_1 and X_2), he chooses from the alternative combinations of X_1 and X_2 represented by cd minus the amount used to produce Q^c represented by k and selects the combination that maximizes his utility. In cases where the employee's budget is partly or wholly cash (with or without a restriction to purchase particular inputs such as X_1 and X_2), or if he is permitted to exchange quantities of inputs or outputs for cash, diversion benefits in cash could be, but are not necessarily, allowed. If so, the employee selects from the broader combination of X_1, X_2 and cash to maximize his utility. If X_1 and X_2 are resources such as the exercise of power that are not readily available to the employee outside of the organization, they may at the margin yield him more utility than their cash value to the employer. In such cases, an employee with the option to take cash would take some benefits from resource diversions in kind.

Although it would usually be very costly for an employer to determine a particular combination of inputs such as at point k, it may not be difficult to prevent employees' uses of resources that are obviously unrelated to production. Such restrictions often benefit an employer by making it harder for third parties to know about his employees' resource diversions. However, although these restrictions could conceivably make the employee's marginal utility derived from personal uses of all inputs go to zero, this result would rarely reduce the resource diversions of an employee under overall value responsibility. The employee can, if other employees are willing and able, exchange such resources for others that yield him utility. He ordinarily has opportunities to invest resources yielding him little or no current utility to increase future benefits from resource diversions (see Chapter 7). If neither of these opportunities should be available, an employee expecting to derive utility at the margin from resource diversions in the future would select an inefficient combination of inputs within his production domain if he suspected that returning part of his budget to his employer would subsequently lead to the employer's attempt to obtain the same rate of output with a lower budget.

Note how unusual it is for an employee under overall value responsibility to lack incentive for efficient resource allocation within his production domain when he is informed about its production possibilities. He must be unable at the margin to derive utility from any personal uses of any productive resources, including his own time and effort, for which other productive resources can be substituted in production. He must find it not worthwhile to invest or exchange any resources at the margin. Also, he must derive no utility at the margin from any activities involved in producing and delivering output in the employer's interest.

Now let us assume that the employee derives utility from personal uses of Q. When personal benefits from resource diversions must be taken in kind, the employee's output of Q exceeds Q' if, within the range of allowable resource diversions, the marginal utility of personal use of the amount of Q produced by a unit of X_1 or X_2 exceeds the marginal utility of personal use of X_1 or X_2. If cash diversion benefits are allowed, his output of Q exceeds Q^r only if the employee derives more utility from Q at the margin than from cash equal to this resource's value to the employer. The combination of X_1 and X_2 that he would use to produce a larger quantity of Q than Q^r remains where the ratio of the two inputs' marginal products equals the ratio of the employer's marginal values of them.

Figure 4.2 illustrates the case where the employee produces two separate outputs with a given budget. The curve ef represents either the employer's best alternative means[1] of obtaining Q_1 and Q_2 or his capability to elicit the employee's outputs via specific responsibility. The amount of resources underlying ef equals the employee's budget minus the employer's amortized transition costs. Depending on his desired uses of the employee's outputs, the employer's indifference curve for Q_1 and Q_2, gj, is derived from the productivities of Q_1 and Q_2 in other production domains, external demands for these outputs, or directly from his utility function. The point i represents the quantities of Q_1 and Q_2 that the employer would obtain via another source or by imposing specific responsibility. The employee must deliver a combination of Q_1 and Q_2 that is on or above the same indifference curve.

The curves ab and cd respectively illustrate the employee's production possibilities with his production domain when he uses his entire budget and when he uses the minimum value of inputs necessary to produce amounts that make his employer as well off as at point i. If the employee derives no utility from personal uses of Q_1 and Q_2 but does derive utility from personal uses of inputs, he delivers to the employer the quantities of Q_1 and Q_2 represented by the point h. This point coincides with point i only if the employee's production possibilities with resources used in the employer's interest should coincide with the employer's alternative opportunities to obtain Q_1 and Q_2.

If the employee derives utility from personal uses of Q_1 and Q_2, the additional amount he produces of one or both of these outputs depends on his marginal utilities derived from them relative to his marginal utilities of his inputs. If he may take benefits from resource diversions in cash, any additional production of Q_1 and Q_2 depends also on his marginal utility of money.

The employer might consider making payments in cash for extra delivered outputs, in effect enabling the employee to exchange extra output for the opportunity to take benefits from resource diversions

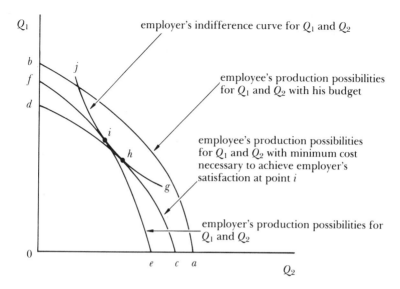

Figure 4.2. An employee's choice of rates of production for two outputs.

in cash. The employee would respond if his marginal utility of the inputs used to produce the extra output, as well as of the output itself, is less than his marginal utility of the payment. Similarly, an employer might make cash payments to employees under IPOR for increased profitability when output replacement is based on a rate-of-return criterion, as often occurs in private corporations. When payments are in cash (or in quantities of highly desired resources), the employer benefits from the employee's preference for them over personal uses of inputs and outputs.

There are two problems in designing a payment schedule that is maximally beneficial to the employer. First, the size of payment for increasing output or profitability should overcompensate the employee's necessary reduction in other benefits from resource diversions by a sum just sufficient to induce him to increase output. This requires the employer both to have information about the employee's preferences and to determine for a given amount of the employee's budget what profitability or output would be without any payment so that rewards (and penalties for sub-par performance) can be scaled from this point. The second problem in designing an optimal payment schedule is that the employer can not rely solely on the payments as prices; all the economically important characteristics of an employee's inputs and outputs should be implicitly or explicitly priced according to the employer's marginal values of them. Berliner's (1957) study of the Russian economy richly describes the behavior of employees under cash bonus schemes, and illustrates both of these problems. However, regarding the second problem, we can see from the analysis of Figure 4.2 that whenever the employee believes that his employer does not hold him accountable for one or more economically important outputs or output characteristics, incentives for the most economically desirable output mix are inadequate in any variant of IPOR or NPOR, whether or not there are cash bonuses.

Similarly, if an input is not attributed to an employee, it does not count as part of his budget and he uses it as if it had a zero price, regardless of whether he is under a cash bonus scheme. If an attributed input is priced implicitly or explicitly below the employer's actual marginal value of it (e.g. because the employer is unaware of the resource's alternative uses that can benefit him), the employee will allocate more of his allowable budget to the input. As a result, the employer's cash equivalent net income will decrease by the difference between the correct and incorrect prices times the quantity of the input that the employee uses. An underpriced or unattributed input increases the apparent desirability to an employer who is determining an employee's output replacement cost of those alternative suppliers who would also find the input underpriced or unattributed. For example, the same input would often be available on identical terms to anyone who works under the same employer or in the same organization. An employer who is not sure that his employee has correctly inferred his marginal values of resources can deal with the pricing problem by basing an employee's cash bonus on an accurate measure of his overall value productivity.

Alternatively, if an input is priced above the employer's actual marginal value of it, the employee, if informed, will explain the error to the employer. If the employer does not correct the price, the employee will decrease the supply of his output; he will regard the total excess charge for the quantity of the input he uses (after appropriately substituting away from it because of the excess charge) as a reduction in his budget. Given his demand for the employee's outputs, an employer will often be worse off with the reduced rate of the employee's supply (see Chapter 5) and will thus correct the price.

The tendency in organizations for employees to use their entire budgets within allotted fiscal time periods can be explained by the incentives of overall value responsibility. An unspent balance at the end of a fiscal period indicates to the employer that the employee has either reduced output or has maintained output at less cost. If the employer suspects the former, he more carefully evaluates the employee's output, and if he decides it is lower (or that he values it less) he reduces the employee's budget. If the employer suspects the latter, he might more carefully evaluate whether output replacement cost or his opportunities to impose specific responsibility in fact permit a lower budget for the same output. If this is not the case, he might believe that the employee will maintain his output in the face of a budget cut because he obviously does not benefit from leftover resources. Thus, as noted earlier, an employee who currently does not derive utility at the margin from resource diversions has an incentive to spend his entire budget if he expects that he will derive a positive marginal utility from resource diversions in the future. Essentially the same phenomenon has been observed in centralized planning systems. Berliner (1957) points out that "a certain universal planning practice . . . operates like a ratchet in the planning mechanism, so that once a new high level of performance has been achieved, the next plan target may not be reduced below that level but must usually be raised above it" (p. 78). He quotes a former Soviet manager as stating, "If you say you cannot [increase output], they show you that you overfulfilled the plan several months last year, without the aid of new capital investment. Therefore enterprises try to overfulfill their plans only by a very little bit" (p. 79).

The simple models represented in Figures 4.1 and 4.2 are readily extended to larger numbers of outputs or inputs or, most important, to the cases where these resources have multiple characteristics. The models can also be extended to include expected variation in the employee's budget and in the employer's expected cost of his best alternative. For example, the employer can assume that his best alternative would have a profile of decreasing costs due to experience with it. The extensions retain the result that the employee applies inputs in production so that the ratio of the marginal products of any two inputs equals the ratio of his employer's marginal values of them. In response to a given budget, the employee supplies a combination of quantities and characteristics of his outputs that is of equal or greater value than the total value of outputs that the employer could obtain with the same budget minus amortized transition costs from another source or by imposing specific responsibility; so long as he meets this condition, the employee has discretion over the particular mix of output quantities or characteristics that he supplies.

Summary of basic hypotheses about economic behavior under overall value responsibility with no spillovers

Under the assumption that the employee derives utility from resource diversions at the margin, we can summarize the basic hypotheses about the employee's demand for information, the implicit prices that guide his uses of resources, his income, and his uses of delegated inputs when overall value responsibility is placed on him. At this point it is possible to state limited hypotheses about efficiency under this type of responsibility.

The employee's demand for information. The employee has an incentive to allocate resources to obtain information both about production possibilities within his production domain and about the employer's marginal values of his inputs and outputs. Insofar as the marginal utility of inputs applied to obtaining information is less than the marginal utility of enhanced personal benefits, additional information enables the employee to increase his welfare. This information can be regarded as additional outputs produced by the employee.

When the employee's expenditures on information do not immediately benefit him, they are among his investments (see Chapter 7).

Implicit prices that guide the employee's uses of resources. The employee attaches an implicit price that is independent of his own utility function to each resource that he believes his employer attributes to him. These implicit prices are his estimate of the employer's conscious marginal values of the resources in uses outside the employee's production domain. They apply whether or not the resource has a market-determined or other explicit price; when there is such a price, the implicit price governs the resource's uses whenever it differs from these other prices. The implicit prices guide not only the employee's uses of inputs and outputs that benefit the employer, but also his uses of these resources that result in resource diversions.

The employee's total income from the organization. The employee's total income is the cash equivalent value to him of the critical budget, including his salary and any other cash income from the organization, at which the employer either switches to specific responsibility or replaces his output, minus his cash-equivalent value of the inputs he must use to produce the quantity of output that is delivered according to his employer's wishes. These inputs include his applications of his skills and efforts that have alternative uses yielding him utility. The employee's total income is thus a residual over which he may be able to exert considerable influence.

When an employee cannot take all of his benefits from resource diversions in cash, he is usually worse off than if he could. Nonetheless, the employee typically has a wide variety of alternative ways in which he can gain utility from resource diversions, and they can yield him substantial welfare.

The employee's uses of inputs and supply of outputs. Unless input uses are obviously unrelated to production, the employer is unconcerned with the employee's particular choices of input uses within the total value of inputs he delegates to an employee. The employee makes efficient uses of inputs in both his own and the employer's interests. When the employer's relative marginal values of inputs change, the employee correspondingly changes the relative intensities with which he uses them for both purposes. Thus the employee's choices contribute to price sensitivity of the organization's market demands for inputs, but these demands are derived from uses of inputs that result in resource diversions as well as those that do not.

The employer is concerned with the employee's overall value productivity, that is, the total value of the outputs that the employee supplies in relation to his total cost of the employee's inputs. Thus, the employee supplies a combination of outputs having the same or slightly higher value than what the employer could obtain either from an alternative supplier (with the employee's budget minus amortized transition costs) or by imposing specific responsibility.

Efficiency. It is not possible to explore fully the effects of resource allocation within an organization on social welfare until we analyze behavior in relation to internal technological spillovers, and deal with interactions between supply and demand – specifically between an employee's supply and a managing employee's demands for his outputs, and between the organization's supply and the final demands for its outputs. However, we can now see that an employee is guided by his employer's marginal values of the inputs attributed to him. Given his information about production possibilities, the employee minimizes his cost of producing his outputs whenever he benefits from resource diversions at the margin. We can also note that when the employee must take benefits from resource diversions in kind, he often prefers cash equal to the resources' value to the employer, resulting in a welfare loss. This preference leads to a related welfare loss due to the reduced motivational effect of in-kind diversion benefits. An employee under overall value responsibility weighs at the margin any loss of utility from the application of his own skills and efforts against his increase of utility from the resulting gain of benefits from resource diversions. When these benefits must be taken in kind and are discounted as described, the employee supplies less effort than if at the margin he were able to take benefits from resource diversions in cash.

B   Resource allocation with a fixed budget and no spillovers under specific responsibility

Specific responsibility influences some of an employee's uses of particular resources and does not hold him accountable for the value of his outputs in relation to the value of the inputs delegated to him. In the analysis of resource allocation under specific responsibility, I maintain the assumption that the employee has a production cost advantage over his employer and assume that the employer has the authority to alter employees' particular uses of resources via *applications* of specific responsibility. These are considered in two categories. In one category are cash or noncash rewards or penalties that attach to an employee's uses of resources and serve as prices to affect his quantities demanded of the uses. In the other category are substitutes and complements that shift the employee's demands for uses of resources in his own and in his employer's interests.

When specific responsibility is imposed the interplay among the quantities of resources available to an employee, his demands for alternative uses of them and any prices attached to the uses, determine how he allocates every resource among its uses. These uses include those that contribute to the production of outputs and delivery of them to the employer, and the employee's supply of his output is thereby determined.

The concern of an employer imposing specific responsibility with his employees' particular resource uses is in contrast to the case where he imposes overall value responsibility; under overall value responsibility, the employee, not the employer, gains from efficiency within the employee's production domain. However, because the income of an employee under specific responsibility is not a residual that increases with his overall value productivity, he does not attach implicit prices to his alternative feasible uses of resources that are equal to his employer's marginal values of the resources. Therefore, the employer can often gain from placing penalties and rewards on employees' feasible uses of resources. In order to analyze the employer's choices in establishing these prices and in using complements and substitutes to shift employees' demands for resource uses, we must look at these demands.

The following subsection addresses the employee's demands for alternative uses of resources delegated to him. Considered next are the two categories of applications of specific responsibility. Subsequently, I analyze the employer's optimal choices in placing specific responsibility on employees. Finally, we turn to the analysis of resource allocation under this type of responsibility.

The employee's demands for alternative uses of resources delegated to him

Consider two uses that an employee might make of an input – one that increases the employer's welfare and one that does not. Of course, there are typically multiple uses of an input that increase the employer's welfare by varying degrees, and there are many uses that do not increase his welfare; but the main issues of specific responsibility can be analyzed with only these two uses. Assume for the moment that the employer takes no action to influence either use of the input. Also, let the employee derive neither positive nor negative utility from his output, all of which he delivers to the employer, and assume that the employer does not directly influence the rate of the employee's output. The use of an input that increases the employer's welfare can be interpreted as the employee's application of it within his production domain (in a specified combination with any other inputs whose usage affects the employee's utility) to produce an output he delivers to the employer. I assume that the two different uses of the same input are not complements or substitutes, that is, an increased application of the input in one use does not affect the employee's marginal utility derived from a given quantity application in the other.

An employee's quantity demanded of a resource in a use can be expressed either as a function of units of the particular reward or penalty attached to the use or of cash prices where in-kind rewards or penalties are converted to their cash-equivalent values to the employee. Cash prices will be used so that demands are comparable when different in-kind rewards or penalties are used. We shall see that where an employer does not find it worthwhile to attach rewards or penalties, the implicit prices that guide the uses of each resource are determined by the quantity delegated to the employee in relation to his demands for uses of it.

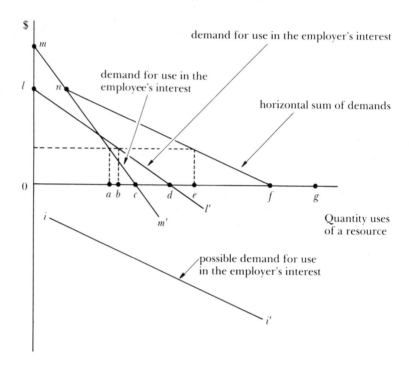

Figure 4.3. An employee's demands for alternative uses of an input delegated to him.

Lines *mm'* and *ll'* in Figure 4.3 illustrate possible demands of the employee for the two uses of an input. The quantity demanded in each use is a function of the cash-equivalent of any rewards or penalties that attach to the use. Line *mnf* is the horizontal sum of *mm'* and *ll'*, representing the employee's total demand for both uses of the input when he always allocates among uses to maximize his utility.

Now consider the employee's uses of the input. Let the quantity *0e* of the input be delegated to the employee. This quantity is small enough in relation to *mm'* and *ll'* so that the employee attaches a positive marginal value to it and applies *0b* of it within his production domain to produce output delivered to the employer and makes personal use of *0a*. When the employer does not know the marginal productivity of an input or does not measure the quantity that the employee places in each use, he cannot base the quantity he delegates on the input's marginal value product in a use benefiting him and further ensure that this is the only use made of the input. Thus, only coincidentally would the employee's cash-equivalent marginal value of the input equal the employer's cash-equivalent marginal value of it outside his production domain. If these values should happen to be equal, the employee would nonetheless make personal uses of the input whenever he thereby gains more utility at the margin.

Consider the larger allocated quantity $0g$ of the input, an amount that exceeds uses from which the employee derives positive welfare. The employee now uses a total quantity of $0f$ of which a quantity $0d$ is applied in the employer's interest and an amount $0c$ is allocated to a personal use. The remaining amount $0g$ minus $0f$ is *wasted*. This term describes an allocation of a resource leading to no welfare for anyone.

The case where the employee would have to be induced to use any quantity of input in the employer's interest is illustrated by the demand line ii' in Figure 4.3 that replaces the demand line ll'. The employee places none of the input in a use benefiting the employer. If the quantity of the input delegated to him is smaller than $0c$, he derives utility from personal use of the input at the margin; none is wasted. Any delegated quantity in excess of $0c$ will be wasted.

The analysis is essentially the same when the employee derives positive or negative welfare from uses of his outputs or when the employer influences these uses. However, in this case his demands for uses of inputs depends on his utility from using or delivering his outputs.

Issues that determine the employer's costs and benefits of alternative applications of specific responsibility

An employer chooses among a wide variety of alternative applications of specific responsibility on the basis of costs and desired behavioral effects. We shall consider these costs and behavioral effects separately for the two categories of specific responsibility's applications.

Applications of specific responsibility that attach prices to an employee's uses of particular resources. By attaching prices to the employee's resource uses, the employer can induce the employee to increase those uses that are in his interest and decrease those that result in resource diversions. The prices can be cash or in kind, and they can be certain or random. They can be paid by the employee as well as to him; when an employee's income from working in the organization exceeds his compensated opportunity cost, penalties, if tied to resource uses and enforced, can influence his choices, as can rewards. Three tasks determine an employer's costs of attaching a price to a particular resource use: (1) measuring the quantity of the resource that the employee places in the use; (2) evaluating the importance of the use; and (3) selecting the rewards or penalties to be applied.

The costs of measuring how much of a resource is placed in a particular use depend on the nature of the use and the characteristics of the resource and of the employee's production domain. The nature of the use determines accessibility for measurement and whether measurement can be performed as a by-product of the employer's other activities. Tangibility and uniformity of a resource's characteristics and its size can affect costs of measuring its usage. When production domains are internally designed, measurement of an employee's resource uses often requires explanation from him about the uses. Indeed, with an intangible resource or an internally designed production domain an employee can often influence a monitor's interpretation of what he observes. Although an employer may be able to economize by randomly measuring employees' uses of resources, they might readily be able to vary resource uses in response if measurement is itself easily noticed.

We now turn to the employer's task of deciding the form that a price will take. His choice between rewards and penalties and whether to make them cash or in kind depends on how opposing factors offset each other in the particular situation. The major disadvantage of rewards is that they directly add to the employer's costs. Penalties, however, run the risk of reducing an employee's income below his compensated opportunity cost, requiring the employer to bear his personal replacement cost. This risk can be large and difficult to predict when the penalty is embarrassing to the employee involved or when it could appear to be arbitrary and is known to other employees. Assessing penalties may also be unpleasant for the employer or adversely affect his relationship with other employees. The widespread practice of "timing" factory jobs enables employers to communicate to employees proper lengths of time to perform tasks. With this information, an employer can defer to those who timed the job when assessing penalties for sub-par performance.

Although employers can usually be certain that cash is important to employees, in-kind rewards can be more costly for third parties to learn about. Granting or withholding such benefits as status or esteem can also have strong motivating effects; and although the employer can keep these benefits scarce, they are economical for him to use. Other rewards or penalties that are often effective include communicating or withholding information (e.g., about demands served by the employer) that is valuable to the employee. An in-kind reward or penalty might also serve the employer as a useful complement or substitute for some of the employee's other uses of resources.

Rewarding an employee's delivered output can increase it by raising the employee's demands for uses of inputs in the employer's interest. Cash rewards elicit especially large output increases when the marginal utility of in-kind benefits from resource diversions is relatively low. In this case, however, unlike the case of overall value responsibility, the employee lacks incentive to use attributed inputs efficiently to produce the additional output. When an employee under specific or overall value responsibility has access to productive inputs that are not attributed to him, he might, in fact, produce the additional output at extremely high cost. If costly characteristics of a priced output as well as the employee's other outputs are also not priced, along with the proper rates of production in progress, these will tend to be more neglected as a result of the employer's attaching rewards to an output. Berliner (1957) provides many examples of such results.

Applications of specific responsibility that affect the utility the employee derives from given quantity uses of resources. We have seen that it is costly to establish rewards and penalties that influence an employee's uses of resources. In many circumstances it is less costly to take two actions that affect the availability of complements or substitutes for these uses. One is to establish work rules to restrict the employee's access both to complements for uses of resources in his own interest and substitutes for resource uses in the employer's interest. For example, requiring an employee to be present in a particular location restricts the availability of complements for leisure uses of his efforts, thereby decreasing his demand for leisure while on the job. Restricting particular on-the-job leisure activities can make substitute uses of effort in the employer's interest more attractive; when idleness is the only alternative to performing a task, the task might be preferred. The employer can also provide the employee with "amenities" or "fringe benefits" that are complements for uses of resources in the employer's interest or substitutes for uses of resources in the employee's interest. Giving an employee a prestigious title or elevating his status might increase his demand for effort in the employer's interest. An example of a substitute is providing convenient rest or recreation facilities for use during work breaks so that work in the employer's interest more quickly becomes competitive at the margin with leisure uses of time.

To influence the employee in this manner the employer must defray the costs of determining appropriate complements and substitutes and then providing them. We can expect that complements and substitutes as well as work rules vary in effectiveness with the amount of resources the employer devotes to them and with the particular employee's preferences. Experimentation with such resources and with alternative work rules can be economical in many situations where it would be very costly to attach prices to employees' uses of resources.

However, the more an employer knows about employees' preferences, the more effectively he can impose specific responsibility. The importance of each employee's own preferences has been aptly characterized by Gross (1964, p. 584):

People who are more interested in leisure or comradeship than in money cannot be readily spurred to action by bonuses or fines. People who are deeply interested in escaping responsibility and in being guided by others cannot be quickly activated by the possibility of a more responsible position. Above all, a satisfied need may cease to be a motivator. Sometimes, before incentives can be used, it is first necessary to stimulate jaded or latent interests.

The high costs of inferring employees' preferences, combined with other costs of specific responsibility, often make it uneconomical for an employer to influence a large number of an employee's resource uses that he wants to discourage. When the employer can readily determine the total amount of resources placed in these uses, it can be constrained by the employee's personal replacement cost, that is, the transitional and any continuing costs of discharging or transferring him and giving his tasks to another employee. This limit on resource diversions reflects specific responsibility, not overall value responsibility, because it does not make the employee accountable for the overall value productivity of his production domain. However, an employee might be "indispensable" in the sense that if he is replaced his production domain is also replaced; the time delay and costs for another employee to acquire enough skill are such that his production domain would no longer be used. Berliner (1957, p. 171) cites an example:

A certain skilled worker had become the virtual dictator of his shop because he was the only one who knew how to make the stems of micrometers. If he failed to show up at work, production had to stop. The foreman toadied to him, which began to go to his head, and when he became completely unreliable the plant had to change its method of making stems so that they could be made by less skilled workers.

The employer's optimal choices in imposing specific responsibility

For each use of every resource, the employer faces two choices: (1) deciding which applications of specific responsibility, if any, to impose on the employee; and (2) if one is imposed, deciding how much to spend on it. The key points can be illustrated under the assumptions that the resources delegated to the employee have been determined and are fixed; that each application of specific responsibility only affects one of the employee's uses of a single resource; and that any one application of specific responsibility does not change the costs or effectiveness of any other. It is also assumed that the employer has enough information to array alternative applications of specific responsibility according to the cost effectiveness of each. The effects of relaxing these assumptions will be examined later.

Figure 4.4 illustrates an employer's optimal choice in placing specific responsibility on a use by an employee of a particular resource. The first and second quadrants respectively illustrate the effect of the employer's expenditures on the intensity of an incentive and the behavioral effect of a more intense incentive on the employee's quantity use of a resource. The solid and dashed lines illustrate two different cases.

An *incentive* on an employee's use of a resource is a price attached to this use or a complement or substitute for it. We are concerned with those incentives that the employer establishes deliberately. An incentive created by specific responsibility is a reward or penalty that the employer establishes, or a complement or substitute he provides for a particular resource use; whereas overall value responsibility leads the employee to attach to all of his feasible uses of a resource an implicit price equal to his perception of the employer's conscious marginal value of the resource. A more *intense* incentive is a larger or more certain price attached to a resource use, a larger quantity of a complement or substitute for the use, or a closer complement or substitute for the use.

The intensity of an incentive in the first quadrant is the variable directly controlled by an employer imposing specific responsibility. The sizes of rewards and penalties and the detail and accuracy of measurements underlying these prices can vary, as can the quantities

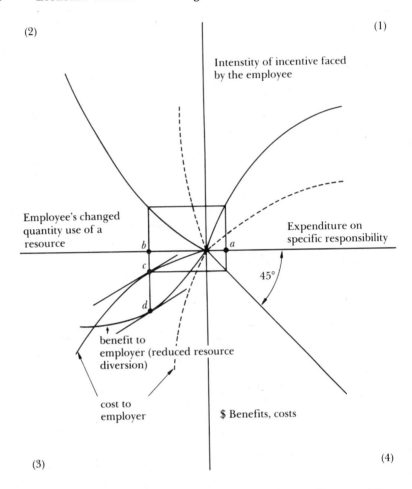

Figure 4.4. The employer's optimal choice in placing specific responsibility on one of an employee's uses of a particular resource.

and characteristics of complements or substitutes provided. Thus, additional expenditures can improve the effectiveness of a given incentive as an influence on an employee's use of a resource. However, beyond some point larger expenditures are normally required to produce equal improvement of detail, accuracy, or enforcement. Also, additional quantities of a given complement or substitute or in-kind reward or penalty will often be drawn from successively more important alternative uses if the resource is not readily available at a constant price. For such reasons, the relationship between the intensity of an incentive and the employer's expenditure on it is shown to be strictly concave. Note that although an incentive's intensity is a quantity or characteristic that can be considered separately from its behavioral effects, these effects influence the employer's optimal ordering of expenditures on the incentive.

If the employer delegates a different quantity of the resource, the relationships in the first quadrant can shift. For example, larger delegated quantities can result in economies in achieving detail or accuracy of measurement of each quantity use of the resource.

The second quadrant illustrates the effect of an incentive's intensity on an employee's changed quantity use of a resource. Successive rises in intensity are shown to have diminishing effects. Larger or more accurately assessed in-kind rewards or penalties have diminishing cash-equivalent value to the employee. Thus, equal increments of in-kind rewards or penalties ordinarily have successively smaller effects on the employee's use of the resource and more units of a complement or substitute produce smaller shifts of the employee's demands for use of a resource. This is not necessarily always the case, however. For example, nonlinear demands for resource uses could make equal increments of in-kind prices that are of diminishing cash-equivalent value to the employee have larger effects on his demanded quantity usage of a resource within a range of quantity values.

The relationship in the second quadrant of Figure 4.4 often shifts when the employer varies the quantity of the resource delegated to the employee. This can be seen by considering the employee's demands for uses of the resource when these uses are not controlled by rewards or penalties. Different delegated quantities of the resource change the point on demand at which the employee is in equilibrium if none of the resource is wasted. In such cases, if shifts of demand due to changed quantities of the complements or substitutes used as incentives are not parallel, the effects of given altered quantities of these complements or substitutes will differ with the amount of the resource delegated to the employee.

An increased quantity of a resource placed in a use benefiting the employer is a reduced resource diversion whenever the resource was not drawn from another use of equal or greater value to the employer. However, a decreased usage that benefits only the employee is not necessarily a reduced diversion; the released quantity of the resource could go to other uses that only benefit the employee or be wasted. For example, consider the cases in Figure 4.3. If the employee's only alternative use of the resource benefits the employer and he derives positive marginal utility from this use, the employer will benefit from a decrease in the use that benefits the employee only. But if the employee derives zero or negative utility from the use benefiting the employer, a decrease in the other use only wastes the resource and does not increase the employer's welfare. (This would imply a horizontal benefit-to-employer relationship in the third quadrant of Figure 4.4.) Thus, it is not sufficient to reduce the employee's personal uses of a resource; the effect on resource diversions depends on resulting usage, if any, in the employer's interest.

The third quadrant illustrates the employer's benefits and costs from an employee's placing different quantities of a resource in a particular use that does affect his welfare. The relationship labeled "benefit to employer" translates altered quantity uses of the resource into the corresponding increases in the employer's cash-equivalent net income (i.e., reduced resource diversion by the employee). Diminishing marginal benefits are illustrated to reflect the typical situation where the employer derives diminishing marginal returns to usage of a resource in his interest. An employer lacking sufficient information about the employee's production domain to estimate marginal products perhaps bases his estimate of an input's marginal value product on some combination of the input's (often diminishing) marginal value to him outside the employee's production domain and his demand for the employee's output. To simplify the figure, the same relationship for "benefit to employer" holds in both of the cases considered next.

The solid and dashed relationships labeled "cost to employer" show two different cases for the employer's costs of placing specific responsibility on one of an employee's uses of a resource. Each expenditure on the horizontal axis of the first quadrant is translated (via the 45° line in the fourth quadrant) onto the vertical axis of the third quadrant and plotted against the corresponding changed quantity use of the resource. The first two quadrants' strictly concave relationships make the corresponding cost relationships in the third quadrant strictly concave; diminishing effects of expenditures on the intensity of incentives and diminishing behavioral effects of increased intensity imply that the employer faces rising marginal costs of changing an employee's quantity use of a resource.

The analysis of Figure 4.4 determines whether it is worthwhile for the employer to impose specific responsibility on a given use of a resource and, if so, this analysis also determines the employer's choice of one or more applications of specific responsibility and the amounts he spends on them. Let the solid-lined relationships represent the employer's most cost-effective available application of specific responsibility. At the changed quantity use of the resource represented by point b, the employer's marginal cost (slope at point c) of changed quantity use equals his marginal benefit of the change (slope at point d). The quantity d minus c produced by expenditure $0a$ is the maximum possible increase in the employer's net income that can be achieved with this application of specific responsibility. A further analysis starting at point b determines whether it would be desirable to supplement this application of specific responsibility with another.

If, instead, the dashed relationships represent the most cost-effective available application of specific responsibility, it is not worthwhile for the employer to influence this particular use that the employee makes of the resource. This can be seen in the third quadrant where for every changed quantity use the (dashed) cost to the employer is always greater than the employer's benefit (same curve as for the solid-lined case).

We can see from the foregoing analysis that the employer's optimal imposition of specific responsibility varies with his demand for the employee's output; when his demand increases, the marginal value products of the employee's inputs increase, as does the marginal value of the output itself. Although an employer frequently lacks information about an input's marginal productivity and thus cannot determine its marginal value product, he may, as noted above, increase his marginal valuation of an input when he attaches a higher marginal value to the output it is supposed to help produce. For the solid lined case, an increased benefit to the employer at every quantity in the third quadrant of Figure 4.4 results in a larger equilibrium changed quantity of the resource in the use analyzed.

Now consider the effects of relaxing the simplifying assumptions that underlie the analysis of Figure 4.4. These include the assumptions that the resources delegated to the employee are given and fixed; that each application of specific responsibility influences the employee's use of only one resource; that imposing one application of specific responsibility does not change the cost or benefits of imposing another; and that the employer orders expenditures on incentives according to their diminishing effectiveness.

Choices in imposing specific responsibility are actually determined jointly with choices in delegating resources to employees; the employer's cost of the employee's output is the sum of his costs of imposing responsibility and of delegated inputs. While increases in expenditure on specific responsibility and on delegated inputs can elicit an increase of an employee's output, either outlay alone will ordinarily have rapidly diminishing returns. Thus the employer selects a combination of these outlays such that the marginal effects of each on the employee's output is the same. In particular, he attempts to delegate inputs and apply specific responsibility to uses of them in such a way as to achieve the following equality. On one side of the equality is the employer's marginal value of the increased supply resulting from an additional unit of an input delegated to his employee, given the employer's optimal expenditures on specific responsibility to influence uses of the input. This marginal supply value is equated to the sum of the input's marginal value to the employer outside the employee's production domain plus the employer's marginal specific responsibility costs of influencing the employee's uses of it. These coordinated outlays can also have rapidly diminishing returns, however, and in a time period long enough to hire additional employees, the number of employees enters importantly into the employer's optimal combination of outlays.

Relaxing the assumption that an application of specific responsibility influences only one use of a single resource requires an analysis identical to that of the first two quadrants of Figure 4.4 for each such use or resource. The employer's optimization is based on his total benefits of all uses affected by the application. Similarly, the analysis is more complicated but not essentially changed when any applications of specific responsibility to one use of a resource affects the costs or benefits of other applications. It becomes necessary to adjust the costs and benefits in the third quadrant of Figure 4.4 to account for these effects.

The employer may not obtain enough information about different intensities of incentives and their behavioral effects to order expenditures on them according to their diminishing effectiveness as is shown in the first quadrant of Figure 4.4. For example, he may randomly experiment only with low-cost applications of specific responsibility. If there were a local maximum of his net income corresponding to relatively small expenditure and a larger maximum corresponding to a substantial expenditure, the employer could fail to maximize his net income.

An important implication of the foregoing analysis is that an employer with an information cost disadvantage nonetheless often obtains information about the employee's production domain as well as about the employee's uses of resources. His incentive to do so can be seen from the undesirability of basing his benefit-to-employer relationship in the third quadrant of Figure 4.4 on values of a resource that are determined outside the employee's production domain. For example, when an input's marginal value product inside the employee's production domain significantly differs from its external marginal value to the employer, the employer would want to adjust the employee's uses of the input (and the quantity he delegates to the employee) to bring these marginal values into closer alignment. The resulting incentive to obtain information about productivity in an employee's production domain can make it partly externally designed in cases where it would have been entirely internally designed under overall value responsibility. An employee under specific responsibility has much less incentive to obtain information about more technically efficient production possibilities in his production domain than if he were under overall value responsibility.

It is interesting to compare the analysis of the employer's optimal choices in placing specific responsibility on employees to Leibenstein's (1975, 1976, 1979) analysis of the influence of "pressure" that makes an employee feel an internal obligation for "adherence to standards of some sort" (1976, p. 79). Leibenstein posits that an employee engages in "selective rationality," meaning that the degree to which he "attends" to his opportunities and constraints depends on the pressure on him. By use of applications of specific responsibility that create pressure the employer can influence in a manner favorable to himself the degree to which the employee engages in selective rationality. In particular, the employer can thereby reduce his cost of the employee's output.

In contrast to Leibenstein's analysis, it is assumed here that the employee always maximizes his own utility subject to his constraints; the employer influences only the employee's constraints (whether specific or overall value responsibility). Although Leibenstein's analysis is more general, the present analysis is more amenable to refutable hypotheses about resource allocation. However, the hypotheses about resource allocation under specific responsibility depend in part on the particular nature of the employee's utility function and are thus reduced in predictive value. This limitation is less important as we broaden the analysis to the nearest aggregation of employees at which overall value responsibility is imposed. At this level of aggregation, the particular ways in which employees benefit from resource diversions continue to depend on the characteristics of each employee's utility function. But, provided that the marginal utility of resource diversions remains positive, the employer's total cost of resource diversions is independent of employees' utility functions under overall value responsibility.

It is not necessary to employ a theory of nonmaximizing behavior in order to derive hypotheses about resource allocation within organizations in short-run and long-run periods and to evaluate the efficiency of this resource allocation. Indeed, testable hypotheses may not occur with a nonmaximizing theory. Nonetheless, a theory based on the assumption that each employee maximizes his utility subject to constraints imposed by others must still be judged on the basis of the validity and usefulness of its hypotheses.

Short-run resource allocation with a fixed budget under specific responsibility

Given the employer's optimal choices in placing specific responsibility on an employee, it is now possible to analyze the employee's short-run resource allocation behavior with a fixed budget. I assume that the employee uses only two inputs to produce (or contribute to) a single output and that all of this output is supplied according to the employer's wishes. Allowing for more inputs or outputs and including the employee's personal use of some of his output does not change the basic results.

Figure 4.5 illustrates the employee's short-run resource allocation. The outermost budget line represents the employer's value outside the employee's production domain of the inputs X_1 and X_2 that are at the employee's disposal, whether or not they are specifically attributed to the employee. Point b illustrates the quantities of these inputs used in the employer's interest, given the effects of the employer's optimal imposition of specific responsibility. The lower the employee's demands for uses of inputs in the employer's interest and the less cost effective it is for the employer to place specific responsibility on these uses, the closer this point is to the origin. The curve ii' represents the isoquant on which the point b occurs; the output corresponding to this isoquant is delivered to the employer. The employee's resource diversions equal the employer's value of the difference between this output and the output of isoquant jj', representing the maximum possible output with the inputs available to the employee.

An important distinction between specific and overall value responsibility is illustrated by points b and a on isoquant ii'. Under specific responsibility, the employee ordinarily gains no residual diversion benefits from increases in the overall value productivity of his production domain and he therefore lacks a general incentive to select point a. Although by coincidence specific responsibility could

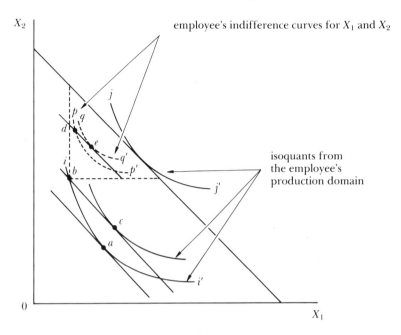

Figure 4.5. Resource allocation under specific responsibility and comparison with that occurring under overall value responsibility.

lead the employee to choose this point, this type of responsibility in fact usually gives him a disincentive to choose it. The employee typically lacks incentive even to obtain costly information necessary to determine point a. Similarly, the employee ordinarily lacks incentive to produce the maximum output possible (point c) with the total cost of the inputs he uses to produce output that is supplied in the employer's interest (taking the employer's marginal values of these inputs). It is helpful to keep in mind, however, that the employer's costs can be lower when he imposes specific responsibility on employees than when he imposes overall value responsibility. The cost effectiveness of available applications of specific responsibility and the employer's alternative opportunities to obtain the employee's outputs, or substitutes for them, determine his relative costs of employees' outputs with these two types of responsibility.

The following incident described to Garson (1979, pp. 234–5) illustrates what is, perhaps, typical of an employee under specific responsibility who derives little or no direct utility from performing the tasks of his job:

The other day I was proofreading an endorsement and I noticed some guy had insured his store for $165,000 against vandalism and $5,000 against fire. Now that's bound to be a mistake. They probably got it backwards. I was just about to show it to Gloria [the supervisor] when I figured, 'Wait a minute! I'm not supposed to read these forms. I'm just supposed to check one column against another. And they do check. So it couldn't be counted as my error' . . . They don't explain this stuff to me. I'm not supposed to understand it. I'm just supposed to check one column against the other. If they're gonna give me a robot's job to do, I'm gonna do it like a robot! Anyway it just lowers my production record to get up and point out someone else's error.

The same forces that usually lead to inefficient input combinations such as point b in Figure 4.5 also have the effect that changes in the relative external market prices of X_1 and X_2 will induce less substitution among these inputs than under overall value responsibility. This results both from distortions in employers' marginal values of employees' inputs and from employers' costs of imposing specific responsibility. A change in the external market price of a resource affects its marginal value to a managing employee who is himself under specific responsibility, only to the extent that the price change brings about a change in specific responsibility on his uses of this resource. Thus, by the argument in the next paragraph, a change in the external market price of an input has less effect on a managing employee's valuation of it if he or any managing employee above him is under specific responsibility rather than overall value responsibility. To the extent that a changed external market price does alter the employer's marginal value of an input he delegates to his employee, we can analyze the resulting input substitution by referring back to Figure 4.4.

We have seen that a change in an employer's marginal value of an input in uses outside the employee's production domain influences his "benefit-to-employer" relationship in the third quadrant when he has an estimate of the input's marginal value product in the employee's production domain that he is willing to rely on. It has been suggested that such a shift can also occur when the employer lacks such an estimate. If there is a shift in the benefit-to-employer relationship in the third quadrant, the resulting change in the employee's relative uses of inputs also depends on the employer's marginal cost of applying specific responsibility to usage of the input. The higher the marginal cost of applying specific responsibility, the smaller the substitutions involving an input in response to a change in the input's price. The employer similarly takes account of the cost effectiveness of specific responsibility in allowing changes in his marginal values of inputs to influence the quantities he delegates to the employee.

Lester (1946) sparked a controversy by presenting questionnaire evidence that firms' employment decisions are not very sensitive to wage rates. In response, Machlup (1946, 1947) and Stigler (1947) argued that this evidence does not imply a lack of applicability of marginal analysis to economic choices within a firm. We can see that the foregoing marginal analysis of employees' optimal choices of resource uses predicts that the sensitivity of an organization's re- source substitutions to price changes is much lower under specific responsibility than under overall value responsibility when it is costly at the margin to influence employees' uses of the relevant resources. When overall value responsibility is imposed, this sensitivity also de- pends on whether the relevant resources are attributed to the em- ployees making choices about their uses.

The employee's uses of inputs that do not benefit the employer and the waste of inputs can be analyzed in Figure 4.5. Consider the dashed vertical and horizontal axes from point b. The remaining quantities of X_1 and X_2 that an employee might put to uses benefiting only himself can be measured along these axes up to the employer's total value of resources delegated to him. Point d on the employee's indifference curve pp' illustrates the quantities that he can succeed in putting to such uses, given the employer's optimal placing of specific responsibility on these uses. The employer's cost of the employee's input uses at point d is the difference between the budgets repre- sented by the lines through b and d. His cost of wasted inputs is the difference between the amount represented by the line through d and the outermost budget line.

Specific responsibility usually makes an employee derive less utility from the same amount of resource diversions than if he were under overall value responsibility. An employee under the latter type of responsibility with an amount of allowable resource diversions repre- sented by the line through d with origin at b would select the combi- nation of resources illustrated by point e where his indifference curve qq' is tangent to this line. His more restricted choice under specific responsibility places him on the lower indifference curve pp' instead. Specific responsibility also commonly leads to waste of in- puts, a result that can occur under overall value responsibility only when the employee derives zero marginal utility from all possible uses of every resource delegated to him.

Summary of basic hypotheses about economic behavior . under specific responsibility with no spillovers

The basic hypotheses about the employee's demand for information, the implicit prices that guide his uses of resources, his income, and his uses of inputs and supply of outputs differ substantially from those for overall value responsibility.

The employee's demand for information. An employee's desire to respond in his own interest to his employer's applications of specific responsibility to him largely determines his demand for information. He devotes resources to learning about what these applications are and how they affect him under alternative actions that he might take. These actions include productive uses of inputs, and thus he does obtain selective information about his production domain. However, the motivation for this information is not to reduce costs as with overall value responsibility, and his preferred responses to specific responsibility can lead him to learn about very inefficient resource uses. An employee will learn about more efficient production possibilities if they release resources yielding him utility, but only if he can prevent his employer from taking the gain for himself. Blauner (1964, p. 104) provides an example of assembly line workers who make their jobs easier or more pleasant as a result of

minor improvements in their tools. By shortening or lengthening the extension of a wrench socket, the assembler may be able to make the movements that he repeats all day long more easily and gracefully than with the standard equipment. Such illegitimate tools will be hidden in tool boxes to delay management detection and the consequent retiming of the job to the worker's disadvantage.

Prices that guide the employee's uses of resources. The implicit prices that guide those of an employee's resource uses that his employer does not influence are determined by the quantities of the pertinent resources available to him and his demands for the uses. Specific responsibility either shifts his demands for uses of resources or attaches (usually nonmonetary) prices to the uses. Because these prices depend in part on the employer's costs of establishing them, and since the employer often lacks an estimate of the marginal values to him of the employee's resource uses, these prices inaccurately reflect the employer's actual marginal values of the uses.

The employee's income from the organization. As in the case of overall value responsibility, the employee's income equals his salary and any other cash income from the organization plus the cash-equivalent value to him of in-kind benefits from resource diversions. However, he has less influence over his income than under overall value responsibility where an employee's income rises as he increases efficiency as long as he derives positive marginal utility from any of the resources delegated to him. Nonetheless, he can benefit from economizing on resources whose uses are not affected by specific responsibility, giving his income a limited residual component.

Because specific responsibility restricts an employee in substituting among personal uses of resources, he derives less utility from a given amount of resource diversions than he would under overall value responsibility.

The employee's uses of inputs and supply of outputs. An employee's choices to place inputs in uses that do and do not benefit the employer depend on his own demands for the uses and the employer's choices in placing specific responsibility on them, that is, his restricting the conditions under which resources can be used, providing complements and substitutes for the uses and attaching prices to them. These choices depend on costs of imposing specific responsibility as well as on the importance of the uses to the employer. When it is not cost effective for an employer to place specific responsibility on an employee's uses of a delegated resource, these uses are influenced only by the utility the employee derives from them. The employer's choices of which resources to delegate are interrelated with his choices in imposing specific responsibility. For example, an employer might not delegate cost-effective inputs that would be intensively used under overall value responsibility because of the costs of influencing employees' uses of them.

Specific responsibility makes employees' quantity uses of inputs less sensitive than they would be under overall value responsibility to changes in employers' marginal values of these resources. Therefore, the organization's resource substitutions are correspondingly less sensitive to changes in external market prices. For example, its demands for inputs purchased in external markets are less sensitive to changes in their market prices. Thus, evidence of price insensitivity such as that found by Lester (1946) can be explained with an application of marginal analysis to economic choices within an organization.

The employee's supply of his outputs is determined by the particular quantities of inputs placed in uses in the employer's interest, given the effects of the specific responsibility imposed on him. The higher the employee's demands for uses of inputs in the employer's interest and the more cost effective it is for the employer to influence these uses, the larger the employee's supply of his outputs with the resources delegated to him.

Efficiency. We have seen that an employee under overall value responsibility is guided by his employer's marginal values of the inputs attributed to him and minimizes his cost of his output. In constrast, an employee under specific responsibility usually selects inefficient input combinations; since input uses are determined by employees' demands for the uses and any applications of specific responsibility to them, and these applications are determined in part by the costs of imposing them, only by coincidence will efficient input combinations, such as point k in Figure 4.1, be selected.

C   The coordination of employees' actions in relation to internal technological spillovers under each type of responsibility

The analysis is now extended to include cases where the application of inputs within one production domain affects the productivity of inputs applied within others or directly affects their outputs. These effects are defined as *internal technological spillovers* or, simply, *spillovers* when the context is clear. Spillovers are encountered frequently, and although they can motivate mergers of production domains in the long run, there are offsetting long-run incentives of information cost savings and benefits from resource diversions to retain or increase the number of separate production domains. Employees' responses to spillovers, referred to as their *coordination* of their actions in relation to spillovers, is usually an important part of an organization's resource allocation in any short-run period.

An employee's productivity and that of the resources delegated to him are often affected significantly by other employees' actions. For example, an employee responsible for sales can be highly dependent on employees involved in product development or providing technical services to customers. The actions of these employees either affect the sales employee's outputs directly, or they affect the productivity of his efforts and other inputs. As another example, productivity in an employee's production domain can be affected by other employees' communication of their specialized knowledge.

For example, information about the employee's production domain provided by employees who use his outputs or make use of the same types of inputs he uses, or by employees who deal with legal, accounting, or regulatory effects on the organization of employees' actions, can increase the employee's output directly or enhance his inputs' productivities. When such information is a product of the other employees' work within the organization, it is an internal technological spillover.

Spillovers can result from employers' placing responsibility on their employees. For example, the specific responsibility imposed by one employer can influence the effectiveness of that imposed by another. With respect to overall value responsibility, output replacement or a switch to specific responsibility for one employee could be costly or beneficial to others.

In order to deal advantageously with spillovers, employees must coordinate their actions with each other. This can be effected by joint decision making or by delegating decision making about the relevant actions. In either case, agreed-upon mechanisms such as schedules and work plans can help. Whatever the means of coordination, it is usually necessary for there to be considerable communication and negotiation among the employees involved. In reference to cases where "workers, whose activities were directly interrelated, were separated from one another by management's formal organization of production," Sayles (1958) points out that "the intimate communications and self-control mechanisms of the work group do not function efficiently ... However, when those who are interdependent work closely together, the informal group itself produces the needed adjustments and interpersonal coordinations" (p. 79). Considering the many possible sources of spillovers in organizations, one might expect that much of the communication and negotiation about them will be among employees lacking authority over each other. Sayles and Strauss (1966) have pointed out that "specialization has increased the relative importance of lateral relationships ... Both managers and nonmanagers alike spend a great deal of their time in contact with other people in the organization ... In one organization, for example, managers had to maintain close working relationships with as many as 70 or 80 people who were not superiors or subordinates" (p. 398).

Perhaps the best known description of possible degrees of interdependence among an organization's subunits is that of Thompson (1967). His simplest case is when units' outputs are not inputs to other units. He suggests that a more interdependent case occurs when a unit's outputs are inputs to others and there is even more interdependence when the relationship is reciprocal. However, such interdependence requires only that demands for inputs be communicated and that responsibility be appropriately imposed. In contrast, spillovers require much more of employees' involvement in each other's activities. Lorsch and Allen (1973) regard an organization's dealing with interdependence as "integration, which we define as the degree of collaboration and mutual understanding actually achieved among the various organizational units" (p. 21). Their research [as well as earlier work of Lorsch (1965) and Lawrence and Lorsch (1967)] deals with devices such as "interunit committees and teams, special coordinating units and/or positions, and measurement and review practices" from which firms select depending on the "pattern of interdependence" (Lorsch and Allen, 1973, p. 17). Although Lorsch and Allen often refer to Thompson's classification, the cases they analyze clearly involve spillovers. Two economists who have analyzed spillovers within organizations are Hirshleifer (1957) and Tullock (1965, pp. 151–6).

In the analysis of the effects of spillovers on economic behavior within an organization, it is useful to make the well-known distinctions applied to externalities among independent economic agents. That is, one can distinguish among internal technological spillovers according to whether they are inframarginal or marginal, potentially relevant or irrelevant, and Pareto relevant or irrelevant.[2] One can also distinguish between separable and nonseparable spillovers.[3]

Moreover, because responsibility creates incentives that differ from the market incentives facing independent economic agents, additional distinctions must be made regarding internal technological spillovers. One such distinction is whether an employee's actions in response to a spillover are in his employer's interest. For example, employees can coordinate their actions in relation to a spillover to their own benefit but not their employers'. Another distinction is whether an employer would intervene to deal with a spillover himself if his employees do not adequately deal with it in his interest. If he would, an employee takes account of his employer's possible responses to them. For example, if an employer has the authority to merge employees' production domains and employees desire to avoid such mergers, inframarginal spillovers are more often Pareto relevant than they would be among independent economic agents.[4]

The type of responsibility facing an employee influences his responses to spillovers because it determines both how his welfare is affected by a spillover and the means by which he can deal with one.

Thus, resource allocation in relation to spillovers is analyzed separately according to the type of responsibility imposed on the employees involved. Except when noted otherwise, the analysis is confined to the case where the employees report to the same employer.

We consider the coordination of employees' actions in relation to spillovers first under CPOR and then when overall value and specific responsibility are imposed.

Coordination of employees' actions in relation to
spillovers under complete pricing overall
responsibility

We have already seen in Chapter 3 that the employer must possess detailed information about the employee's production domain in order to impose CPOR. However, the additional requirements for information created by spillovers can be elucidated by making the artificial assumption that the employer need not possess information about production domains in the absence of spillovers. Consider two employees reporting to the same employer who have a Pareto relevant spillover among their production domains. If the employees coordinate actions in relation to the spillover in a manner that initially makes one better off without the other being worse off, the employer will by assumption receive the benefit by subsequently taxing the benefiting employee. In general, the employer receives the benefits from employees' coordination in dealing with all Pareto relevant spillovers. Thus, employees lack the motivation to carry out the coordination on their own.

One possibility would be for the employer to use the scheme proposed by Davis and Whinston (1966) in which the employees propose alternative levels of each others' outputs and the employer sets prices that the employees must correspondingly pay each other. If the intention to maximize his own profits underlies each employee's proposals, the employer can, without information about employees' production domains, establish a set of prices that leads employees to coordinate their actions in relation to spillovers in such a manner that his net income is maximized.[5] However, consider the requirement that each employee must maximize his own net income. In order to focus on the additional information costs imposed by spillovers, assume that the employee already possesses information about his production domain, but only that information needed for efficient production at an initial rate of the output (or particular input application) of the other employee that directly affects his output or the productivities of his inputs. If the other employee's output should vary it would often be costly for the employee to obtain the necessary information about his production domain to maximize his pretax net income. For example, it may be necessary to induce the other employee to vary his output (or one of his input applications) experimentally and then undergo the costs of attempting different input applications within his own production domain.

Because employees lack incentive to obtain costly information about effects of spillovers in their production domains, the employer imposing CPOR must have detailed information about the production possibilities that are affected by spillovers in order to ensure that employees' pretax net incomes are maximized. Of course, the employer must also have detailed information about the other parts of employees' production domains; this discussion has pointed out how spillovers impose additional requirements for information.

Coordination of employees' actions in relation to
spillovers under overall value or specific responsibility

Under specific and overall value responsibility, employees frequently can coordinate themselves in the face of spillovers in a manner that increases their own welfare at the expense of their employer, and they sometimes do not deal with spillovers at all. The following sections first analyze the employer's behavior in obtaining information about spillovers among his employees' production domains and his choices of when to intervene to ensure that employees are coordinating themselves in his interest. Subsequently, we analyze the behavior of employees in relation to the remaining spillovers that the employer does not deal with.

The employer's behavior in obtaining information about spillovers and his choices to intervene. An employer imposing overall value responsibility will not benefit from intervening to deal with spillovers among his employees' production domains unless the spillovers extend beyond these employees or intervention would also lower the employees' allowable resource diversions, that is, reduce output replacement costs or the overall productivity levels at which the employer would switch to specific responsibility. Lorsch and Allen (1973, p. 114) provide an example:

[Firm 3] had undertaken a bold effort to get three divisions to collaborate in providing a complex system of products to the government ... The program immediately ran into the parochial interests of each division ... Basically, each division manager was more motivated to focus on his own differentiated goals than those of the total corporation. In effect, this is what the control and reward system told him he should do. While the president occasionally gave off signals about the importance of interdivisional collaboration, they were not sufficiently strong.

Although an employer imposing overall value responsibility lacks an incentive to coordinate his employees' actions in relation to spillovers per se, a spillover might lead him to suspect that he could reduce his employees' allowable resource diversions. For example, he might believe that by intervening to coordinate employees in relation to a spillover he would learn about reorganization possibilities that lower output replacement costs or about more cost-effective ways of imposing specific responsibility that reduce the costs of employees' outputs at which he would switch to this type of responsibility. If so, lower allowable resource diversions would take effect regardless of whether the spillover is in fact dealt with effectively. If a spillover affects the productive activities of employees who are under other employers, and the employer is rewarded or penalized for it, he treats it as one of his employees' outputs and accordingly prices it implicitly or explicitly.

Employees under specific responsibility cannot make compensating adjustments that maintain the employer's cost of their outputs after he intervenes to coordinate their actions in relation to spillovers. Thus, an employer imposing specific responsibility has an incentive to deal directly with his employees' spillovers whenever the direct cost reduction exceeds the costs of intervening. Such intervention is often a modest extension of his other applications of specific responsibility.

Employees' behavior in relation to spillovers that the employer does not deal with himself. We now consider employees' benefits and costs from coordinating their actions in relation to those spillovers that the employer does not deal with. The potential gain to employees from such coordination depends importantly on whether they are under overall value responsibility or specific responsibility. Benefits from resource diversions are a residual for an employee under overall value responsibility deriving positive marginal utility from any of the resources available to him; and thus, a spillover that affects the marginal productivities of any of his inputs or directly affects his output at the margin is potentially relevant. Inframarginal spillovers can also be potentially relevant, since employees often find it economical to coordinate their entire applications of inputs.

Potentially relevant spillovers under specific responsibility are confined to those that (1) affect the available quantities of resources whose uses directly give the employee utility; (2) affect the quantities of complements or substitutes for these uses; and (3) raise the employer's costs of imposing specific responsibility. Other spillovers are not potentially relevant no matter how much they affect the combined productivity of employees' production domains. As an example of a spillover that yields an employee a larger quantity of a desired resource, consider a case where specific responsibility allows an employee to make personal use of a given fraction of his output. A spillover that directly increases the rate of his output yields him more output for his own use. If a spillover increases the productivity of one of his inputs, and specific responsibility allows personal use of this input, the employee can benefit from the released quantity of this resource. Spillovers can affect an employer's costs of imposing specific responsibility as, for example, when they make an input more jointly productive with another input.

Employees' costs of coordinating their actions in the face of spillovers derive from costs of information about their own production domains and about other employees' production domains and preferences, and also from negotiation costs. An employee's costs of relevant information about his own production domain can be especially high when spillovers affecting his outputs are nonseparable (that is, marginal productivities of his inputs are affected) and when the most cost-effective means to obtain information about changes in marginal productivities is to induce other employees to vary their input uses experimentally. An employee under specific responsibility usually faces higher costs of coordinating his actions in relation to spillovers, because he starts with less information about his own production domain. The means by which employees coordinate their actions to economize on resources devoted to information and negotiation are analyzed in Chapter 7.

Employees under specific responsibility must have information about each others' production domains to achieve Pareto optimal coordination of their actions in relation to spillovers. However, it might appear that employees under overall value responsibility could avoid obtaining this information because it is theoretically possible for them to coordinate themselves via a cooperative Davis–Whinston scheme. Unlike the case of CPOR, these employees do find it worthwhile to minimize their costs when they benefit from resource diversions at the margin. Nonetheless, if benefits from resource diversions have to be taken in kind, the employees managing the scheme need information about preferences to set the payments employees make to each other. Additionally, they have to obtain enough information about production domains to prevent the coordinated employees from being able to " 'bluff' in hope of obtaining a better solution from their private point of view" (Davis and Whinston, 1966, p. 317). In Chapter 7 I argue that employees do delegate to specialized employees the task of coordinating their actions in relation to spillovers. However, these employees effect coordination by issuing instructions that are based on information they obtain about the coordinated employees' production domains. They reduce the costs of this information by including among their numbers "representatives" from groups of coordinated employees having production domains with similar characteristics.

> *Summary of basic hypotheses about economic behavior in the face of internal technological spillovers*

The following two subsections present summaries of how the type of responsibility imposed affects employers' and employees' behavior in relation to spillovers. Then, Section D includes a summary of the influences of spillovers on demands for information in an organization.

Employers' differential incentives under overall value and specific responsibility to deal with spillovers. We have seen that an employer imposing overall value responsibility leaves more spillovers to be dealt with by employees than if he were imposing specific responsibility. He intervenes himself to deal with spillovers only when they extend beyond his own employees or when the intervention enables him to reduce employees' output replacement costs or the cost at which he switches to specific responsibility. In contrast, an employer imposing specific responsibility deals with spillovers whenever he has an available application of specific responsibility that is cost effective in the particular circumstance.

Employees' differential incentives under overall value and specific responsibility to coordinate their actions in relation to spillovers. Employees under overall value responsibility have a much stronger incentive to coordinate their actions in relation to spillovers than if they were under specific responsibility. Whenever employees derive utility from resource diversions at the margin, overall value responsibility makes potentially relevant all spillovers that affect marginal productivities of inputs, and many spillovers that affect productivity inframarginally are also potentially relevant. The only potentially relevant spillovers under specific responsibility are those that directly release resources whose uses give the employee utility, or that release complements or substitutes for these uses, or raise employers' costs of imposing this type of responsibility.

D   Summary of demands for information and implications for the dispersion of information within the organization

The demands for information within an organization can be considered in relation to the concept of informational decentralization that grew out of the early debates on the feasibility of centralized planning. We have seen that information costs lead employers to delegate to employees discretion over resource allocation and then impose resource responsibility on them. Each type of responsibility in turn creates its own incentives for employees and employers to devote resources to obtaining information. These resources can amount to a large part of an organization's social cost. However, the cost of information in an organization can vary substantially depending on the degree to which demands for information are aligned with information cost advantages.

Recent research, most notably that of Hurwicz (1960b, 1969, 1972), has given operational significance to the concept of informational decentralization by formally analyzing the implications of any resource allocation mechanism for the types of costly information that are held by its participants. The early debates and the subsequent research have thus focused attention on the costs of information held and interpreted by participants in competing economic systems as one of the key evaluation criteria for choosing among the systems. Economic systems can have differing numbers and sizes of organizations, and these organizations can select among alternative suborganizations and types of responsibility. It is therefore worthwhile to take information demands within organizations into account when comparing economic systems whose organizations differ.

In the spirit of the concepts of information cost advantages and informational decentralization, I consider two categories of demands for information. The first includes an employee's demand for information about his own production domain. Because of the presence of resources in organizations that are not competitively priced in external markets, I also include in this category the employee's demand for information about the marginal values to others, whether inside or outside the organization, of his inputs and outputs. Included in the second category is additional information about how the employer places responsibility on him and about other employees' production demans and preferences beyond what is needed to infer these marginal values. Also in this category are the employer's demands for information in order to impose responsibility. We have already considered these demands both in the absence and presence of spillovers, and the following discussion focuses on their relationships to information cost advantages.[6]

*The employee's demand for information about his
production domain and the values of his
inputs and outputs*

We have seen that an employee under overall value responsibility gains from information that enables him to reduce his costs whenever he derives utility at the margin from using any of his inputs or outputs. In contrast, CPOR and specific responsibility both give employees weak incentives to obtain information about their production domains in spite of their major differences in resource allocation. Because the employee's income is taxed to his compensated opportunity cost under CPOR, he does not benefit from information leading to more technically efficient applications of inputs. An employee under specific responsibility gains from information about only those potential uses of inputs that either directly increase his utility or raise the employer's costs of imposing specific responsibility on him.

Information about his employer's marginal values of his inputs and outputs is available at no cost to an employee under CPOR via the required explicit prices of all economically important characteristics of his inputs and outputs. Under the other types of responsibility, the employee bears many of the costs of obtaining this information and he decides how much of it to obtain. An employee under overall value responsibility who derives utility at the margin from using any of the resources delegated to him has an incentive to learn about his employer's conscious marginal valuation of each of the inputs and outputs that he believes the employer attributes to him. In contrast, an employee under specific responsibility infers only the employer's applications of specific responsibility to his uses of resources. Because these applications are also influenced by his employer's costs of imposing them, the employee does not infer the employer's marginal values of his inputs or outputs.

An employer imposing overall value responsibility will often take advantage of an employee's incentive to ascertain his marginal values of the inputs and outputs he delegates in order to reduce his own communication costs or to raise third parties' information costs. However, an employee may have an information cost disadvantage that exceeds the avoided communication cost for the employer, such as when the valuation of a resource depends on the employer's preferences. In contrast, in cases such as when an employee directly provides multiple outputs (or output characteristics) to a client and the employer is concerned only with the client's overall satisfaction, there are cost savings from the employee's incentive to determine a combination of outputs that achieves a given level of the client's satisfaction at minimum cost; it is unnecessary for the employer to have information about the separate contribution of each output to the client's satisfaction.

Of course, any informational economies created by incentives on employees do not necessarily benefit the funding authority or the organization's clientele.

Other demands for information

Each type of responsibility creates its own incentives for employees to have demands for information not pertaining to their own production domains or the marginal values to others of their inputs and outputs. Each type of responsibility also provides different incentives for employers to obtain information about their employees' production domains and preferences.

The employee's demands. An employee's demands for information about the responsibility placed on him are considered first. Subsequently we shall consider the employee's demands for information about the production domains and preferences of other employees. Under CPOR all information about resource responsibility is contained within the prices of the employee's inputs and outputs and the tax on his income. In contrast, it is necessary for an employee under one of the other types of responsibility to acquire information about how responsibility constrains him and what are his preferred responses. An employee under overall value responsibility infers the cost of his output at which his employer would replace it or place specific responsibility on him. His willingness to pay for information is limited only by his loss of rent from the employer taking one of these actions. He attempts to learn about his employer's perceived gains from making these changes. The employee also values information about the employer's actual gains in order to be able to correct the employer's perception whenever he appears to have overestimated the potential of a change. This information often includes details about more costly sources of his output or data about the availability of less cost-effective substitutes.

An employee under specific responsibility has a demand for information about each particular application of this type of responsibility, for example, his work rules, the monitoring of his uses of resources, and the applicable rewards or penalties. In each case, his willingness to pay for information depends on the resulting increase in his estimated capability to make preferred uses of resources. If personal replacement cost limits some of the employee's resource diversions he also infers his employer's estimate of this cost and learns what the cost actually is.

Overall value responsibility provides stronger incentives than specific responsibility for an employee to coordinate his activities with those of other employees. Such coordination often leads employees to obtain information about other employees' production domains and preferences. We have seen that in order to implement a cooperative Davis–Whinston scheme it would in fact be necessary for the employees managing the scheme to have some of this type of information. Such information is obtained by the specialized employees suggested in Chapter 7 to have key roles in coordinating employees' actions in relation to spillovers.

Although employees under specific responsibility have less incentive to deal with spillovers, their coordination to raise employers' costs of particular applications of specific responsibility lead them to obtain information about each other's production domains and preferences.

The employer's demands. In order to impose CPOR the employer must have detailed information about an employee's preferences, labor market opportunities, production domain, and his particular uses of the resources delegated to him. His motivation for imposing other types of responsibility is to economize on information. Nonetheless, he spends on information whenever it reduces his costs of employees' outputs by a larger amount.

An employer imposing overall value responsibility has a demand for information about an employee's production domain only insofar as it helps determine the critical cost at which he would switch to specific responsibility or replace the employee's output. An employer planning to take the latter course learns about alternative supply opportunities when the alternative suppliers do not themselves communicate this information to him. The employer has a demand for information about the total values to him of the employee's delegated inputs and supplied outputs in order to determine the employee's overall value productivity.

An employer imposing specific responsibility learns about an employee's preferences and production domain to facilitate his selection of cost-effective applications of this type of responsibility. However, the employer's selective information about production domains usually does not enable him to determine least-cost input combinations. If resource diversions are cumulatively attributable to individual employees, the employer has additional demands for information about personal replacement costs. When an employee who would be replaced has specific skills or if his replacement would disrupt other production, the employer has additional demands for technical information about his production domain.

CHAPTER 5

Short-run resource allocation in response to demand: the cases of an employee, a private corporation, and a private nonprofit organization

This chapter separately analyzes the short-run resource allocation in response to demand of an employee, a private corporation, and a private nonprofit organization. The external demands for private organizations' outputs are taken as given and a managing employee's demand for his employee's output is derived. Based on the analysis of Chapter 4, Section A derives the employer's and the employee's costs of each rate of the employee's delivered output. Section B analyzes an employee's supply behavior in response to a managing employee's demand. Sections C and D respectively analyze the supplies of private corporations and private nonprofit organizations in response to their external demands.

A Costs to the employer and to the employee of the employee's delivered output and simplifying assumptions about these costs

This section applies the analysis of Chapter 4 to derive the costs to an employer and to his employee of each rate of the employee's delivered output. Although the employee might not supply part of his output to his employer or to other parties whose receipt of this output benefits his employer, I ignore such quantities (i.e., amounts put to personal use, wasted, or supplied to other parties) in order to simplify the exposition. The exposition is also facilitated by the assumption of a single output. An employee's output can either be a separate intermediate or final output or his determinate contribution to such an output.

   The employee's cost of a given rate of output is defined to be the quantities of the inputs he actually uses to produce this output times the employer's cash equivalent marginal values of these inputs. Using the employer's marginal values of inputs in this definition enables us to compare the employee's cost with that of the employer and thus determine his cost advantage. The employer's cost of the same output equals his value of all the inputs he must delegate to the employee, given the resource diversions allowed by the responsibility facing the employee, plus his costs of imposing this responsibility.

The determination of an employer's and his employee's cost of the latter's output varies with the type of responsibility placed on the employee. The employer's costs of imposing responsibility are the sole source of difference between the employer's and employee's costs under CPOR. An employee under CPOR selects combinations of inputs within his production domain and, along with all other employees who are under CPOR, deals with spillovers in such a way as to maximize the net income of the lowest level employer to whom they commonly report (disregarding his responsibility costs). Because resource allocation under CPOR is efficient if we disregard the costs of imposing responsibility, an employee's costs under CPOR provide a useful contrast with costs under the other types of responsibility that are actually placed on him. For this reason, the figures for supply behavior in this and later chapters show the employee's costs under CPOR. (These costs do not include what would be the employer's costs of imposing CPOR.) In these figures it is assumed that CPOR is placed on all the organization's employees and that there is no monopoly pricing of the organization's intermediate outputs.

An employee under overall value responsibility selects the most efficient combination of inputs within his production domain, and his cost for a given rate of output is, in this sense, minimized. (This cost minimization is illustrated by the tangency of a budget line to the employee's isoquant at point k in Figure 4.1.) However, his costs usually differ from those under CPOR because of inadequate incentives for employees to coordinate their actions vis-à-vis internal technological spillovers in their employers' interests. Although an individual employee's own costs could as a result be lower or higher than under CPOR, the figures always illustrate higher costs, because these inadequate incentives raise the combined costs of all employees.

Under specific responsibility there are inefficiencies within the employee's production domain brought about by the absence of benefits from resource diversions as a residual net income to him. Therefore, the employee's cost of each rate of his output typically exceeds what it would be under overall value responsibility. (For a given rate of output and disregarding spillovers, the difference between the employee's costs under specific and overall value responsibility is illustrated by the difference in the amounts corresponding to the budget lines through point b and point a in Figure 4.5.)

The total cost of his employee's output to an employer imposing overall value responsibility is limited by the sum of (1) the employer's cost under a different supply arrangement. This is the cost of his best alternative supply of the employee's output, or the minimum compensating amount that would make him equally well off without this output (our example being his obtaining a quantity of a substitute and adjusting resource uses so he is as well off using it), or his cost of obtaining the employee's output via imposing specific responsibility on him, whichever is lowest; (2) the employer's amortized one-time cost of making one of these changes; and (3) the employer's responsibility costs, that is, the cost of determining the employee's overall value productivity and deciding on the cost at which he will replace the employee's output or switch to specific responsibility. Under specific responsibility the employer's total cost of the employee's output exceeds the employee's total cost by his value of all resources used in the employee's interest or wasted, given the employer's choices in imposing specific responsibility, plus his costs of this responsibility. Despite the inefficiency within the employee's production domain under specific responsibility, the employer's total cost can be lower than when overall value responsibility is imposed; we have seen that the relative magnitudes of these costs depend on relative allowable resource diversions and responsibility costs under the two types of responsibility in the particular situation.

The employer's and the employee's costs of the employee's output both have components that are fixed and vary with the rate of the employee's output. Fixed costs can, of course, result from the infeasibility of varying inputs in the short run. But employers can also treat costs as fixed because of employees' discretion over the application of inputs that would be feasible to vary. When it is not in an employee's interest to vary an input and it is not economical for his employer to induce him to vary it, the input can be regarded as being, from the employer's perspective, fixed. Further, the costs of imposing responsibility constitute part of the employer's cost of the employee's output, and we have seen that these costs have components that do and do not vary with the rate of the employee's output.

For an employer imposing overall value responsibility, his fixed and variable costs of an employee's output are determined by the fixed and variable components of his responsibility costs and the fixed and variable costs he would face if he replaced the employee's output or imposed specific responsibility on him. I only consider cases where the employer's fixed costs, and his total variable costs for each rate of output, respectively exceed the employee's fixed and variable costs.[1] The employee's fixed allowable resource diversions equal the following: the fixed component of the employer's critical total cost at which he will replace the employee's output or switch to specific responsibility, plus the employer's transitional cost of making the change, taken as fixed,[2] minus the employee's fixed production costs under CPOR. Similarly, the employee's variable allowable resource diversions are determined by the component of this critical total cost that does vary with the employer's desired rate of the employee's output; this variable quantity, minus the employee's total variable cost of his output under CPOR, equals his variable allowable resource diversions.

The employer imposing specific responsibility makes choices concerning the intensity of incentives on employees and the quantities of inputs he delegates to them that determine the quantities of each input and output placed in each use in the employer's and the employee's interest and the quantities wasted. Some uses of resources and wasted quantities do not vary with the rate of the employee's output and others do, thus establishing the employer's fixed and variable costs. Given these costs and the employee's fixed and variable costs under CPOR, his fixed and variable resource diversions are determined.

Because fixed production and responsibility costs and fixed resource diversions do not influence short-run resource allocation, they are not taken into account in the analysis of the short run in this chapter and Chapter 6. The derived rate of a private corporation's short-run profits is a gross value before subtraction of these fixed quantities. Similarly, the derived rate of the funding authority's welfare from other types of organization is a gross amount from which these fixed quantities are subtracted. To simplify the figures, fixed costs and fixed resource diversions are not shown. However, they become important in the long run. (See Chapter 8.)

Under overall value responsibility, the employer's marginal cost of the employee's output equals either marginal output replacement cost or the marginal cost of obtaining the employee's output via specific responsibility, plus marginal responsibility costs. For some ranges of output in particular cases, the employee's marginal cost could exceed the employer's marginal output replacement cost based on the marginal cost he would face if he obtained the employee's output from an alternative source or used a substitute (while making the necessary adjustments of resource uses to be equally well off with it). However, I only consider cases where the employee's marginal cost is less than the employer's marginal cost for all rates of output.

The employer's marginal cost under specific responsibility equals the marginal cost of resources used in his interest (the employee's marginal cost) plus the sum of his marginal costs of resources used in the employee's interest, marginal wasted resources, and the sum of marginal costs of his applications of specific responsibility.

The separate components of the employer's marginal costs could have been shown separately in the figures (in later sections and in subsequent chapters), but have not been because their total is what affects output determination in response to demand. The amount by which the employer's marginal cost exceeds the employee's marginal cost under CPOR equals marginal resource diversions plus marginal costs of imposing responsibility.

To simplify the figures, the employer's and employee's marginal costs are treated as constants. The assumption of constant marginal costs is frequently unrealistic and can be relaxed without changing the results. It is interesting to note, however, that economies in imposing responsibility on larger amounts of economic activity should often result in decreasing marginal responsibility costs. These decreasing marginal costs added to rising marginal production costs might help explain the many findings of "constant returns to scale" in production function estimates.

The employer's cost shown is that which results from his choice between overall value and specific responsibility.

B Short-run resource allocation when an employee responds to a managing employee's demand

The demand of a managing employee for an output of his employee is straightforwardly derived. The managing employee can make uses of his employee's output that do not result in resource diversions vis-à-vis his own employer, say, by efficiently using it as an input to produce an output delivered to his employer. Alternatively, he can make uses of it that do result in resource diversions and these uses may or may not benefit him personally.

I assume that a managing employee attaches diminishing marginal value to his increased quantity uses of an employee's output that do not result in resource diversions; this would result from the employee's output having diminishing marginal productivity as an input or from its diminishing marginal value to his own employer or to a client that is reflected in the responsibility facing the managing employee. Similarly, let the managing employee derive decreasing marginal benefits from placing his employee's output in uses that do result in resource diversions vis-à-vis his own employer. These include any inefficient uses that benefit his employer and efficient or inefficient uses that only benefit himself such as personal uses or uses in producing outputs not demanded by his employer. Whether or not inefficient uses of his employee's output benefit the managing employee, we shall assume that he pays increasing penalties (via the responsibility imposed on him) if he places larger quantities of the employee's output in them; he will thus add more of this resource to such uses only when it is compensatingly less costly to him. Under these assumptions the managing employee's demand for his employee's output is a decreasing function of its cash equivalent price to him.

It is worthwhile to consider the managing employee's possible uses of his employee's output in more detail. Under CPOR his demand for his employee's output reflects only uses that do not result in resource diversions. In response to an exogenous decrease in his cost of the employee's output, the managing employee might substitute larger quantities of this output as an input. If the employee's output is sold to a third party, the buyer's demand determines the price sensitivity of the managing employee's demand.

Under other types of responsibility, however, resource diversions can also underlie the managing employee's demand for the employee's output. These include uses that do and do not benefit him. If the managing employee is under overall value responsibility, his benefits from resource diversions are a residual, and his demand for his employee's output weighs the productivity of inputs in his production domain against any utility he derives from them in personal uses or gains from trading them. If he is instead under specific responsibility, his employer will at some point limit any uses of a resource that result in resource diversions because they cost him more as larger quantities of the resource are placed in them. Similarly, either his employer or other employees will at some point induce a managing employee under overall value responsibility to limit his uses of resources that are not attributed to him or that have undesired spillover effects. A managing employee under specific responsibility has much less incentive to make resource substitutions in his production domain and is restricted in making substitutions among personal uses of resources that would benefit him. Thus his demand for his employee's output is less price sensitive than if he were under overall value responsibility.

Before proceeding to the employee's supply to his managing employee, we must consider the managing employee's personal costs of replacing an employee's output or imposing specific responsibility on him. Such tasks as "monitoring," "penalizing," "motivating," "reprimanding," "firing," and "reorganizing" employees are often unpleasant, and we have seen that they are risky and can adversely affect the managing employee's relationships with other employees. A managing employee under overall value responsibility directly benefits from imposing responsibility. But if he is working under specific responsibility, his benefits from imposing responsibility depend on the particular ways in which specific responsibility is imposed on him. If the managing employee under either type of responsibility must receive the benefits of imposing responsibility in kind and these benefits are worth less to him than their cash value to his employer, he will allow his employee larger resource diversions than if he could take the benefits in cash.

We shall consider the simplified case where the employer is aware of the total value to him of the resources delegated to his employee, and thus knows his entire cost of the employee's output.[3] Figures 5.1 and 5.2 illustrate the employee's supply behavior in the respective cases where he delivers his output to the managing employee and to a client. In both figures it is assumed that when CPOR is placed on the employee it is also placed on the managing employee, and vice versa. The middle demand line of Figure 5.1 represents what would be the managing employee's demand for the employee's output under CPOR. The typical demand of a managing employee under overall value responsibility for his employee's output is represented by the highest demand line, while the demand of a managing employee under specific responsibility is often represented by the lowest, as well as the highest, demand line. These demand lines are horizontal sums of the managing employee's demands for uses of his employee's output that do and do not result in resource diversions vis-à-vis his own employer. Because of inadequate incentive for employees under overall value responsibility to deal efficiently with spillovers, the latter demand could conceivably be low enough to make the combined demands lower than under CPOR. This outcome would be unusual. However, if the managing employee is under specific responsibility, his demand for uses of the employee's output not resulting in resource diversions is often substantially lower, and whether this lower demand would offset his demand for uses involving resource diversions is problematic. Thus, the demand of an employer under specific responsibility can as easily be lower as it can be higher than it would be under CPOR.

The highest two cost lines represent the managing employee's

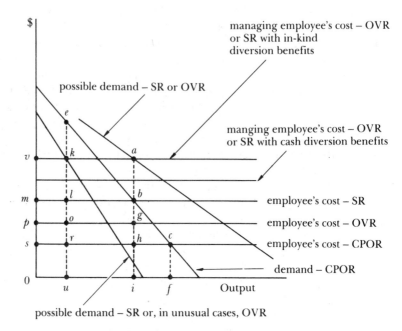

Figure 5.1. Short-run price, budget, and output of an employee. The employee's output is not directly sold to a client. When CPOR is imposed on the employee, it is also imposed on the managing employee, and vice versa. Marginal and average variable cost is shown. (OVR = overall value responsibility; SR = specific responsibility; CPOR — complete pricing overall responsibility.)

marginal and average variable costs of the employee's output, including the employee's allowable variable resource diversions. The difference between these lines is the employee's extra allowable resource diversions at each rate of output due to the managing employee's reduced net return to imposing responsibility when his benefits from doing so are in kind and he derives less utility from in-kind benefits than from cash equal to the resources' value to his employer. Regardless of whether the managing employee's benefits from imposing responsibility are in cash or in kind, his marginal cost of the employee's output equals the employee's marginal production cost under CPOR, plus the employee's marginal allowable resource diversions and the managing employee's marginal costs of imposing responsibility on the employee. The lowest cost line represents the employee's marginal and average variable cost under CPOR, and the next two cost lines respectively indicate his marginal and average variable cost under overall value and specific responsibility. Recall that the employee's costs are higher under specific responsibility than overall value responsibility because he lacks incentive for efficiency within his production domain.

The managing employee's total variable cost for any quantity of the employee's output includes the exact amount of his employee's allowable variable resource diversions for that quantity; he can elicit any particular output rate that he desires by spending that quantity's total variable cost. Thus, he selects the rate of the employee's output at which his marginal value of the output equals his marginal cost. In the case illustrated in Figure 5.1 where this output is delivered to the employer, the equilibrium rate of the employee's output would be $0f$ if the employer had no variable costs of imposing CPOR and thus his marginal cost under this type of responsibility equaled the employee's. Equilibrium output determination under the other types of responsibility is shown where the managing employee's benefits from resource diversions must be taken in kind. The relationships in Figure 5.1 are such that in the case with higher demand, equilibrium output $0i$ is lower than it would be with CPOR. At this rate of output, the amount $0iav$ is the managing employee's total variable cost, comprising the employee's total variable costs under CPOR plus his total allowable variable resource diversions and the employer's total variable responsibility costs. However, depending on the offsetting effects of higher costs and demand, output could easily be higher than it would be under CPOR. Equilibrium output is always less in the case with lower demand and is the amount $0u$ in Figure 5.1. In this case the managing employee's total variable cost equals $0ukv$.

That $0i$ and $0u$ are equilibrium rates of output can be seen from the analysis of employees' allowable resource diversions in Chapter 4. It is more costly than worthwhile to reduce the resource diversions of employees under specific responsibility below the allowable amount. An employee under overall value responsibility can reduce his rate of nondiverted output in response to a reduction in his budget because the rate of output that is available to the employer with this amount from an alternative source or via specific responsibility is correspondingly lower. Therefore, if an employer with demands depicted at $0i$ or at $0u$ reduced his variable expenditures below $0iav$ or $0ukv$, he would either be spending a suboptimal amount on responsibility for that output or he would be reducing the variable component of the employee's budget and thus reducing the employee's resource diversions below those allowed by responsibility for output $0i$ or $0u$. In the latter case, the employee would have to redeploy resources out of uses that yield him benefits from resource diversions in order to maintain his output at $0i$ or $0u$. Thus, the employee minimizes his loss of these benefits by reducing the quantity of output he delivers to the employer to that rate where the resource diversions allowed by responsibility are covered by his budget; as a result, the employer's welfare would decrease by the excess of his demand over his marginal cost for the reduced output quantity.

Total variable resource diversions plus the managing employee's variable responsibility costs are represented in Figure 5.1 by the quantity *shav* in the case of the higher demand. The amounts *shgp* and *shbm* are always welfare losses due to inefficient uses of resources under overall value and specific responsibility, respectively. The remaining amounts *pgav* and *mbav* are made up of the employer's total variable responsibility costs and the employee's total variable cost advantage; the latter quantity potentially benefits the employee (more so when he is under overall value responsibility than in the case of specific responsibility). The comparable values for the lower demand case are *srkv* (total variable resource diversions and responsibility costs), *srop* and *srlm* (welfare losses due to inefficient resource uses), and *pokv* and *mlkv* (total variable responsibility costs plus employees' total variable cost advantage).

There are several components to the welfare loss that result from the high costs of CPOR inducing employers to place other types of responsibility on employees. To the welfare losses already mentioned, are added the welfare losses of *rce* and *hcb* in the lower and higher demand cases that result from differences in the rate of the employee's output from what it would be under CPOR. We must of course also add the welfare loss due to employees' discount from cash value of many of the benefits from resource diversions that are taken in kind. If CPOR should become costless to impose, there would be Kaldor-Hicks efficiency gains, not Pareto efficiency gains, in the typical case where employees would not be compensated for their losses of benefits from resource diversions.

Now consider the case illustrated in Figure 5.2 where the employee's output is directly sold to a client. Line *ae* illustrates the client's demand. The same five categories of costs as in Figure 1 are shown. If the managing employee is under overall value responsibility, with profits from the sale of the employee's output treated as his output, he must pass on to his employer a critical rate of profits to avoid replacement or having the employer switch to specific responsibility. Any profits beyond this critical amount that he must pass on

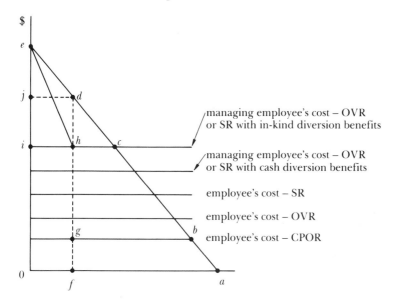

Figure 5.2. Short-run price, budget, and output of an employee. The employee's output is directly sold to a client. When CPOR is imposed on the employee, it is also imposed on the managing employee, and vice versa. Marginal and average variable cost is shown.

accrue to him (although often in kind rather than in cash), and if he derives utility from resource diversions at the margin, he will maximize profits by equating marginal revenue (line *he*) to marginal and average variable cost at point *h*. Marginal revenue to the managing employee is thus the demand to which the employee responds, and he produces output 0*f*. The welfare loss component represented by *gbd* consists of an amount *hcd* due to monopoly pricing and an amount *gbch* due to the high costs of imposing CPOR. The profit *ihdj* includes the critical rate of profits that the managing employee must pass on.

It would not be in the managing employee's interest to delegate control to the employee over pricing of the output unless he were to place overall value responsibility on the employee based on profit from sale of his output. When the employee's allowable resource diversions instead keep increasing with the quantity of output he delivers to the client (as shown in the figure), he will charge the lowest price he can get away with in the case where he keeps none of the profit. In the extreme opposite case where he may keep all of the profit in cash (in addition to the other resource diversions shown in the figure), his price would be determined by the point on demand where marginal revenue is below his own cost of the output by the amount of his cash-equivalent gain from his other variable resource diversions at the margin. In more realistic cases where the employee keeps smaller shares of profit, he would find it in his interest to charge even lower prices and produce even higher rates of output.

If the managing employee's employer should fail to regard his output as the profit from the sale of his employee's output, and if the managing employee's own allowable resource diversions should be a positive function of the amounts of this output delivered to clients, he would charge a lower price than $0j$ and his employee's output would exceed $0f$. As a result, pricing decisions tend to be centralized at points of a corporation where it is possible to place employees under overall value responsibility with profits treated as their outputs.

It is interesting to note that the supplying employee can have entrepreneurial incentives with respect to the managing employee's or a client's actual or potential demand for his output. These incentives are especially strong when there are large differences in his and the managing employee's marginal costs of his output and he derives substantial utility from increased resource diversions. An example is the frequently observed tendency for technical personnel to anticipate future demands for their services and communicate these possibilities to their employers.

*Summary of basic hypotheses about the short-run
demand for and supply of an employee's output*

The foregoing analysis implies the following specific hypotheses.

The employer's demand. The responsibility placed on a managing employee determines the degree to which his demand for an employee's output derives from uses of this output that do and do not result in resource diversions. When the managing employee is under overall value responsibility, he makes efficient uses of his employee's output, both involving and not involving resource diversions, within his production domain. Thus, except in unusual cases of inadequately coordinated actions in relation to economically important spillovers, his demand for the input is higher than if he were under CPOR. Because of inefficient uses of his employee's output in his own production domain, a managing employee under specific responsibility can have a demand for this output that is, in typical cases, higher or lower than if he were under CPOR.

A managing employee under overall value responsibility weighs the productivity of inputs in his production domain against any utility he gains from them in personal use or in exchange with other employees. But if he is under specific responsibility he cannot as generally benefit from such substitutions or exchanges and thus his demand for his employee's output is less sensitive to price.

The employee's supply. The marginal cost to the employer of each quantity of the employee's output constitutes the employee's supply schedule. For any quantity, this cost includes the employee's marginal resource diversions allowed by responsibility and the employer's marginal responsibility costs. The equilibrium output quantity occurs where the employer's marginal cost equals his marginal value of the output. The crucial role of resource responsibility in determining supply and demand within an organization does not imply a reduced role of the nature of production functions; technology affects the choices of delegation of discretion over resource allocation and the cost effectiveness of alternative types of responsibility on those holding discretion. Thus, Woodward's conclusions (1965) about the influence of technology can be extended to the determination of an employee's equilibrium rate of output.

Efficiency. At the equilibrium rate of an employee's output, welfare losses derive both from divergences of the managing employee's demand from what it would be under CPOR and from divergences between the managing employee's costs and those his employee would face under CPOR. There are also welfare losses from inefficiency within the employee's production domain under specific responsibility and from inadequate coordination of employees' actions in relation to spillovers both under specific and overall value responsibility. The employee's discount of in-kind benefits from resource diversions below the employer's cash value of the resources involved results in another welfare loss.

When an employee delivers all of his output to his employer, his equilibrium rate of output is determined by the equality of the employer's marginal cost, not his own, to demand. The employee's marginal cost is usually lower than the employer's. We have seen in Chapter 4 that under overall value responsibility in the absence of spillovers the ratios of marginal products of the employee's inputs equal the ratios of their marginal values to the employer. Thus, the marginal value product of every input exceeds its marginal value to the employer by the same proportion. Inadequate incentives for employees to coordinate their actions in relation to spillovers can alter this condition, which holds only coincidentally under specific responsibility. When the employee makes personal use of some of his output, he produces more of it but he typically attaches less cash equivalent value to this extra output than would the employer.

C   Short-run price, income, and output of the private corporation

In the analysis of price and output determination of private corporations, private nonprofit organizations, and public organizations, one or more top managing employees reports directly to the funding authority (or to a governing board, which reports to the funding authority). All of the organization's other employees report to top managing employees directly or through other managing employees. The costs faced by top managing employees include the resource diversions allowed by the responsibility facing those employees who report to them directly, plus the resource diversions that these employees must allow their employees, and so on, plus all costs of imposing responsibility within the organization. The top managing employees of a private corporation are assumed to exercise discretion over the pricing of its outputs. The analysis can be extended to cases where top managing employees delegate this discretion (see the previous section).

It is assumed that a private corporation's short-run profits do not come at the expense of long-run profitability; the effects of relaxing this assumption are considered in the analysis of the long run. Whereas stockholders prefer that top managing employees select rates of output that maximize short-run profits, these employees may prefer other output rates. For example, they might have "managerial" motivation to increase sales at the expense of profitability (for a survey see Marris and Mueller, 1980). In what is perhaps the best-known model (Baumol, 1959), the corporation's top managing employees maximize sales subject to the constraint that the corporation's profits must meet a minimum goal. However, an analysis of the profitability achieved by a top managing employee should take into account the responsibility facing him. For example, top managing employees may be able to use the resource diversions allowed by this responsibility to finance marketing expenditures that achieve unprofitable sales increases. In this case, there could be the same profits at a higher rate of sales as in the case where allowable diversions are used in other ways. Alternatively, if top managing employees and any other willing employees increase sales by reducing their resource diversions below those allowed by responsibility, short-run profits would increase.

What determines the responsibility placed on top managing employees? Whereas large stockholders can find it economically worthwhile to impose overall value responsibility on these employees based on the corporation's profitability, small stockholders usually depend on the choices made by directors and large stockholders. When there are no concentrated stockholdings, it can be that stockholders impose no responsibility on the corporation's top managing employees. However, it has often been suggested (see Marris and Mueller, 1980) that takeover threats effectively impose responsibility on top managing employees on stockholders' behalf. Among some types of firms top managing employees can transfer their experiences and skills with little loss of their own productivity. Fama (1980) points out that labor market competition can cause resource diversions attributed to these employees to be "settled up" in their future wages. Top managing employees held accountable in this manner will increase resource diversions at the expense of profits only insofar as they are willing to sacrifice future wages as a result.

If a corporation's top managing employees were not under any overall value responsibility based on the corporation's profits or did not have to face labor market competition based on profitability, they might choose to increase sales at the expense of profits, that is, choose between sales and profitability according to their own objectives. However, these employees would still face a constraint on resource diversions – that of the corporation's funding limit. This limit is the reduced supply of equity capital that results when the firm's current profitability decreases. The responsiveness of employees' resource diversions to the supply of external funding is hypothesized in Chapter 8 to result in a positive relationship between a corporation's profitability and its growth.

In the analysis of the short run, I assume that stockholders and directors impose overall value responsibility on each top managing employee where his output is the corporation's short-run profits or the identifiable contribution of his part of the organization to profits.[4] When stockholdings are concentrated or directors are seriously concerned with profitability, stockholders or directors can become "actively" involved in management – in effect, imposing specific responsibility on top managing employees – and they can reorganize the production domains of these employees or find suitable replacements for them. When stockholdings are diffuse and directors are relatively unconcerned with profitability, takeovers can replace top managing employees' managerial outputs. Under these assumptions, there is a critical rate of profits that top managing employees must maintain and pass on to stockholders (in dividends and demonstrably reinvested in the firm in ways that enhance profitability) to avoid large stockholders or directors replacing their managerial outputs or the corporation becoming a takeover target. Profits beyond this amount that are not passed on to stockholders can contribute to top managing employees' benefits from resource diversions. For example, these profits can be used to augment corporate overhead expenditures or fund investments in the firm of sub-par profitability that reflect the preferences of top managing employees.

A top managing employee maximizes his own welfare by selecting rates of output that maximize short-run profits provided he attaches enough cash-equivalent value at the margin to increased benefits from resource diversions to offset his personal cash-equivalent costs of taking the necessary managerial actions. The marginal cost to which the firm's marginal revenue is equated includes all of the marginal allowable resource diversions of those reporting to top managing employees. Top managing employees pass on to stockholders the critical rate of profits. When these employees must take benefits from resource diversions in kind and derive less utility from them than from equal amounts of cash, directors can increase the amount of profits passed on to stockholders by attaching cash bonuses to the amount by which passed-on profits exceed the critical amount. Also, to the extent that top managing employees believe that higher profits will increase their future wages as suggested by Fama (1980), the profits passed on to stockholders can be higher, depending on these employees' time preferences.

However, at some point top managing employees may not benefit enough from increases in profits beyond those passed on to stockholders to offset their personal costs of the managerial actions required to achieve them. If not, they do not necessarily price the organization's outputs in such a way as to maximize its gross profits or even to increase them beyond the critical amount. Also, top managing employees will devote fewer resources to imposing responsibility than if they did derive utility from increases in their allowable diversions. Thus the costs to them of their employees' outputs will be higher. Whether or not top managing employees derive utility from resource diversions at the margin, the position of demand for the corporation's output is problematical because it can include the effects of employees' cost-ineffective expenditures (within their allowable diversions) to increase sales.

Winter (1964) has suggested that "the firm that purchases information and maximizes profit on the basis of that information can be regarded as a profit maximizer behaving *as if* the information expenditure were optimal" (p. 263). Winter and other authors such as Simon (1961), and Cyert and March (1963) imply that top managing employees make only those expenditures to increase information that are expected to be justified by increased profits passed on to stockholders. However, it is suggested here that a reduction in costs resulting from increased information held by any employee, including a "top" managing employee, increases stockholders' profits only insofar as employees are induced by the responsibility placed on them to pass the benefit on.

In the following analysis, it is helpful to keep in mind that top managing employees find it in their interests to permit the resource diversions allowed by the responsibility facing their employees. We have seen that any managing employee's failure to do so results either in less desirable rates of their employees' outputs or in uneconomical expenditures on responsibility.

Analysis of price, income, and output determination

The lowest cost line in Figure 5.3 applies where CPOR is imposed on all of the corporation's employees and where intermediate outputs are priced at marginal cost. This line represents the lowest possible marginal and average variable cost (disregarding responsibility costs) of the organization's externally demanded output. The next two lines represent the marginal and average variable cost faced by the corporation's employees who report to top managing employees under the respective assumptions that they are all under overall value and specific responsibility. These cost lines are derived from individual employees' cost lines such as those shown in Figures 5.1 and 5.2. If, as is ordinarily the case, the corporation's employees other than top managing employees are not all under the same type of responsibility, their marginal and average variable cost of the organization's output lies between these lines. The highest cost line represents the marginal and average variable cost faced by the corporation's top managing employees. In Figure 5.3, unlike

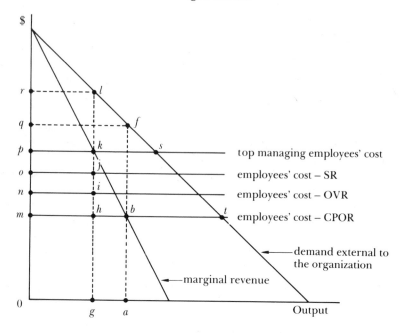

Figure 5.3. Short-run price, income, and output of a private corporation. Marginal and average variable cost is shown.

Figures 5.1 and 5.2, there is only one line for top managing employees' marginal and average variable cost to simplify the presentation.

Marginal revenue is the demand of top managing employees for the corporation's output when these employees' marginal cash-equivalent values of resource diversions exceed their personal cash-equivalent marginal costs of the managerial actions necessary to increase profits. Top managing employees' marginal cost constitutes their employees' supply of this output. Top managing employees maximize profits subject to all their employees' allowable resource diversions by selecting the rate of output $0g$, where marginal revenue equals their marginal cost (point k). Since marginal responsibility costs and marginal allowable resource diversions are part of this marginal cost, they affect the corporation's equilibrium rate of output. Note that employees would have to reduce variable resource diversions to increase output with a given demand. They may be able to make unprofitable expenditures within allowable diversion limits to increase sales, and these can increase demand and output.

At the equilibrium rate of output, the corporation's income is $0glr$

and its gross profits (before subtracting fixed responsibility costs, all resource diversions of top managing employees, fixed resource diversions of other employees, and other fixed costs) are *pklr*. Top managing employees' total variable cost including variable responsibility costs and their employees' variable resource diversions is 0*gkp*. There is a loss of potential profits as a result of the cost of placing CPOR on employees leading to other types of responsibility being imposed. If CPOR were imposed (ignoring the required variable costs of placing it on employees), the corporation's output would be the larger rate 0*a* and gross profits would equal *mbfq*, a higher amount than gross profits of *pklr* at 0*g* partly because marginal revenue exceeds marginal cost under CPOR over the range 0*g* to 0*a*.

It is interesting to note that Baumol's (1959) solution in which top managing employees maximize sales subject to a profit constraint is most likely to exist in a particular circumstance that can be expected to occur frequently. Consider the case where the employees reporting to top managing employees can readily coordinate themselves to raise top managing employees' costs and that the responsibility facing them allows them to do so. Assume that they can increase these costs to a point where profits would fall below the critical value at which top managing employees' managerial outputs would be replaced or large stockholders or directors would impose specific responsibility on them. When top managing employees derive little personal benefit from profits beyond the critical amount, they devote fewer resources to imposing responsibility, thus making this situation more likely. Assume also that top managing employees are convinced that the employees raising costs would not themselves be adversely affected by such actions. If the latter employees' allowable resource diversions rise with the corporation's output (as shown in Figure 5.3) and they gain significant utility at the margin from them, they could find it in their interests to force top managing employees to increase output at the expense of gross profits. Unless the lower-level employees feel they would be better off under a different top management, the corporation's output (and sales) would rise until top managing employees' allowable resource diversions become very small or go to zero, that is, the corporation's gross profits minus fixed costs and fixed resource diversions other than those of top managing employees are reduced to the critical amount that must be passed on to stockholders.

Chapter 8 analyzes how employees' roles in the determination of a corporation's growth can raise a corporation's short-run output and profit above the respective amounts 0*g* and *pklr* derived previously.

The traditional analysis of welfare loss due to monopoly takes account only of the quantity *ksl*, the potential gain from operation at the rate of output where top managing employees' marginal cost equals demand. However, employees' resource diversions create another welfare loss vis-à-vis demand, as can be seen by comparing with *ksl* the welfare gain *htl* that is achieved by operating at the rate of output where employees' cost under CPOR (ignoring the costs of imposing CPOR) equals demand. Of this amount, *hbfl* would be gained with CPOR while retaining the corporation's monopoly pricing policy. The additional gain *btf* would result from competitive pricing.

The welfare losses of *mhin* under overall value responsibility and *mhjo* if specific responsibility is imposed result from inefficient uses of resources within the corporation. The quantities *nikp* and *ojkp* represent total variable responsibility costs plus employees' total variable cost advantage under overall value responsibility and specific responsibility. There is a welfare loss within employees' total variable cost advantage to the extent that employees derive less utility from these resource diversions than they would from cash. If CPOR could be imposed without cost, there would be a Kaldor-Hicks welfare gain, not a Pareto welfare gain, if employees were not compensated for their losses of benefits from resource diversions.

Although the foregoing analysis can apply to a monopolistically competitive corporation as well as to a monopoly in the short run, it would, of course, be necessary to drop the simplifying assumption of constant marginal costs to apply it to a perfectly competitive corporation. The effects of employees' resource diversions on long-run cost relationships is analyzed in Chapter 8.

Leibenstein (1966) has interpreted a number of studies that suggest that newly introduced incentive systems and other managerial improvements might have large effects on labor productivity. These studies typically show measured labor productivity increases that are 30 percent or more, and the increases often exceed 100 percent.[5] One suspects that in many cases the new incentive system or managerial changes accompanied changes in the relative demands that employees faced for different outputs and that only those outputs with increased demands were measured. Another possibility is that a new incentive system is not in fact economical because of its costs but that it does increase output during the experimentation period. Nonetheless, Leibenstein raised an important question of whether economic theory based on constrained maximization behavior could explain the possibility of very large increases in measured production as a result of such incentive and management systems. He argued that these increases could have resulted from a greater willingness to produce (i.e., "X-efficiency"). In his later work, Leibenstein analyzed how "pressure" on an employee can affect his "constraint concern." (See the discussion in Chapter 4 of this book.)

Changes in suborganization or the responsibility placed on employees can increase the equilibrium rates of employees' outputs when they reduce marginal responsibility costs or enhance the effects of responsibility on marginal resource diversions and thus lower the marginal costs that employers face. The resulting increases in employees' outputs depend on the sizes of the cost reductions and the slopes of employers' demands.[6] At present it is possible only to speculate on the cost reductions achievable by changes in suborganization or responsibility. In the following discussion I consider possible increases in the corporation's total output that result from alternative assumed reductions in its costs. Using the relationship MR (= MC) = $[(E - 1)/E] \cdot P$, where P is price and E is elasticity, if marginal cost decreases by a given percentage, P changes by the same percentage provided that elasticity remains constant. The corresponding percentage change in output is the elasticity multiplied by the percentage change in price. For example, assume that top managing employees' marginal cost decreases 25 percent as a result of a new incentive system or managerial improvement, and let elasticity of demand be -3 and remain constant (notwithstanding the linear demand of Figure 5.3). Then the percentage change in price is -25 and the percentage increase in output is $+75$. Table 5.1 gives other examples of output increases that result in productivity increases in the range of the data used by Leibenstein (1966).

Summary of hypotheses about resource allocation of the private corporation

Stockholders as the funding authority. Although stockholders desire to maximize profits, their information cost disadvantage usually leads them to delegate to top managing employees discretion over the pricing of the corporation's outputs. Employees' allowable resource diversions prevent the corporation from achieving the highest feasible profits.

Equilibrium price, income, and output. The analysis applies in the case where top managing employees exercise discretion over the pricing of the corporation's output. Marginal revenue is these employees'

Table 5.1. *Examples of percentage increases in output under different assumed elasticities of demand and different assumed decreases in top managing employees' marginal cost resulting from a new incentive system or managerial improvement*

Percent decrease in top managing employees' marginal cost	Elasticity of demand			
	−1	−2	−3	−4
10	10	20	30	40
20	20	40	60	80
30	30	60	90	120
40	40	80	120	160

demand for the corporation's output when their personal benefits from increasing gross profits (beyond the critical amount they must pass on to stockholders) exceed their personal costs of achieving profitability at the margin. Their employees' supply of this output, that is, top managing employees' marginal cost, includes variable allowable resource diversions and all marginal responsibility costs. The equilibrium rate and price of the corporation's output are determined where marginal revenue and top managing employees' marginal cost are equal, and by demand at this point. Because top managing employees' marginal cost includes all their employees' allowable resource diversions at the margin, only by reducing variable resource diversions or using resource diversions for cost-ineffective expenditures to increase sales would employees be able to increase the firm's output beyond this rate. The allowable resource diversions of top managing employees, the fixed resource diversions of other employees, and fixed costs, including fixed responsibility costs, are deducted before profits are passed on to stockholders.

Efficiency. The evaluation of efficiency depends on an analysis of resource allocation within the firm as well as the traditional analysis of excess of demand over marginal cost. This analysis identifies separate welfare losses due to inefficient resource allocation and employees' discount of in-kind diversion benefits. Because top managing employees' marginal cost exceeds that which holds under CPOR, inadequacy of the corporation's rate of output in relation to the demand for this output is attributable to resource allocation within the firm as well as to any monopoly power it may have.

D   Short-run resource allocation of the private nonprofit organization

Consider a group of individuals having a demand for an output to be provided to themselves or to others. Assume that the output cannot be competitively supplied and that government does not provide demanded quantities of it.[7] These circumstances might lead the group to form a private nonprofit organization and act as its funding authority. Such an organization enables the group to avoid monopoly charges by a private firm. The output of such an organization typically has public characteristics common to the group, and this mutual interest helps offset costs of acting as a funding authority. However, the output does not necessarily have any public characteristics; the mutual interest to avoid monopoly charges can motivate the choice to form a private nonprofit organization.

The private nonprofit organization's "top" managing employees report directly to donors or to a board that represents donors and imposes responsibility on these employees. The analysis can be extended to include the means by which board members are selected, the responsibility facing each of them, and their allowable resource diversions (which, for simplicity, are assumed to be zero in the following discussion). Such an extension of the analysis has similarities to the analysis of legislatures in Chapter 6. All other employees directly or indirectly report to top managing employees.

Analysis of price, income, and output determination

The output of a private nonprofit organization will be taken to be a public good, although it can have differing degrees of publicness.[8] The output can be directly provided to individuals who have demands only for its privately capturable benefits to them; in such cases, beneficiaries of the organization's output include others than these direct recipients. Because donations to a private nonprofit organization are voluntary, the schedule showing incremental donations at each rate of output is lower than beneficiaries' actual demands.[9] Tailoring outputs to the preferences of large beneficiaries does not succeed in making their donations equal to demand when the outputs have other beneficiaries. Smaller beneficiaries can usually easily avoid having to make donations, and what they give largely results from the satisfaction they derive from providing personal support for what they feel to be important. In this sense, small beneficiaries are like some individual voters. However, unlike votes,

donations can vary with intensity of preference. Perhaps small beneficiaries give amounts that are less than but positively related to their
demands for the private nonprofit organization's output.

When increases in a private nonprofit organization's output raise
the allowable resource diversions of its employees (as shown in
Figure 5.4) and these employees benefit from resource diversions at
the margin, they gain from outward shifts of the organization's incremental donation schedule. Employees can often achieve such shifts by
either of two means. First, by altering outputs and their characteristics
they may be able to bring in additional donors or increase the sizes of
donations. Second, they can reduce interdependence of beneficiaries'
donations by tailoring some outputs to preferences, especially those
of the largest beneficiaries. (Information costs can reduce interdependence of smaller beneficiaries' donations.)

In the first case considered, the organization does not charge its
clients for its output because the output lacks privately capturable
benefits or because it would be more costly than worthwhile to assess
a charge. Figure 5.4 illustrates the private nonprofit organization's
equilibrium behavior in this case. The schedule of incremental donations is shown below actual demand. Four lines representing marginal and average variable cost are shown. The lowest line represents
employees' cost when CPOR is imposed on all employees and intermediate outputs are priced at marginal cost. The highest line represents donors' cost under other types of responsibility, and the next
two lines represent employees' costs under specific and overall value
responsibility.

Even though incremental donations are below beneficiaries' demand, they represent the actual funding responses to alternative
rates of output. Thus, the private nonprofit organization's output is
determined by the equality of incremental donations to donors'
marginal cost. In Figure 5.4, the organization's equilibrium rate of
output is $0d$ and its income is $0dbp$. The excess of this income after
all costs, including fixed responsibility costs and fixed resource diversions, is available for uses desired by donors or their board, such
as additions to the organization's capital. The sum of total variable
responsibility costs and employees' total variable cost advantage is
mfbr under overall value responsibility and *ngbr* under specific
responsibility.

The welfare loss that results from the costs of imposing CPOR
leading to other types of responsibility being placed on employees is
the following sum. There is a loss to donors of consumers' surplus
vis-à-vis the incremental donation schedule (*eab*) to which we must

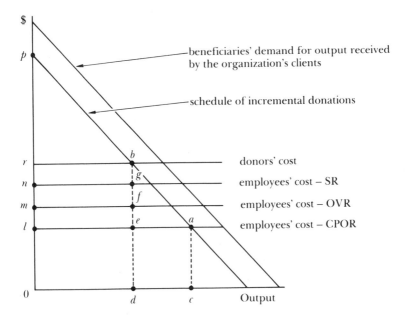

Figure 5.4. Short-run price, income, and output of a private nonprofit organization. The organization's clients are not charged for the output. Marginal and average variable cost is shown.

add the losses due to inefficient resource allocation within the organization (*lefm* under overall value responsibility and *legn* under specific responsibility), and employees' discount below the cash value of in-kind benefits from their cost advantages. Note that beneficiaries would lose welfare even under CPOR due to inadequate donations. For example, the output $0c$ leads to a welfare loss equal to the area under demand above the incremental donation schedule up to $0c$ and beyond $0c$, the area under demand above employees' cost under CPOR.

Now consider the case where it is cost effective to assess charges to clients directly receiving privately capturable benefits from the organization's output. In the top portion of Figure 5.5 both the schedule of incremental donations and the clients' demand are shown. (Total beneficiaries' demand, including that of indirect beneficiaries whose demands are for clients' receipt of the output, is omitted.) The same four lines for marginal and average variable cost are shown as in Figure 5.4. The rising line in the bottom portion is donors' net marginal cost of providing the organization's output to clients. This cost is determined by subtracting from donors' marginal

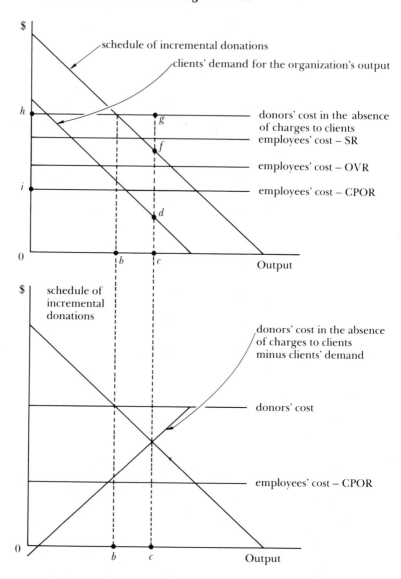

Figure 5.5. Short-run price, income, and output of a private nonprofit organization. The organization's clients are charged for the output. Marginal and average variable cost is shown.

cost ($0h$) in the absence of charges to clients, the price that clients are willing to pay at each quantity. In the absence of a charge to clients, incremental donations equal donors' marginal cost at output $0b$, and this is the equilibrium rate of the organization's output. However, with a charge that clients must pay, incremental donations equal donors' net marginal cost at the larger rate of output $0c$. Here the price for clients is cd and the donors' effective price is cf; these two prices sum to cg, the donors' marginal cost (which the clients help defray).

Analysis of resource diversions and welfare losses is analogous to the case where there are no charges to clients.

Summary of hypotheses about resource allocation of the private nonprofit organization

Donors as the funding authority. By forming a private nonprofit organization, a group of individuals can avoid monopoly charges for a good or service that is insufficiently supplied by government and unavailable from competitive suppliers. However, the voluntary nature of this organization's funding creates divergences between beneficiaries' demand and the organization's incremental donation schedule. Donors also face costs of imposing responsibility and of employees' allowable resource diversions.

Equilibrium price, income, and output. The private nonprofit organization's equilibrium rate of output is determined by marginal donors' cost equalling incremental donations, not beneficiaries' demand. The organization's income equals cumulative donations at this rate of output. Any charges to direct recipients of the organization's output depend on clients' demands for privately capturable benefits of the output. Such charges reduce donors' net marginal cost and thus increase the equilibrium rate of the organization's output.

Efficiency. The analysis of efficiency depends both on the amount by which beneficiaries' demand exceeds incremental donations and on resource allocation within the organization. Employees have incentives to make inefficient uses of resources in this as well as in any other type of organization, and they also derive benefits from resource diversions that represent a transfer of welfare to them. To the extent that they discount any in-kind benefits from resource diversions below cash-equivalent value, there is a welfare loss associated with this transfer.

CHAPTER 6

Legislative demand and short-run price and output of the public organization

Although the behavioral postulates underlying demands of private citizens for an organization's outputs are well established, the analogous demand of a legislature cannot be derived from existing theory. Therefore, before analyzing short-run price, income, and output determination for a public organization, it is necessary to consider how a number of important contributions in the political science and public choice literatures can be extended in order to derive a legislature's demand function for a good or service. This analysis also enables us to determine the role of a legislature as the funding authority of a public organization.

An analysis of legislative behavior may seem a detour in a book about economic behavior within organizations, but a legislature is an organization whose funding authority consists of citizens eligible to vote. These citizens' willingness to provide funds to a legislature depends in part on the welfare they derive from public goods, although legislatures find it in their interest also to provide private goods. The analysis will determine the allowable resource diversions that derive from a legislature's capability to tax citizens and then provide economic benefits to them, as well as establish the shares of these resource diversions that go to legislators and to employees in organizations supplying legislative demands. Legislators face costs of negotiating with each other as do employees in other types of organizations. The analysis here of how a legislature minimizes these costs is similar to the analysis in the next chapter of how employees in other types of organizations coordinate their actions to invest, to deal advantageously with spillovers among their production domains, and to hold their combined resource diversions within funding limits.

We now proceed to an economic analysis of legislative behavior, followed by the analysis of public organizations in the short run.

A   Economic behavior within a legislature that
        underlies legislative demand

The analysis of legislative behavior is in four parts. First, a brief
discussion of existing work clarifies the assumptions of the present
analysis. I next analyze the economic behavior of voters and the
candidates for a legislative office, while taking as given the amount
of legislative spending that each individual legislator can direct to his
constituents. The analysis then turns to the determination of each
legislator's influence over legislative expenditures. Finally, a legislature's demand for a good or service is derived, and this demand is
compared with citizens' demands for the same resources.

*Existing analyses of legislative behavior and
assumptions about voter preferences and information costs*

Three important bodies of research are pertinent to the present
analysis of legislative behavior. One includes empirical investigations
of the influences of constituents on legislative outcomes. For example, a number of studies (see Turner, 1951; MacRae, 1952; W.
Miller, 1970) have measured the influence of a legislator's party and
his constituents on his voting behavior and particularly his party
loyalty. The present discussion of this first body of research owes a
large debt to Fiorina's (1974) excellent review of this literature. Fiorina points out that the early studies of constituency influence have
contradictory results due to deficiencies of both theory and data. For
example, MacRae's and other early studies found that representatives from "competitive" districts tended more to be subject to constituency influence than those from "safe" districts. Miller found the
opposite. These conflicting findings could result from the "safety" of
a legislator's district deriving from his responsiveness to constituents
as well as vice versa. Later studies, including those of MacRae (1958),
Kessel (1964), Jackson (1967, 1971), and Clausen (1973), improved
on the earlier ones by explaining legislators' actual votes rather than
overall measures of their party loyalty. Fiorina (1974) points out,
however, that "for the most part these studies report fairly weak
relationships between constituency characteristics and voting behavior" (p. 19).

The following three issues in this literature are important for our
purposes. First, the studies employ ad hoc measures of constituency
characteristics, such as numbers of voters in districts owning houses

or being "blue collar" or tabulations of voters' subjective attitudes. An implication of the theory presented here is that it is not specifically the characteristics of constituent groups, but the costs and benefits to individuals within them resulting from particular collective actions, that determine votes for candidates. Thus, measures of the numbers of beneficiaries of such actions and of the costs and benefits that directly or indirectly accrue to them are important in the proper specification of equations explaining voting behavior. The second issue is that these studies take political parties as given rather than explain party affiliations as responses to the informational and fund-raising economies that parties can achieve, as suggested in this discussion. The third issue results from the very interesting contradictory findings of Stokes and Miller (1962) and Miller and Stokes (1969) that, even though interviewed voters are poorly informed about legislative issues generally, congressmen believe that the votes they receive from constituents are strongly influenced by their own legislative voting records. The analysis presented here helps resolve this paradox by focusing on the incentive for those voters who find it in their interests to deal with legislators to be much better informed about the small subset of issues that directly affect them than about other issues.

Spatial analysis of constituency influences on electoral outcomes constitutes the second body of research relevant to the present analysis. Under specific assumptions about the behavior of constituents and candidates, spatial analysis provides hypotheses about whether each candidate in an election has an equilibrium platform of promises to constituencies, whether these platforms are identical, and whether identical platforms reflect the median voter's most preferred outcome. Downs's (1957) work is the seminal contribution to spatial analysis. His work is thoughtfully interpreted and extended by Tullock (1967). There have been a number of theoretical extensions of the earlier spatial analysis that have been summarized by Riker and Ordeshook (1973) and Mueller (1976, 1979).

By applying the techniques of game theory to spatial analysis, Riker and Ordeshook provide general conditions for the combinations of assumptions about voters and candidates that must hold in order for there to be equilibrium platforms for two candidates equal to the median voter's most preferred outcome. These assumptions are in four categories: (1) One assumption specifies whether all citizens vote and, if not, whether their abstention is due to the perceived unimportance of the election, the distance of candidates' positions from their own most preferred ones, or a combination of these two reasons. When a combination of both reasons is responsible for abstention, the authors allow for the possibility that citizens might vote for a less preferred candidate, that is, where "nonspatial considerations affect citizens' choices, or where our measurement of spatial considerations is imprecise" (p. 328). (2) Citizens' utility functions defined on the deviations of candidates' policies from their own most preferred policies are assumed either to be concave or they are assumed to be symmetric and concave or symmetric and quasi-concave. Symmetry implies, for example, that equally more "liberal" or "conservative" deviations from one's most preferred policy produce the same decreases in utility. When citizens' utility functions are assumed to be symmetric concave or symmetric and quasi-concave, an additional highly restrictive assumption is made. While different citizens can have diverse preferred policies on issues, all citizens must attach the same weights to the issues. (3) The distribution of voters' most preferred positions is either assumed to be an unspecified density or is restricted to being a symmetric unimodal or bimodal density. (4) Finally, candidates are alternatively assumed to maximize pluralities or votes.

For our purposes, the most important assumptions are those pertaining to the utility functions of voters and the distributions of voters' most preferred policies. Perhaps the best known result of spatial analysis is that, if the utility functions of citizens and the distributions of voters' most preferred policies are symmetric and if all citizens vote, both candidates' equilibrium platforms are equal to the most preferred position of the median voter. However, Riker and Ordeshook point out (p. 343) that whenever it cannot be assumed that the distribution of voters' most preferred policies is symmetric, an equilibrium under majority rule either does not exist (when those citizens who vote always vote for their most preferred candidate) or cannot be specified (when nonspatial considerations permit votes for the less preferred candidate).[1] Also, when it is not assumed that citizens' utility functions are symmetric (and that they give equal weights to all issues), there is no equilibrium unless votes for the less preferred candidate are allowed. In those cases where no equilibrium under majority rule exists each candidate puts together coalitions of minorities.[2]

Consider, however, the density functions of citizens' most preferred policies when some citizens derive net economic benefits (whether private or public) from a collective action and other citizens bear a net economic loss because they derive less utility from the action than from their share of the cost. If only a minority of voters derives net economic benefits (whether all members of this group directly receive benefits, or the gains for some of these members are benefits to others in the minority group), the majority will be opposed. This situation will result in an asymmetric distribution of voters' most preferred positions with the larger mode at zero or very small benefits and the smaller mode at some substantial positive level of benefits. For reference in the immediately following discussion, note that members of the minority desiring the benefits will have relatively intense demands for them, whereas the opposition will be less intense. In such situations, it of course cannot be assumed that all citizens attach the same weights to all issues.

How can minorities succeed in having policies enacted that benefit them at the expense of majorities? The third body of research relevant to the present analysis of legislative behavior analyzes the effects of the costs of information and of coordination on voter behavior. This work includes Stigler's (1971) analysis of the demand and supply of regulation and Peltzman's (1976) extension and refinement of Stigler's work. The authors point out that the regulated parties stand to gain individually large benefits at the expense of individually small costs to their customers. Thus, the gainers view the issue as important, but the losers may not feel the costs are high enough to devote resources to opposing it. In another example, Weingast and colleagues (1981) note that geographically earmarked government expenditures drive up prices of factors that are geographically fixed during a given time period. The gains to individual factor owners are usually much larger than the individual losses to other citizens. These authors point out that losers' opposition is further reduced because "the illusion may be such that pecuniary losers are unable to distinguish the source of their losses from general price inflation" (p. 649). In these and similar cases, particular groups of citizens can obtain benefits at the expense of other groups when there are two types of imbalances. First, the group seeking benefits is more willing to determine their benefits than the other groups are to evaluate the resulting costs to them. Second, this group has stronger incentives to organize itself as a political force. Underlying these imbalances is a combination of asymmetry of density functions of voters' most preferred positions and differences in intensity of preferences. When minorities can turn information and coordination costs to advantage because of greater willingness to defray them, they can often receive benefits for themselves at the expense of majorities via the political process instead of paying for them in the marketplace.

The same two imbalances of incentives underlie the present theory of legislative behavior. Specifically, I assume that it is costly for citizens to obtain information about their costs and benefits of many of the expenditures that a legislature might make and that it is costly for them to organize themselves to vote in a coordinated manner. The larger the potential for individually received benefits, the greater the incentive for citizens to defray these information and coordination costs. It is thus possible for benefits to members of minority groups to be provided collectively whereas smaller benefits to each member of a majority of voters are not provided. If information were costless and if everyone were to vote, there would be no minority benefits at the expense of majorities,[3] but with information costs such benefits can occur frequently.

Economic behavior of voters and candidates

Costly information presents significant economic choices for voters and candidates alike. Instead of spending for private goods in the marketplace, citizens can spend on information to increase the public or private goods provided by government. Candidates must spend on information to determine the votes that would result from alternative benefits in their platforms, and to communicate about benefits they would provide if elected. If the votes that correspond to different benefits remain stable indefinitely, the same candidates' information costs would decrease with time. But if votes shift somewhat from election to election, candidates must continually allocate resources to information.

The analysis applies to a legislature whose members are periodically elected from a geographic district[4] not bound by referenda about individual issues. An incumbent's information cost advantage about citizens' preferences, resulting from his providing benefits to citizens as a legislator, gives him an edge in his competition with a challenger. However, the challenger is more flexible in the positions he can take. I initially assume that each candidate has an identical budget of economic benefits to provide to voters, contingent on his being elected, but we shall see that advantages of skill or information within the legislature can give an incumbent candidate a larger budget than his opponent.

A legislator or his challenger maximizes utility subject to the constraints of the productivity of information to his election probability and his financial and other resources available for defraying information costs. A legislator or challenger derives enough utility from remaining in or obtaining office to be willing to undergo the costs of time and effort and any necessary personal financial costs of competing for it. This utility may be derived from presence in the legislature when all of his actions would be in the interest of constituents. However, a legislator can also derive utility from resource diversions vis-à-vis his constituents.

A legislator or his opponent can allocate commitments of legislative spending to groups of citizens in such a way as to maximize expected election probabilities. Alternatively, he can exert an influence on legislative spending that is independent of his constituents' votes. That is, he can have expected benefits from resource diversions vis-à-vis marginal voters by committing less spending than he could and thereby also reducing his election chances. He thus faces a trade-off between expected resource diversions and his election probability.[5] An experienced politician with advantages over his opponent of skill and information about the voting consequences of alternative allocations of a given amount of legislative spending may be able to take substantial benefits from resource diversions vis-à-vis his constituents while continuing to be reelected by comfortable margins. The more risk averse a legislator, the fewer his resource diversions.

A citizen's decision whether to vote for a candidate is determined by one of the following: the size of the candidate's commitment of a single benefit that results from legislative spending; the total value to him of the candidate's commitment of multiple benefits of legislative expenditures; the candidate's position on one or more issues not involving legislative spending; or a combination of such issues and benefits from legislative spending.[6] We are concerned with citizens whose votes are influenced by one or more benefits that result from a legislature's expenditures. These benefits can be goods or services provided gratis or at subsidized prices to citizens. They can directly benefit the citizens whose votes are influenced by them or, alternatively, these citizens' benefit can be other citizens' receipt of goods and services. The benefits of legislative spending can also include income transfers and increases in demand for labor or other owned resources that result from legislative spending. When a citizen is additionally influenced by issues not involving expenditures by the legislature, his vote is determined by the sum of his cash equivalent value of these and the spending issues important to him.

In deciding whether to allow the amount of one or more committed legislative spending benefits to influence his vote, a citizen takes account of his perception of how his vote influences the probability of the benefit being provided. A citizen's expectation of the number of other votes for a desired benefit can have offsetting effects on his own voting choices. While a larger number raises the likelihood of the benefit's being taken seriously by a candidate, individual citizens have an incentive to be free riders with respect to other citizens' votes. The practical importance of such free riding can be seen by noting that when legislators have the option to provide privately capturable benefits and collective goods benefiting small groups of citizens, the votes of citizens that are influenced by these benefits are correspondingly less influenced by their gains from broadly beneficial public goods. Thus, to the extent that citizens have a lesser incentive to act as free riders with respect to more narrowly received benefits, there is a greater tendency for the former benefits to be supported by voters at the expense of the latter.

I assume that higher taxes reduce a citizen's utility ceteris paribus. A higher legislative deficit usually (but not necessarily) also has this effect through increasing expected future taxes and, in the case of a national deficit, through creating an expectation of increased inflation or interest rates. Thus a citizen's utility is ordinarily reduced when other citizens receive benefits that he does not share in or desire. However, he may face high costs of opposing these benefits or even learning about them.

A legislator's commitment of an increased benefit from legislative spending can influence five categories of citizens:

1. citizens who had not intended to vote, some of whom now decide to vote for the candidate;
2. some of those who had intended to vote for his opponent who now decide to vote for him;
3. voters who will change their reason for voting for him – if the candidate should reduce the benefits that previously elicited these votes, he will still receive them and can use the savings to obtain additional votes;
4. some citizens who will not vote for him because they specifically oppose the benefit;
5. citizens whose votes will be lost when the increased benefit results in higher overall legislative spending funded by increased taxes or deficits.

The fourth and fifth categories can also be decomposed into those voting for the opponent or not voting at all. The change in the number of votes from each category that results from an increased legislative spending benefit is determined by its density function of individual citizens' critical values of the benefit at which they will switch their voting choices.

Changes in election probabilities that result from variation in benefits to constituents are a function of the composition of affected votes as well as the numbers of them. Thus, in estimating the effect of alternative ways of allocating benefits among constituents on his election probability, the candidate is interested in the proportion of affected voters in each category. Those who would not otherwise vote represent increased votes, while his opponent's votes remain the same. However, the candidate benefits doubly from those who would otherwise vote for his opponent; not only does he receive their votes but his opponent loses them. Of similar importance is whether vote losses go to his opponent. The candidate's net vote gain (or loss) from the voters who change their reasons for voting for him depends on the relative costs of providing the increased benefit and that which previously attracted their votes, as well as on the votes obtainable through expenditure of the reduced funding of the latter benefit. The candidate also seeks information about "vote-complementary" benefits that provided in combination produce more than the sum of votes from each benefit provided alone. Such complementarity results from underlying consumption or production relationships and from economies in communication between citizens and legislators when citizens base their votes on multiple issues.

Although candidates have the incentive to devote resources to determining the votes that result from providing alternative benefits to constituents, groups of voters with high benefits relative to coordination costs find it worthwhile to inform candidates of their vote potential and, perhaps, to take "bids" of benefits from different candidates. (Employees in public organizations can assist voters in this respect; see Chapter 7.) Other citizens directly make campaign contributions in return for benefits and these, combined with any funding provided by the candidate's party and personal funds, determine the financial resources available to a candidate. Campaign contributions can come directly at the expense of votes; but these funds can be spent on obtaining information about citizens' preferences or on conveying information about positions that yield other votes. The candidate thus obtains additional campaign funds whenever the vote gain from spending them exceeds the direct vote loss they cost him. The candidate similarly obtains personal assistance for his campaign.

Each candidate allocates his time and the financial and other resources available to him between obtaining information about the votes that result from alternative benefits to his constituents and providing information to constituents about benefits they receive. Given the information he obtains and provides, a candidate allocates the budget of legislative spending that he can direct to his constituents in such a manner as to maximize his expected utility; and as noted earlier, he is not willing when in equilibrium to sacrifice at the margin any expected resource diversions vis-à-vis marginal voters in order to increase his estimated election probability.

An incumbent ordinarily has more experience in dealing with constituents than his challenger and usually faces lower costs of the information necessary to explore the vote consequences of alternative allocations of benefits. Also, because citizens can compare his past promises with performance, an incumbent's promises may receive less discount for uncertainty about whether they will be carried out. However, some marginal voters are discouraged from voting for a candidate because benefits for other voters or the candidate's support for issues not involving legislative spending displeases them. Whereas a legislator may be forced to shed some of these voters over time, a challenger may be able to retain them during his first campaign because he lacks previous commitments and because voter groups lack comprehensive information about all of his positions. Although incumbent legislators' information cost advantages seem formidable and perhaps explain why incumbents are so often re-elected, this advantage is reduced when there are changes in the composition of voters or in their preferences. Thus challengers' best chances for winning are when these changes occur.

A candidate allocates legislative spending among different benefits so that the contribution of every benefit to his utility from resource diversions or from increased probability of reelection is equal. It is thus not the median of all voters but marginal votes (differently weighted for each voter category) for individual benefits, along with candidates' utility functions, that determine amounts of legislative spending. Note that there need not be a majority of votes influenced by any particular benefit. The preferences of intramarginal voters, no matter how intense, have no direct influences on benefits. Intensity of preferences can, however, lead citizens to make campaign contributions in return for benefits.

Subsidies can be provided for private as well as public goods and services, and those seeking rents such as suppliers to an organization providing a legislatively demanded good or service can be a source of votes for above-market compensation. Enhancing the likelihood of votes based on broadly beneficial public goods is a legislature's frequent competitive advantage over private markets in providing them, as well as the relative absence of opposed voters. However, private goods and public goods benefiting a small part of the population can yield large personal benefits to citizens; they, in turn, can find it worthwhile to bear costs of forming groups of citizens who base votes on their obtaining these benefits and to provide campaign contributions in return for them.

Both candidates' platforms are partly identical when some benefits are sufficiently important to groups of voters that any difference would immediately make them switch candidates. The real differentiation between candidates lies in the provision of benefits whose net vote support is costly to identify. The costs of information about such benefits makes citizens' voting choices vulnerable to manipulation via the spending by others on information. When groups of citizens are unwilling to bear the costs of information about potential benefits, their votes become dependent on whether a candidate or other interested party, such as the employees of an organization supplying the benefit, finds it worthwhile to bear these costs.

High information costs can prevent some citizens from knowing about any possibilities for them to benefit from basing their votes on legislative spending. Such citizens can be among Downs's (1957) "rationally ignorant" voters. Some of these citizens will be well informed about other legislative issues. Others, however, will not, and when these citizens cast votes based on noneconomic issues that are relatively ephemeral, they contribute a random element to election results that can make it worthwhile to run against an incumbent legislator possessing a large information cost advantage vis-à-vis other voters' preferences. By increasing the randomness of election results, these citizens also lead risk-averse candidates to reduce their expected resource diversions vis-à-vis citizens who do base votes on government spending.

Determination of each legislator's influence over legislative spending

We now turn to an analysis of how each legislator's influence over legislative spending is determined. If the legislature were to vote separately and independently on every item in each legislator's platform, it would face two problems. First, it would most likely fail to achieve some of the potential gains from trade. Although each legislator would have a vote on all issues, some issues would be unimportant to him but important to others. However, the information and negotiation costs of effecting ad hoc vote trades could prevent desirable trades. The second problem is that the independent votes on each issue would have to be repeated frequently[7] in order for the legislature's total spending to stay within its income constraint determined by its votes on taxes and other financing measures.

By having a subset of legislators specialize in arranging vote trades, the remaining legislators would require much less information in order to participate in them. Individual legislators vary in skill at negotiation and at acquiring and usefully applying the necessary information for this task. However, an election within the legislature would not necessarily select the most able legislators because votes might also be based on candidates' stands on particular issues. For this reason, and since the information held by the selected legislators can be valuable to the legislature as a body, there is also an incentive to use longevity as a criterion when past longevity is perceived to portend future longevity. By whatever combination of voting and longevity, the legislature delegates to a subset of its members the tasks of arranging vote trades and minimizing the number of separate votes required to align spending with income. These members, referred to as *coordinating legislators*, include committee chairmen and the leadership who coordinate the proposed legislation of the committees. The subdivisions of legislative committees are specializations that further economize on information and negotiation.

Coordinating legislators in substantive committees in particular specializations solicit information and proposals from interested citizens about relevant issues and, except when there are overlaps of jurisdiction, usually perform most of the legislature's analysis of each proposal's likely impacts on constituents. Most important, appropriations committees make actual budgeting decisions for the legislature. These and other coordinating legislators schedule the legislature's consideration of issues and can set before the legislature the issues to be voted upon (and not voted upon) by the legislature as a body and the combinations of issues that are voted on together. (The rules of different legislatures allow widely varying amounts of open debate about issues included in or excluded from these bills.)

When other legislators can independently propose legislation or make independent vote trading agreements, they face the disadvantage of competing with proposed legislation that is based on coordinating legislators' often very large information advantages and which involve trades among all issues of interest to every legislator. In regard to appropriations committees of the U.S. Congress, Wildavsky (1964, p. 57) points out that:

The bulk of Congressmen are busy with other things. They can hardly hope to become knowledgeable in more than a few areas of budgeting, if that. Some way of reducing their information costs must be found unless they are to abdicate their powers. And the way they have adopted of doing so is to accept the verdict of the appropriations committees most of the time, intervening just often enough to keep the committees roughly in line.

Individual legislators may "rebel" against a system in which the shape of legislation is determined through skillful negotiation within and between committees. However, they are unlikely to be successful because of the system's overall gains to all legislators. The following quotation from Keefe and Ogul (1968, p. 267) is instructive:

The "effective" senators, defined as those who are most successful in getting their bills passed, are distinguished by their adherence to the unwritten code of the Senate. They abide by apprenticeship rules and treat their colleagues with deference. Their policy interests are narrow and particularistic, and their contribution to debate is measured and infrequent. The nonconformists . . . are least "effective" in the Senate.

By some specified majority, a legislature or a designated committee may withdraw the authority granted to one or more coordinating legislators. However, legislators must take account of these legislators' personal replacement costs, which are largely based on information cost and skill advantages. The larger the required majority for replacement, the more likely replacement would be based on diversions vis-à-vis other legislators being in excess of the value of these advantages rather than individual legislators' perceptions that a new coordinating legislator would tilt outcomes to their particular interests.

The resource diversions of coordinating legislators vis-à-vis other legislators are much more commonly limited by possibilities for replacing their outputs: passing independent legislation, changing committee jurisdictions, or giving overlapping assignments to other committees. Within these limits, each coordinating legislator's own information cost and skill advantages determine his own benefits from resource diversions. These benefits include legislation that he personally desires, for example, to increase his election chances or to further his ideological preferences, as well as legislation desired by other legislators who promise future support in return. Legislation representing coordinating legislators' resource diversions increases the incentive for other legislators to introduce legislation that would replace their outputs. Thus, a coordinating legislator aims to keep such potential initiatives short of success by an amount depending on his risk aversion; any fewer votes than this amount represent unrealized benefits from diversions.

Many observers believe that the influence of committee chairmen in the U.S. Congress has declined in recent years (see, for example, Farney, 1979). This phenomenon can be attributed to reduced information cost advantages. Economical data processing facilities and improvements in statistical methodology have increased general access to demographic and budgetary information useful in evaluating the vote consequences for individual legislators of alternative legislation. Within committees, this information has reduced the resource diversions of chairmen vis-à-vis other members, and perhaps it has also reduced the resource diversions of some committees vis-à-vis the legislature.

Given coordinating legislators' allowable resource diversions, each legislator's influence over the remaining legislative spending is determined by the value of his vote. Coordinating legislators have a strong incentive to arrange vote trades as efficiently as possible because any inefficiency costs them benefits from resource diversions. With an equal right to vote in an efficient market for votes, every legislator has an equal base influence over legislative outcomes plus whatever diversion benefits he receives as a coordinating legislator or are given to him by these members. If all legislators attach the same relative importance to issues that do and do not involve legislative spending, the equal base influence implies equal spending influence.[8]

It is conceivable that a party or other group of legislators could obtain the required majority on all votes. In this case, the remaining legislators would only bring to their constituents benefits of broadly beneficial public goods or those benefits the other legislators find economical to base on generally defined (e.g., demographic, farm, "small business") characteristics that can apply in each district. Brennan and Buchanan (1980) argue that a majority of legislators can "exploit the maximal minority to the maximal extent feasible" (p. 21). This result can occur when there are overriding issues of intense and uniform concern within a majority that produce stable coalitions. For example, tension of racial or national identity could produce this result in a representative legislature of a colonized country. Such a result is much less likely when legislators within any potential majority group formed around a given set of benefits to constituents differ significantly in the relative importance they attach to these and other benefits provided by the legislature. For example, individuals within a potential majority of legislators agreeing on benefits for metropolitan areas at the expense of nonmetropolitan areas may attach quite diverse relative importance to these benefits and subsidies to different industries that are concentrated in separate parts of the country. In such cases, the votes of legislators in potential minority groups can contribute to efficient vote trades with legislators in potential majority groups. Diversity of interest groups across legislative districts adds to this diversity in the relative importance that individual legislators attach to different legislative outcomes.

For the crucial legislative votes on taxation, each legislator weighs his loss of votes for each increment in taxes against the increased votes he receives for expenditures. The more effectively he and coordinating legislators work out a utility-maximizing combination of subsidized benefits within his platform and the more efficient the vote trading within the legislature, the higher each legislator's desired level of overall taxes.[9]

Political parties play three roles in achieving informational and fund-raising economies, all of which derive from the tendency for the same sets of issues to influence portions of the voting from each district. Parties' economizing roles come into play in the following circumstance: (1) some citizens' votes are influenced by several of these issues; (2) other citizens are influenced by fewer of these issues or even only one of them; and (3) these latter citizens tend not to be opposed to the legislative actions desired by those interested in the broader set of issues. This situation can result from widely held preferences about issues and from commonly held ideologies about the types of governmental actions that are appropriate in particular events. The first of political parties' economizing roles is to provide coordination and shared resources for the groups formed around combinations of issues. The second role is to communicate information about voting behavior within these groups to individual candidates and especially to coordinating legislators. A given party gains from one of its members being a coordinating legislator whenever he would use some of his allowable resource diversions to make legislative outcomes more responsive to the combination of issues that the party represents. The third role of political parties is achieving economies in obtaining campaign contributions from voters that are influenced by these issues. Because each district's voting is unique, candidates have incentives to stray from party positions and a party's allocation of its campaign funds is a means of enforcing party "discipline."

As with committee chairmen, the roles of political parties decline as information becomes less costly to individual candidates due to data processing and the increased availability of polls and technical expertise at inferring voter preferences.

B   Legislative demand as a function of price

It is now possible to derive a legislature's demand for a public or private good or service that it provides to citizens.[10] This is done separately for the cases where private citizens can and cannot obtain the same good or service in private markets. In both cases, it is taken as given that there are no direct charges to the direct recipients of goods or services provided by a legislature; a legislature's choices in assessing such charges is considered later in the chapter.

Legislative demand for goods and services not available
to citizens in private markets

The legislature and each legislator are initially assumed to be in equilibrium with respect to every legislator's influence over legislative spending and the funding of all items in his utility-maximizing platform. Each such item yields utility to a legislator by contributing to his election probability or his benefits from resource diversions. Ignoring indivisibilities and jointness of voting or supply, a legislator's equilibrium allocation of spending for constituents is such that his marginal utility from providing each benefit divided by its marginal cost to the legislature equals the comparable ratio for any other benefit in his own platform; any inequality in these ratios enables him to increase his utility by redirecting from the benefit with the lower ratio to that with the higher ratio.

In deciding whether legislative provision of a good or service unavailable in private markets should influence his vote, a citizen has no incentive to take account of what the legislature pays for it but only his own demand for it. Assume that the price the legislature pays for such a resource decreases. The same quantity of the resource provided on identical terms elicits the same votes as before, and the legislature has additional funds to provide other benefits. These funds are allocated among all legislators according to their base shares plus their individual incremental allowable resource diversions vis-à-vis other legislators.

To simplify the discussion on the manner in which election probabilities affect legislative demand, I make the simplifying assumption that individual legislators have no allowable resource diversions.

Under this assumption, each legislator allocates any additional funds under his influence so as to maintain equality of all ratios of marginal election probability to price.[11] The change in expenditures on each item depends on three forces: (1) A larger quantity provided of a good or service can increase votes from each of the first three of the five categories of citizens mentioned in the previous section of this chapter. These votes can result from citizens' receipt of a larger benefit or from the benefit being newly available to them. (2) When a good or service provided by a legislature is a complement or substitute for another, the increased availability of one can increase or decrease votes based on the other. (3) Finally, an increased benefit for some citizens (or a new benefit for an additional category of citizens) can result in larger losses of votes from other citizens not desiring the benefit.

The net vote response to increased quantity provision of an individual good or service in legislators' platforms will vary with the particular resource involved. This varying responsiveness is due to differing density functions of citizens' critical values of benefits from individual legislatively provided goods and services at which their votes are influenced by the benefit, and the effects of changed quantities of other legislatively provided goods and services that are complements and substitutes for the resource in question and thus shift its density function. However, a legislature is more likely to provide an increased quantity of a good or service if its price has decreased. As a legislator allocates expenditures among items in his platform to equate ratios of marginal election probabilities to prices, a reduced price for a good or service elicits a further adjustment on his part. We may decompose this effect of a price change on a legislature's quantity demanded of a good or service into substitution and income effects analogous to those of consumer demand behavior. However, in determining the compensated substitution effect we must take account of the possible losses of votes from citizens not desiring this benefit. It is conceivable that these vote losses can be large enough at the margin that the compensated substitution effect for a given good or service would be positive. Barring this presumably unusual possibility, the compensated substitution effect for a legislatively provided good or service contributes to a larger quantity demanded in response to a decrease in its price. The influence of diversion benefits on legislators' choices among quantities of goods and services always provides a negative component to the substitution effect. The income effect can increase or decrease the responsiveness of quantity demanded to price.[12]

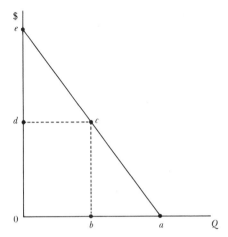

Figure 6.1. Legislative demand for a good or service that is not available to citizens in the private market.

Line *ae* in Figure 6.1 illustrates a legislature's demand for a good or service that is not available to citizens in a private market. The height of legislative demand at each quantity is legislators' combined willingness to pay for the resource's marginal net contribution to election probabilities and for its marginal contribution to benefits from resource diversions. This willingness to pay is influenced by the following: the substitutability of different resources in contributing to election probabilities and legislators' diversion benefits; legislators' individual marginal willingness to trade reduced diversions for increased election probabilities and vice versa; and the marginal effects of taxes and other financing on election probabilities. The mix of votes from the first three categories of marginal voters also influences a legislature's willingness to pay for particular goods and services; for example, the larger the fraction of marginal voters from the second category who would otherwise vote for opponents, the more the legislature is willing to pay. However, recall that no matter how much intramarginal voters are willing to pay, their voting behavior does not directly affect legislative demand at the margin. As noted, these citizens can affect legislative demands for goods and services that they desire by making campaign contributions; the resulting increased willingness of legislators to pay for these goods or services depends on how effectively they can use the contributions to increase election probabilities.

If a legislature is required to pay only a single price times the total quantity provided, its expenditures of $0bcd$ are the highest at quantity $0b$ where elasticity equals 1; if vote losses from those not receiving benefits are based on expenditures instead of quantities provided, they tend to make the quantity demanded less responsive to price where demand is elastic and to increase this responsiveness where demand is inelastic. However, a legislature often has to pay more than price times quantity demanded (see Chapter 8).

Legislative demand for goods and services that are available to citizens in private markets

A legislature's demand for a good or service that is available to citizens in the private marketplace will now be derived. Many resources not available in private markets have important characteristics in common with goods or services that are. Whether they should be treated analytically as available in private markets depends on the degree of substitutability to citizens and in practice is somewhat arbitrary.

When a good or service is available in private markets, the votes of citizens willing to pay the going market price for the quantity provided for free are based on the size of the subsidy, rather than the welfare these citizens derive from the good or service itself. That is, the value of the benefit to these citizens is the unit subsidy multiplied by the quantity of the good or service they receive. Thus changes in market conditions for this resource affect the votes that result from providing a subsidized quantity of it. Those who are willing to pay less than the market price attach correspondingly lower values to their subsidies depending on their demands for the good or service.

Assume a decrease in the market price of a good or service that a legislature makes available at a given below-market price. Unlike the case where the legislature is the only source of supply, the lower price reduces many citizens' valuations of the benefit. Some may decide to purchase the item in the market as a result of the price decrease and of these citizens, those having based votes on the benefit will no longer do so; there may, for example, be some costs of qualifying for the benefit that are worthwhile at the higher price but not at a lower one. Among those continuing to take advantage of the subsidy, some discontinue voting and the benefit has less influence on the votes of others.

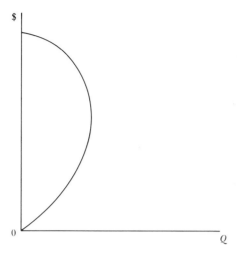

Figure 6.2. Legislative demand for a good or service that is available to citizens in the private market.

Because a decrease in the price of a good or service available to voters in the market reduces votes based on it, it is not possible to derive a legislative demand that would be downward sloping throughout its entire range; the decreased votes due to citizens' reduced valuations of the benefit can easily offset the income effect of the decrease in price, if positive, and the usually negative substitution effect of the price change. However, under reasonable assumptions one can generalize about the shape of legislative demand. Assume that voters' information and coordination costs and their opportunities to obtain other benefits with their votes do not vary with the market price of the resource. Starting from sufficiently high market prices, these costs continue to be justified for most citizens when their own demands are high also. However, successive decreases in market price make the voting and opportunity costs of larger numbers of citizens no longer justified. Thus, the higher the price, the more likely legislative demand is negatively sloped, and we expect legislative demand to become positively sloped when the price becomes lower than most citizens' information and coordination costs along with their opportunity costs of basing votes on this benefit. Figure 6.2 illustrates such a "backward bending" legislative demand for the case where the resource is provided at no charge to those receiving it.

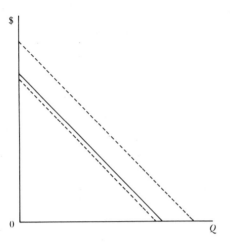

Figure 6.3. Shifts in legislative demand.

*Influences of information costs and types of voters
on legislative demand*

Using negatively sloped portions of demand, this discussion analyzes
the influences of information costs and types of voters on the position of a legislature's demand for a good or service to be provided to
citizens. Consider first a decrease in a group of citizens' costs of
knowing their common interest in coordinating their votes to obtain
an economic benefit from a legislature (e.g., because an organization's employees defray these costs). The cost decrease produces
more votes for individual legislators in response to their providing
the benefit in their platforms. In turn, the additional votes raise the
legislature's quantity demanded at each price, illustrated by a shift
from the solid line to the higher dashed line in Figure 6.3.

Next, consider an increase in citizens' costs of knowing about a
benefit to other citizens that they would oppose. (A public organization can bring about such an increase in information costs; see
Chapter 9.) By reducing awareness of the benefit, this cost increase
reduces losses of votes from the provision of the benefit and thus
increases legislative demand, again illustrated by a shift to the upper
dashed line in Figure 6.3.

Finally, consider the possibility that many citizens derive a very
small gain from an economic benefit provided by a legislature that

only slightly affects their voting because, for example, many other benefits also influence their voting. Assume also that a smaller number of citizens base their votes entirely or almost entirely on the benefit and are thus the major determinant of the shape and position of legislative demand (illustrated by the solid line in Figure 6.3). The smaller group might, for example, be the direct recipients of the benefit, plus the employees and suppliers of the organization providing it. The broader group having a mild interest in the benefit might perceive that it confers modestly desirable externalities. Let the members of this broader group change their minds so that the benefit has no influence at all on their voting, while the voting behavior of the smaller group remains unchanged. The lower dashed line in Figure 6.3 illustrates the resulting small inward shift of legislative demand. This example helps explain why programs often continue to receive the same or nearly the same public funding in spite of reduced support in public opinion polls.

Commitments of present legislatures that increase future legislative demand

By committing future legislatures to provide economic benefits to citizens, a legislature can increase votes for its members without having to use tax revenues or other current financing.[13] Individual citizens often derive significant gains from commitments of future economic benefits and, in fact, they prefer a substitution of committed future benefits for present benefits that exceeds the rates at which they personally substitute future for present consumption, if they are equally certain of receiving both. Legislators can increase their election probabilities by making additional commitments on future legislatures when only the benefiting minorities are aware of the commitment or when other citizens do not find it worthwhile to withdraw enough votes to have offsetting effects on election probabilities. The resulting constraints on future legislatures would be faced equally by a legislator having made the commitment and his opponents in the next election. The opponent may not even criticize the commitment to avoid losing support of those benefiting from it.

The presently imposed commitments on future legislatures can be enforceable contracts, but statements of promised future benefits can be so costly in terms of votes to terminate that they would be just as assured; once the future benefit is promised, the prospective beneficiaries and those dealing with them take this benefit into account in their plans. Thus, if the commitment is not honored, blocs of voters much larger than those originating the commitment will vote for opponents. As long as a benefit promised in the past is provided, it need not even influence current voting.

Comparison of legislative demand with citizens' demand for public and private goods

Whenever an organization supplies a good or service demanded by a legislature, an analysis of economic efficiency requires comparing this demand with citizens' demand for the resource. A legislature's willingness to pay for a resource derives from votes and resulting impacts on election probabilities, from legislators' benefits from resource diversions, and from constraints on its total spending; thus, the connection between legislative demand and citizens' demand for the same good or service is not a close one. Although the influence of an economic benefit on a citizen's voting is determined partly by his demand for it, his vote also depends on his perceived possibilities for receiving other desired legislative outcomes, his perception of the influence of his vote on each legislative outcome, and his information and coordination costs of basing his vote on this benefit. The influences of legislators' benefits from resource diversions tends to make legislative demand more independent of citizens' demand. The constraints on a legislature's total spending, discussed below, are largely independent of citizens' demands for particular goods and services.

The fact that it can be more economical to vote than to pay for a resource tends to make legislative demand for particular goods and services exceed citizens' demand. Votes based on supplier rents can contribute to excesses of legislative demand over citizens' demand. Citizens' perceptions that their votes have more influence on relatively unimportant outcomes can make legislative demand exceed citizens' demand for the less important outcomes and can make it be less than citizens' demand for the more important outcomes. Although a citizen's willingness to pay for a resource beyond the amount inducing him to base his vote entirely on it does not add further weight to his vote, we have seen that campaign contributions can augment legislative demand in this case.

A legislature's total spending[14] is constrained by individual and collective responses of citizens to its taxing and spending policies. Individuals' own adjustments to these policies (for example, their relative emphasis on taxed and untaxed activities) place limits on a legislature as do individual choices to emigrate from a legislature's jurisdiction. However, the costs of making these adjustments give a legislature latitude to impose net costs on individual citizens, that is, to impose taxes that exceed their valuations of benefits received from the legislature. Citizens also have the option to act concertedly with others to impose responsibility on a legislature. For example, citizens can form the necessary coalitions to ensure passage of constitutional amendments that limit the amounts or composition of a legislature's spending or income or that change the type of representation in a legislature. To do so requires individual citizens to bear the negotiation and coordination costs and the risks that the outcomes will not be as they desire. These costs also contribute to a legislature's capability to impose net costs on individuals. In contrast to constraints on actual legislative spending, the efficient rate of a legislature's spending is the minimum amount necessary to elicit the welfare maximizing quantity of each public good, including those income transfers that citizens regard as public goods. This quantity is determined where the vertical sum of citizens' informed demands for each public good equals the public good's marginal cost in the most economical forms of supplying organizations where CPOR is imposed on all of their employees. It should be noted, however, that it would be difficult or impossible to design compensating payments so that an efficient rate of legislative spending could be achieved without making some individuals worse off.

The following incentives on citizens tend to make total legislative spending exceed the efficient rate. Citizens' gains from basing votes on privately received benefits and their costs of knowing about undesired privately received benefits accruing to other citizens contribute to the collective funding of these benefits. Such funding contributes to an excess of legislative spending over the desirable rate except, of course, when private goods have public characteristics or when efficiency is otherwise enhanced (e.g., subsidies for marginal cost pricing in decreasing cost industries). Resource diversions of legislators and of employees supplying legislative demand can raise legislative spending above the efficient rate but do not necessarily do so because of the welfare these individuals derive from the resource diversions and because the increased spending can be for undersupplied public goods. A legislature's committing future legislative spending also can but does not necessarily make this spending exceed the efficient rate, as can voting based on supplier rents.

There are forces, however, that tend to reduce legislative spending below the efficient rate. As noted, the preferences of intramarginal voters for public goods do not directly affect legislative spending, although these voters can make campaign contributions that do increase spending. Downs's (1957) argument that citizens are uninformed (due to "rational ignorance" of the benefits of collective expenditures) implies that legislative demand for public goods can be below the proper level. This argument may be offset somewhat by the incentive felt by employees supplying public goods to inform voters of the benefits that result from them (see Chapter 7). But employees are perhaps considerably less effective in providing information about broadly received benefits from public goods than they are in comcomitantly providing information about private or public benefits to smaller groups while keeping information costs high for the public at large. Finally, we have seen that Downs's argument can be augmented: the opportunity to gain private benefits from the government makes citizens give less weight than otherwise to public goods in their voting.

In conclusion, broadly beneficial public goods are often underfunded and private goods and public goods that benefit small parts of the population are frequently overfunded.

Summary of basic hypotheses about legislative demand

Legislative demand as a function of price. It is possible to derive from the behavior of voters and legislators in the face of information costs a legislature's demand as a function of price for the goods and services that it provides to constituents. The effects of changes in price on quantity demanded by a legislature can be decomposed into substitution and income effects analagous to those of consumer demand behavior. However, the opposition of voters not desiring benefits makes it theoretically possible for the compensated substitution effect to be positive. Nevertheless, a legislature's quantity demanded of goods and services that are not available from private suppliers will usually be inversely related to price. In contrast, legislative demand for goods and services that citizens can obtain from private suppliers will ordinarily be positively related to price up to some price above which it will become negatively related.

Types of goods and services demanded by a legislature. The influence of broadly beneficial public goods on citizens' voting choices is reduced when legislatures can provide goods and services to citizens whose benefits are privately capturable, or public goods that benefit small parts of the population.

Legislative and citizens' demands compared. A legislature's demand for a good or service can exceed or be less than citizens' demand for the same resource, depending on the constraints on total legislative spending, citizens' alternative opportunities to receive benefits from a legislature, each citizen's perception of his vote's influences on legislative outcomes, and the information and coordination costs of basing votes on particular legislative outcomes. Legislative demand is most likely to be less than citizens' demand in cases of public goods benefiting a broad segment of the population.

C   The legislature as the funding authority of a public organization and the public organization's short-run price, income, and output

As a public organization's funding authority, a legislature prefers a public organization's income to be no larger than necessary to elicit a desired rate of output;[15] any larger income would reduce legislators' election probabilities and diversion benefits. However, the same forces that give employees of private organizations cost advantages over stockholders and donors give a public organization's employees cost advantages over a legislature. That is, a public organization's income must include employees' allowable resource diversions. In the short-run analysis the legislative demand facing a public organization is given and fixed, and the legislature's choice whether instead to purchase a good or service from private or other public organizations is not examined. (This choice is analyzed in Chapter 9.)

The following discussion examines only the situation where the public organization's output is not available in private markets. It separately analyzes the cases where citizens are not charged for the public organization's output and where these charges are made. The absence of a charge can result from an output lacking privately capturable benefits, costs of assessing charges, or votes gained thereby. Figures 6.4 and 6.5 respectively illustrate short-run price, income, and output determination when legislative demand exceeds and is less than citizens' demand. Four lines representing marginal and average variable cost of the organization's output are shown. (See Chapter 5.) The highest line represents the legislature's cost of the public organization's output, including employees' marginal and average variable allowable resource diversions and all marginal and average variable costs of imposing responsibility on employees. The lowest line represents employees' cost when CPOR is placed on all

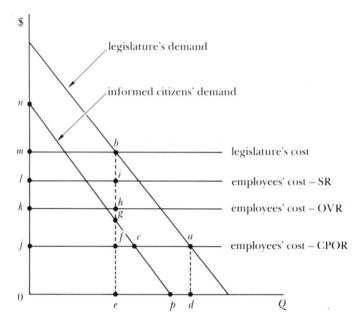

Figure 6.4. Short-run price, income, and output of a public organization. The legislature's demand exceeds citizens' demand, and there is no charge to clients. Marginal and average variable cost is shown.

employees and intermediate outputs are priced at marginal cost. (Employers' costs of imposing CPOR are not included in this line.) The next two lines represent employees' costs under overall value and specific responsibility.

The public organization's equilibrium rate of output is determined where the legislature's marginal cost of output equals its marginal value of the output, that is, point b corresponding to output $0e$ in Figure 6.4 and point g corresponding to output $0c$ in Figure 6.5. In the short run analysis, one can determine only the public organization's variable income that corresponds to its equilibrium rate of output. This income, $0ebm$ in Figure 6.4 and $0cgk$ in Figure 6.5, includes all allowable variable resource diversions and variable responsibility costs. The determination of fixed income is analyzed in Chapter 8.

That $0e$ and $0c$ are equilibrium rates of output for the demands shown in the figures can be seen as follows. If the legislature having these demands reduced its variable expenditures below the respective amounts $0ebm$ and $0cgk$, it would either be spending a subopti-

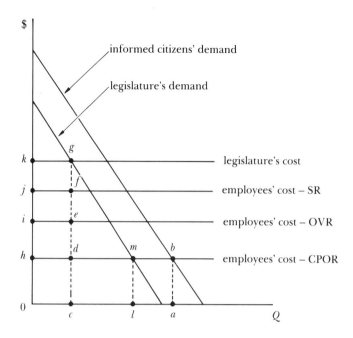

Figure 6.5. Short-run price, income, and output of a public organization. Citizens' demand exceeds the legislature's demand, and there is no charge to clients. Marginal and average variable cost is shown.

mal amount on specific or overall value responsibility for output rates $0e$ and $0c$, or it would be reducing the resource diversions of employees under overall value responsibility below those that are allowed by the optimal imposition of this responsibility for these rates of output. In the latter case, employees would respond by reducing the organization's nondiverted output until their allowable diversions for their output rate would equal those available to them. In turn, legislators would be worse off by the excess of legislative demand over the reduced output quantities. Wildavsky (1964, pp. 102–3) points out that:

A major strategy in resisting cuts is to make them in such a way that they have to be put back. Rather than cut the national office's administrative expenses, for instance, an agency might cut down on the handling of applications from citizens with full realization that the ensuing discontent would be bound to get back to Congressmen, who would have to restore the funds.

The effects of a public organization's supply behavior on economic welfare depends on divergences between legislative and informed citizens' demand as well as on economic behavior within the organization. This can be seen in the figures, where under CPOR an excess of legislative over citizens' demand would make marginal cost be greater than citizens' demand at the equilibrium rate of output (0d) and, when the demands are reversed, marginal cost would be less than citizens' demand at this output (0l). By considering welfare as a function of citizens' demand only, this discussion ignores the welfare within legislative demand for a good or service that legislators personally derive from resource diversions involving this resource.

The lower rate of output brought about by other types of responsibility than CPOR tends to mitigate the welfare loss attributable to excess of legislative over citizens' demand. Depending on the positions of legislative and citizens' demand, output could be less, more, or coincidentally equal to the rate of output necessary (but not sufficient) to achieve the maximum (*jcn* less fixed costs) net welfare gain for citizens in Figure 6.4. A smaller output is shown in the figure, leading to a modest loss of *fcg*. Of course, there are additional welfare losses of *jfhk* (under overall value responsibility) and *jfil* (under specific responsibility) due to inefficient resource allocation within the organization. The quantities *khbm* and *libm* respectively equal the sum of total variable responsibility costs plus employees' total variable cost advantages under overall value responsibility and specific responsibility. The degree that employees discount below cash value or waste the amounts within their cost advantages determines the respective portions of these amounts that are transfers of welfare to employees and social welfare losses.

In contrast, when citizens' demand exceeds legislative demand as in Figure 6.5, the effects of demand and types of responsibility other than CPOR reinforce each other in leading to an inadequate rate of output. Legislative demand leads to an output of 0l under CPOR that is further reduced to 0c by the other types of responsibility. Note, however, that the smaller rate of output implies reduced social welfare losses within the organization and smaller transfers to employees; the welfare losses of *hdei* or *hdfj* due to inefficiency within the organization are smaller than if legislative demand exceeded citizens' demand, and the amounts within *iegk* or *jfgk* that represent welfare losses and provide income to employees are also smaller.

It is frequently proposed that public organizations be made more "efficient," by which is usually meant an increase in the rate of an organization's output with a given budget or a reduction in its budget with no decrease in its output. We have seen, however, that when legislative demand exceeds citizens' demand, an increase in the rate of output could decrease efficiency. Assume for a moment that by making resource responsibility more effective, a new management technique reduces the legislature's cost of a public organization's output. At an extreme consider the output rate $0d$ corresponding to point a in Figure 6.4 where marginal cost under CPOR equals legislative demand. If citizens' demand equals zero between $0p$ and $0d$, a welfare loss of $pdac$ (minus fcg) resulting from the excess of marginal cost over citizens' demand must be weighed against efficiency gains within the organization. In contrast, in Figure 6.5 where citizens' demand exceeds legislative demand, a higher rate of output via a decrease in the legislature's cost always adds to efficiency. Here, the output $0l$ determined by marginal cost under CPOR equaling legislative demand at point m increases welfare vis-à-vis citizens' demand by the amount dmg, and there are efficiency gains within the organization. However, even this output is short of the welfare maximizing rate $0a$ determined at point b. Of course, any efficiency gains due to a new management technique are Kaldor-Hicks gains, not increases in Pareto efficiency, in the case where employees are not compensated for their personal losses of benefits from resource diversions.

In fact, new management techniques often fail to reduce the legislature's cost, because they would require employees to take less than the amounts of resource diversions that are allowed by the responsibility facing them. The time or released workload allotted to employees to implement an ineffective technique can fund other activities, including employees' cooperation to increase future benefits from resource diversions. Apparent "success" can result from one demanded output simply being increased at the expense of others.

We now turn to the situation where there is a charge to the citizens directly receiving a public organization's output. It is useful to distinguish two types of outputs. For one type, referred to here as an *income equivalent output*, the votes underlying subsidies would be the same if the recipients of the output instead received cash giving them the same utility. This situation frequently occurs when the recipients and the voters supporting the benefit are largely the same. The in-kind benefit is provided instead of cash because information costs to other citizens are higher or these other citizens are somewhat less inclined to withdraw votes in response to the in-kind benefit. There is little incentive for a legislature to require charges for such an output because the underlying votes are based on recipients' total economic gains.

The votes underlying the other type of output, referred to as an *object output*, derive from the particular quantities received, often by other citizens, rather than the size of the economic benefit to the recipient. A legislature has an incentive to coordinate its expenditures for these outputs with private demands for them and, in particular, to charge clients when the costs of assessing charges are smaller than the revenues received.

Figure 6.6 illustrates the case where the organization provides such an object output. It is necessary here to introduce the demand of the clients who directly receive an object output. Two client demand relationships, one higher and one lower than the legislative demand relationship, are shown. The dashed lines through points k and f represent the vertical sum of legislative and clients' demand for the alternative client demands. Citizens' demand, which encompasses clients' demand and the demands of other citizens for clients' receipt of the output, is not shown in order to simplify the figure.

The solution for the organization's equilibrium price and rate of output is similar to that of the private nonprofit organization when there are charges to clients. The rising lines in the lower graph represent the difference between the legislature's marginal and average variable cost in the absence of charges to clients, and the price that clients are willing to pay for each rate of output. The lower graph's downward sloping line repeats the legislature's demand. The lower graph shows that at outputs $0g$ and $0b$ in the two cases, the legislature's marginal value of the output equals its net marginal cost after subtracting the amounts paid by clients. The upper graph shows that when clients' demand is less than legislative demand the output $0g$ is financed through price gh paid by the client and the per unit amount gj paid by the legislature. Alternatively, be is paid by the client and bc by the legislature when clients' demand exceeds the legislature's demand. The relative shares paid by the legislature and clients depend on the relative positions of their demand curves at the equilibrium output. The organization's total variable resource diversions and variable costs of imposing responsibility are $likm$ at output $0g$ and are $ldfm$ at output $0b$, and its total variable income is $0gkm$ and $0bfm$ at these rates of output. To simplify the diagram employees' cost of the public organization's output is not shown.

It is possible to analyze the welfare implications of the output rates $0g$ and $0b$ by imagining a citizens' demand relationship (including clients' demand) that is above, below, or coincident with the combined legislative and client demand relationship in Figure 6.6. The separate components of welfare loss attributable to divergence of

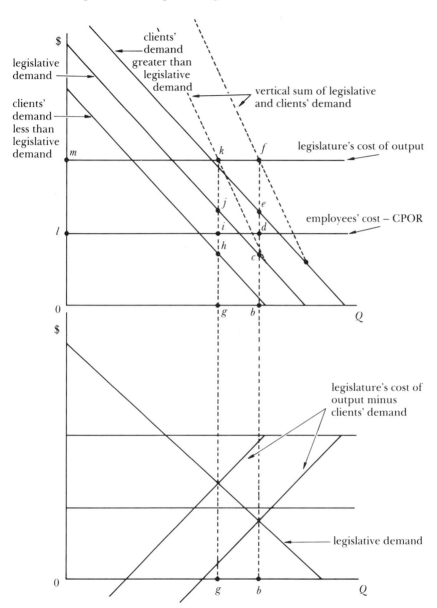

Figure 6.6. Short-run price and output of a public organization. The public organization produces an object output for which clients are charged. Marginal and average variable cost is shown.

legislative and citizens' demands, on the one hand, and excess of legislative cost over employees' cost under CPOR, on the other, can be calculated in the same manner as in the case where there are no charges to clients.

Summary of basic hypotheses about a public organization's supply

The legislature as a funding authority. Because of each member's desire to maximize his utility from election probabilities and resource diversions, a legislature attempts to make a public organization's income no larger than necessary to elicit any given rate of its output. However, the resource diversions of a public organization's employees that are allowed by the responsibility facing them make the legislature's cost exceed employees' cost of this output.

Equilibrium price, income, and output. In the absence of charges to clients, the equilibrium rate of a public organization's output is determined by the equality of the legislature's marginal cost and its demand for this output. The organization's income includes the legislature's variable costs of obtaining the organization's output plus the legislature's fixed costs (analyzed in Chapter 8). When there is a charge to the direct recipients of the organization's output, the organization's rate of output is determined where its net marginal cost, that is, the difference between its marginal cost in the absence of such charges and clients' demand, is equal to the legislature's demand. Clients' demand at this rate of output determines the price the organization charges for its output.

Efficiency. The analysis of efficiency requires taking account of divergences between legislative demand and citizens' demand for the public organization's output, as well as determining the efficiency of resource allocation within the organization. As in other types of organization, a part of employees' resource diversions represents transfers of income to them and are thus welfare losses only insofar as employees discount in-kind benefits from this income below its cash equivalent value to them.

CHAPTER 7

Employees' investment behavior and implications for suborganization

This chapter analyzes employees' investment behavior. Investments, such as additions to plant and equipment, improvements in employees' skills, reorganization affecting production domains, and changes in responsibility on an organization's employees are typically believed to reflect the interests of the funding authority. However, an employee often can use resource diversions to make investments that increase his future welfare. Thus, the long-run analysis of economic behavior within organizations should take into account employees' investment behavior as well as the funding authority's.

Employees' investment behavior is determined by: individual employees' time preferences and utilities derived from particular resources; the nature of investment opportunities and their returns; and constraints on the resource diversions available for investment. The constraints on resource diversions of course include responsibility, which also can restrict the particular investments that employees may make. Another constraint is the funding limit on the total resource diversions of an organization's employees in any time period, to be analyzed in Chapter 8. Employees' investments are often directed to increasing the future resource diversions allowed by responsibility. Here, it is assumed either that the resource diversions presently allowed by responsibility sum to less than the funding limit or that employees seek alternative benefits from diversions within this limit that yield them more utility.

This chapter focuses on the nature of employees' investment opportunities, particularly those that influence suborganization and the coordination of employees' activities. The discussion first illustrates how investments can provide returns both to employees and to employers. Next, we explore investment opportunities that directly involve employees in altering an organization's economic activities. Such investments are described in separate categories for those that do and do not alter the division of the organization's production functions into production domains, that is, suborganization. Employees' investments to facilitate the coordination of their activities are then analyzed, and resource allocation under voluntary modes of coordination is contrasted with that occurring under coordination via authority. A brief section evaluates the roles of employees as investors in corporate adoptions of multidivisional suborganization. A subsequent section considers investments that directly involve employees with their organization's external constituencies. Finally, we consider how managing employees and funding authorities respond to employees' investments.

A   Returns to employees and employers from investments of the organization's resources

One who initiates an investment plans the specific activities involved. The funding authority has discretion over whether an investment he initiates takes place, although one or more employees may have enough influence over its expected returns to determine whether in fact it does take place. In contrast, an investment initiated by an employee may require approval, and thus he does not necessarily have discretion over whether it takes place.

Figure 7.1 illustrates expected returns to the feasible investments that are available to an employee and his employer. The vertical axis measures the net (cash equivalent) expected present value returns to the employer of investments initiated either by him or by the employee within a given time period. Similarly, the horizontal axis measures net (cash equivalent) expected present value returns to the employee of investments initiated either by him or the employer within the same time period. Either party's return to his own investment is his expected stream of future benefits from it. A party's return to an investment initiated by the other party is his expected stream of impacts on him that can have a net negative or positive cash equivalent present value. The returns shown for each party are assumed to be net of any effects of the other party's returns.

The investments indicated in upper case letters are those that the employer (managing employee or funding authority) initiates.[1] One might argue that the funding authority (as opposed to a managing employee) never actually initiates investments – rather his investment role is restricted to approving or disapproving investments initiated by employees. For example, Penrose (1955) has noted: "Both general reasoning and discussions with businessmen confirm the hypothesis that a firm would never have a high degree of confidence in any extensive plan for expansion drawn up and executed exclusively by men with no experience within the firm itself" (p. 534). For

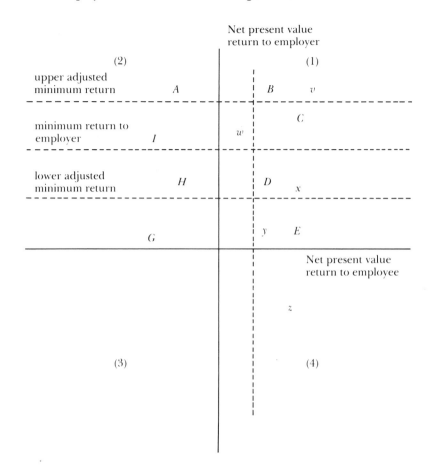

Figure 7.1. Overview of investment opportunities in an organization.

generality, however, the discussion allows for the possibility that the funding authority initiates investments.

The investments that the employee initiates are shown in lower case letters. Two categories of employee-initiated investments are those requiring and not requiring the employer's approval. An employee's need for the employer to provide resources beyond those already under his discretion, whether in-kind or in the form of a capital budget, constitutes one reason for the employer's approval to be required. Another reason would be the employer's imposing specific responsibility on some of the employee's particular investment activities. Investments not requiring approval are those for which the necessary resources are already at the employee's discretion and are not prevented by the responsibility imposed. Our main concern is with those investments initiated by employees that do not require the employer's approval. However, Bower's (1970) important study of decision making about investment projects within firms suggests that lower level employees' discretion over resources and their information cost advantages often largely determine the content of investment projects that must be approved by top managing employees.

The employee is assumed to have an estimate of the returns to himself from the investments that might be initiated by the employer. These investments must have positive expected returns to the employer and are thus confined to the first and second quadrants, where they can respectively produce either positive or negative returns to the employee. For example, an investment can increase or decrease the output replacement cost of an employee under overall value responsibility, or it can raise or lower the costs of monitoring the activities of an employee under specific responsibility. If the net expected returns to himself are high enough, an employer will be willing to make investments yielding higher allowable limits on his employee's resource diversions.

Investments initiated by an employee must yield him positive returns and can have either positive or negative returns to the employer. These investments are thus confined to the first and fourth quadrants. The employer is not necessarily aware of the returns to him resulting from particular investments that the employee initiates; if not, the expected return shown for the employer would be zero. However, if the investment requires the employer's approval, those effects of the investment of which the employer is aware must produce a net positive expected return. The illustrated returns on investments the employee initiates are assumed to be conditional on the employer's investments and the responsibility imposed.

For illustrative purposes, assume that each party's present value cash equivalent cost of every investment he might initiate is equal. Under this assumption, the dashed lines parallel to the axes illustrate minimum expected returns below which an initiated investment would not go beyond the planning stage.[2] This minimum return is the cash equivalent present value cost of each investment.[3] Either party's expected investment costs are assumed to be conditional on the current or expected actions of the other party that influence these costs. When the employee must take benefits from resource diversions in kind, his required minimum return will typically be smaller as a result; although internal opportunities for investing cash benefits would have to compete with investment opportunities outside the organization, in-kind benefits ordinarily must be used on the job. Thus, the illustrated required minimum expected return is smaller for the employee than for the employer.

Three dashed lines are shown for the employer. The middle line represents his minimum required expected return. The employee may be able to use his discretion over the resources delegated to him and his control over the information he communicates to raise or lower the employer's expected costs or returns from the investments he initiates. The upper and lower lines illustrate the range of this influence over the employer's expected present value cost or benefit of an investment. Specifically, when the employee influences the employer's expected costs, the lines show the compensating change in the employer's minimum return. When the employee influences the employer's expected benefits, the distances of these lines from the minimum return show the present value of this influence. The two lines imply that the employee has the same influence over expected costs and benefits and that this influence is uniform over all investments; alternatively, varying influences could be characterized.

Among investments initiated by the employer, the employee wants to discourage investments yielding him negative expected returns, shown in the second quadrant. However, the one labeled A has a high enough expected return that the employee cannot use his influence over the employer's expected costs or benefits to remove this investment from consideration. Such investments are *dominated* by the employer. In contrast, the employee can use his influence over expected costs and benefits to prevent further consideration of the investment labeled I. He will exercise this influence if his cost is low enough in relation to the avoided negative return to himself and if he believes the employer would otherwise make the investment. The investment D in the first quadrant yields the employer an expected return smaller than the required minimum, but the employee could reverse this relationship and might do so because of the investment's positive return to him. Although investments such as I and D would be initiated by the employer, they are dominated by the employee.

Investments H and C are dominated by the employee, but he would not want to encourage the former and may not need to encourage the latter. Investment E, like A, is one the employee might want to influence but cannot. The employee cannot bring G into consideration, nor can he prevent B's consideration, and he would not take these actions if he could.

Among investments initiated by the employee, those requiring the employer's approval must, like v or w, have estimated returns larger than the employer's minimum return to qualify for approval. Bower (1970) found that employers tend to base their estimates on the employee's estimate plus the employee's reputation for accuracy. One managing employee stated: "What it really comes down to is your batting average . . . I decide the degree of optimism incorporated into the estimates" (p. 59). Another managing employee, a chairman of the board, remarked, "Some groups in the corporation are such that you just know their numbers are optimistic. In others you know that they are pessimistic" (p. 60).

However, an investment must also yield above the employee's minimum expected return for him to submit it for approval. Although investment v meets both requirements, investment w yields an insufficient return to the employee. An employee will not submit for approval an investment giving him a negative expected return or a positive expected return smaller than his minimum, no matter how favorable to the employer. For example, Bower (1970) states, "a general manager sponsors a project when he believes it will be in his interest to do so rather than not to do so, given his understanding of the 'rules of the game' " (p. 59).

Employee initiated investments not requiring the employer's approval need only yield expected returns above the employee's minimum to qualify. In particular, these can include investments such as z in the fourth quadrant representing negative returns to the employer. When these investments do yield positive returns to the employer, such as in the cases of y and x, the positive return counts as part of the output of an employee under overall value responsibility and the employee may not be discouraged if he is under specific responsibility. The employee has the option to raise the employer's returns to x and submit it as an investment requiring approval.

We now turn to the behavior of employees as investors.

B   The employee as an investor

An employee can use resource diversions directly for investments not requiring the employer's approval and also to alter the employer's expected returns and costs on investments he initiates or that require his approval. The employee's supply of resources to investments is determined by his estimated cash-equivalent present value benefits and costs of available investments, his cash-equivalent marginal values of noninvestment uses of the resources available to him, and the total resource diversions allowed by the responsibility facing him. Estimated present value returns depend on the employee's estimated length of employment as well as his time preference.

An employee is much more likely to make investments when his only alternative is to take current benefits from resource diversions in kind. As noted in the previous section, an employee typically is restricted to using in-kind benefits while on the job, and he thus has little incentive to take account of opportunities for using such income outside the organization. For example, although an investment can represent a much better use of an employee's time than aimless socializing, it may not yield him a return competitive with the time's cash value. The restriction of in-kind benefits also enhances returns on investments that give employees access to particular resources that they especially desire.

The discussion deals with employee initiated investments that increase either the resource diversions allowed by responsibility or the nature of resources available to an employee so that he derives more utility from given diversions. Such investments are considered separately in the cases when overall value and specific responsibility are imposed, and in both cases the focus is on investments not requiring the employer's approval. Many potentially desirable investments require the cooperation of multiple employees; in Section C we consider the means by which employees coordinate themselves.

Three important cases of employees' investments are not analyzed. In one case the employee uses resource diversions to fund investments that increase his future value in the labor market through, for example, the acquisition of skills and experience valued by other employers. The present discussion largely applies to an employee whose expected future utility during the long run from remaining within the organization considerably exceeds that from employment outside the organization. He may nonetheless value qualifying for higher-paying cohorts of employees (see Chapter 3). However, if so, he does not direct all investments to future labor market opportunities at the cost of investments to increase benefits from resource diversions. Another reason for an employee to be concerned with labor market opportunities is the contingency of making inaccurate estimates of allowable resource diversions and losing his job, or much of his total income from his job, as a result.

The second case not dealt with is where an employee works very hard on his employer's behalf early in his career and then "lets up" after establishing some seniority in his organization. By reducing his resource diversions below those allowable to him, he can prove his "dedication" or "loyalty" and thereby earn promotions. Such investments will occur until the employee reaches a position at which he values increased benefits from resource diversions more than the opportunities for promotion that he believes he is foregoing. Thus, by providing more promotion opportunities, an increase in an organization's growth can reduce some of its employees' resource diversions.

The third case not analyzed here is where an employee's social environment enables him to earn the esteem of other individuals who are important to him by establishing a record of reducing his resource diversions below those allowed by the responsibility imposed on him.

The nature of investments to increase benefits from resource diversions when overall value responsibility is imposed

Investments initiated by employees are considered separately according to whether or not they alter divisions of production functions into production domains (i.e., suborganization).

Investments not altering divisions of production functions into production domains. Employee-initiated investments not altering divisions of production functions into production domains are those that reduce the employee's costs of producing his output, yield him information about the demands for his outputs or increase these demands, and alter the employer's choices in placing responsibility on him.

An employee under overall value responsibility directly benefits from lower costs of producing his output except when benefits from resource diversions must be taken in kind and the marginal utility of every available resource is zero. Although the employee's incentive to reduce costs tends to increase economic efficiency, the employee is often the only gainer. We have seen in Chapter 4 that cost reduction can result from experimenting both within one's own production domain and with alternative coordinations of actions in relation to spillovers. Both of these investments are reflected in employees' demands for information.

Uncertainty about the availability of new production techniques, whether or not their adoption would require the employer's approval, can motivate employees to initiate investments. New production techniques can lower an employee's costs of his outputs and, by changing the types of resources available to him, can increase or decrease his cash-equivalent gain from in-kind diversion benefits.

Further, new production techniques can raise or lower employees' output replacement costs or the critical costs at which their employers would switch to specific responsibility. Thus in an environment of frequent technological change that is expected to affect his production domain, an employee will have a demand for information about these changes and the resulting costs and benefits not only to himself but to other employees if investments require their cooperation, and also to his employer if related investments require his approval or are initiated by him.[4]

An employee's investment behavior with respect to demand depends on the nature of the demands facing him and his employer. It is often not necessary for an employer to disclose his demand for his employee's outputs, and in many situations he need not let the employee know how these demands derive from the demands to which he himself responds. For example, he often does not have to involve the employee in dealing with his employer, higher employers, or clients inside or outside the organization having broader demands. All that is essential is that the employee know the employer's desired output rates.

When the managing employee takes his employee's outputs, he may subsequently process them or combine them with other outputs or he may simply pass them on to his employer or a client within or outside the organization demanding them, with or without recognition for the employee's contribution. In the former case the employer makes an additional productive contribution, but in the latter case his employees could readily displace his role. In either case, an employer will not involve his employees in dealing with his employer or with clients when they would thereby displace some of his role and his welfare would decrease as a result. Alternatively, an employer can gain from such involvement when his employees are unable to displace his role and they possess cost advantages in obtaining information about demand. Such cost advantages can occur, for example, when employees have the capability to tailor their outputs to clients' preferences.

In response to employers' restricting information about demand, employees may find it worthwhile to learn about demands for their outputs and the broader demands to which they contribute. Efficiency gains result when employees' outputs are thus more closely tailored to demands and when the information enables employees more rapidly and with less communication cost to respond to shifts in demand. Thus these investments can produce positive returns to clients and the funding authority and possibly to the managing employee, but they can also enable employees to displace managing employees.

Uncertainty about future demands, especially in an environment of large shifts due to Schumpeterian competition, creates especially strong incentives for employees to learn about the demands that they serve directly or indirectly. Such an environment also gives employees incentives to invest in information about alternative means of dealing with the shifts, for example, introducing new products or diversifying outputs, and to cooperate with other employees to this end. (Some of these incentives are discussed in the next subsection. Employees' investments related to demands for an organization's final outputs are analyzed later in this chapter and in Chapters 8 and 9.)

An employee's investments that influence the way his employer imposes responsibility include inferring the employer's estimate of his output replacement cost or the cost at which it is worthwhile to switch to specific responsibility; providing information to the employer that induces him to raise these estimates; increasing output replacement cost through adding unique characteristics to his output; and providing incentives for the employer to impose another variant of overall value responsibility or change over to specific responsibility.

It is possible for an employee to infer interest of his employer in replacing his output or switching to specific responsibility by keeping track of the employer's perceptions and attitudes about his performance. However, the employer may be able to give the impression that the critical cost of the employee's output at which he will take one of these actions is lower than it actually is. Thus, the employee can find it worthwhile to estimate the actual cost at which the employer would be better off taking each of these actions. He would then communicate these estimates whenever the employers' estimates seem to be lower.

By adding unique characteristics to his output, an employee may be able to increase his output replacement cost. For example, he might acquire information about the preferences or production domains of his employer or clients within or outside the organization and tailor his output accordingly. Employees may be able to increase their combined output replacement costs by agreeing to coordinate their actions so as to create the appearance of more spillovers among production domains than actually exist or reduce combined outputs in response to budget cuts for any one party.

Investments initiated by employees can induce employers to alter the type of responsibility imposed. If the employee were able to substitute inputs or outputs that are more costly to measure or value, the employer might, for example, be led to prefer NPOR over IPOR. At some point such substitutions on the employee's part could make specific responsibility preferable to overall value responsibility. Substituting outputs with different characteristics requires the employee to obtain information about potential demands for his outputs inside or outside the organization as well to negotiate with internal or external clients. Substituting inputs requires obtaining the relevant information about production possibilities, may require convincing employers to delegate different inputs, and might depend on the cooperation of other employees.

Investments that alter divisions of production functions into production domains. Information cost advantages often give employees discretion over suborganization, that is, the way an organization's production functions are divided into production domains as well as over resource allocation within production domains. That employees can have such discretion is well established. For example, Chandler's (1962) classic study of corporate adoptions of multidivisional suborganization thoroughly documents the roles of employees in these changes. In her study of British firms, Woodward (1965) found that "formal organization can arise imperceptibly and gradually from informal organization and spontaneous relationships" and that "approximately only half the firms studied show any organization-consciousness, and in many of these its effects were limited to a few aspects of formal organization" (pp. 74–5).

Researchers have analyzed the nature of employees' discretion over suborganization and the conditions under which suborganization is formally planned. Management practices have been classified as "mechanistic" and "organic" (Burns and Stalker, 1961), depending on how formally job roles are defined and the importance of direct communication among employees. Lorsch (1965), Lawrence and Lorsch (1967), and Lorsch and Allen (1973) have analyzed organizations' choices between formal and informal approaches to suborganization. Each of these studies found that employees' information cost advantages and uncertainty – especially that resulting from technological change – are positively associated with their exercise of discretion over suborganization.

The influence of employees over suborganization can be analyzed via employee initiated investments that alter employers' choices in dividing production functions into production domains. When

CPOR is imposed, employees cannot benefit from nor have they the means to effect changes in suborganization that are not in the funding authority's interest. However, under other types of responsibility, many of the investments determining suborganization can be dominated by employees. For example, inputs differ in individual employees' cost advantages derived from experience in applying them and in the amount of cooperation required to apply them. By using their discretion over relative applications of inputs, employees can thus change the advantages to the employer of delegating discretion over inputs and whether this discretion is individual or shared. Employees can cooperate to reduce resource diversions under particular suborganizations and thereby make them more attractive to employers. Frequently, employers face such high costs of evaluating alternative suborganizations that they must rely on employees' recommendations. Employees can thus help bring about forms of suborganization that reflect their interests at the expense of their employers.

An employer's optimal choices of responsibility and suborganization are interrelated. For example, an employer will choose a suborganization that takes less advantage of potential information cost advantages about production possibilities if it yields him sufficiently lower costs of imposing responsibility. In turn, employees can often alter an employer's choices of suborganization when they can influence his responsibility costs.

Aside from actual reorganization that changes the boundaries of production domains, employees can make tacit or explicit agreements, referred to as effectual reorganization, under which they involve specific additional employees in their choices about resource substitutions. Actual reorganization requires employees to bear larger initial costs, and the investments leading to it are more likely to be dominated by employers. An effectual reorganization can have results comparable to an actual reorganization, but it usually imposes higher continuing costs on employees.

There are several different motivations for employees under overall value responsibility to reorganize actually or effectually. These include reorganizing to increase the resource diversions allowed by responsibility; to ensure that some inputs are not counted as part of budgets; to alter the type of responsibility imposed; to reduce individual accountability and diversify risks; and to adapt favorably to Schumpeterian competition or technical change.

By combining their production domains, employees under overall value responsibility may be able to raise the allowable limits on their resource diversions. For example, when there are spillovers among production domains, an actual or effectual combination of them can increase the employer's cost of switching to specific responsibility or raise output replacement cost for any one output. However, employees under overall value responsibility have an incentive to weigh any increases in their own costs due to actual or effectual reorganization against any increases in the employer's costs of making one of these changes.

It is advantageous for an employee working under overall value responsibility to have the use of productive resources that are not attributed to him and thus not counted in his employer's cost of his output. Multiple employees often dominate investments that substitute shared indivisible resources or resources that are costly to measure or value. The organization's funding limit on employees' diversions constrains the total value of resources that are not attributed to employees.

Employees' investments in reorganization can alter employers' choices in imposing responsibility. For example, when productive activity is arranged so that individual employees' contributions to outputs are costly to measure or value, the relative desirability of placing specific responsibility on these employees is increased. Alternative suborganizations can vary the costs of observing individual employees' contributions to output, thus affecting the number of employees who are under overall value responsibility together. Similarly, varying suborganizations can alter the actual or apparent interaction effects among different inputs in producing given outputs or change the number of different outputs jointly produced by given inputs, thus affecting allowable resource diversions under both types of responsibility.

Employees desiring not to be held individually accountable for their overall value productivity or their specific uses of resources can benefit from reorganizing to be under the same overall value responsibility with other employees, whether or not justified by actual joint productivity. In the situation described by Alchian and Demsetz (1972) in which there are high costs of attributing the productivity of each individual, the consequences of one employee's reduced productivity to pursue other ends are spread over all the employees involved. If a potential switch to specific responsibility is what limits resource diversions under the overall value responsibility imposed in this situation, high costs of assessing each employee's productivity may translate into reduced potential effectiveness of available applications of specific responsibility and thus raise the employees' combined allowable diversions. Employees under the same overall value responsibility can delegate to specialized employees the tasks of coordinating themselves and maintaining performance standards. (See Section C of this chapter.)

Perhaps the most commonly desired benefit from being under the same overall value responsibility with other employees is diversified risk. For example, production domains might be actually or effectually combined to share risks vis-à-vis the demands facing each employee. For two reasons, employees are willing to pay more at the margin to reduce job related risk than the funding authority when both are equally averse to risk. Employees' investments in their jobs are ordinarily much less diversified than the funding authority's investments. Specifically, the organization usually represents only a small part of an investor's stock portfolio or a legislator's platform. However, an employee usually cannot capture all the benefits of his actions that increase returns to the organization's capital.

Of particular interest is actual or effectual reorganization in the face of Schumpeterian competition or expected changes in technical knowledge that can affect production domains substantially. The employee faces the following conflict when such changes can affect him directly. On the one hand, if he were personally accountable for an output he could reduce delays in adjusting to the changes, minimize his costs of eliciting the cooperation of others, and avoid having to share favorable outcomes. On the other hand, if he were under combined overall value responsibility vis-à-vis this and other outputs, he would have more diversification. [Schumpeterian competition occurs when the organization's competitors introduce new products, technologies, supply sources, or modes of organization (see Schumpeter, 1950, p. 84). In contrast, technological change can originate from sources other than the organization's competitors.]

Employees capable of dealing advantageously with Schumpeterian competition or technological change find themselves inadequately compensated for risk when personally accountable for outputs because they share benefits of favorable outcomes with others. Thus, they merge their production domains to be under combined overall value responsibility for one or more other outputs, or they start new companies where risk is even greater but the potential rewards better compensate risk. The tendency for being under combined overall value responsibility might, for example, result in fewer product-oriented subdivisions within the divisions of a multidivisional firm. Top managing employees' desires to be diversified in the face of technological change and Schumpeterian competition help explain the increased diversification of American firms in the postwar period.

Another hypothesis is that both Schumpeterian competition and technological change lead employees to seek flexible suborganization that, for a given amount of risk, allows decision-making authority to focus on the parts of production functions expected to be affected by the changes. When demand and technological knowledge are expected to remain stable, an employee's predominant investment interest is long-run static income from the organization. But expected changes in demand or technology make him willing to sacrifice income to be able to react favorably to the changes – both to be able to maintain his income from his job and to reap whatever rewards that accrue to him. Thus an environment of Schumpeterian competition or technological change tends to make the employee's interests in suborganization more closely aligned to those of the funding authority. Woodward (1965) commented, "It was found too that as technology became more advanced, the chief executive seemed able to control an increasing number of direct subordinates successfully" (p. 71). In their summary of the results of Lawrence and Lorsch (1967), Lorsch and Allen (1973) stated that "units which dealt with relatively uncertain parts of the environment tended to use less formalized approaches to organizing their activities" (p. 15).

The nature of investments to increase benefits from resource diversions when specific responsibility is imposed

Three types of investments can increase the diversion benefits of an employee under specific responsibility: those affecting his production domain and the resources delegated to him; those affecting his personal replacement cost; and, if there is an aggregation of production domains including his own at which overall value responsibility is imposed, those investments related to this combined responsibility. The investments of employees under specific responsibility usually require the cooperation of multiple employees. The first two types of investments ordinarily affect multiple similarly situated employees, and the third type by definition requires coordinated behavior. The following discussion separately considers each of the three types of investments.

Investments directed to the employee's own production domain. We have already seen that an employee under specific responsibility invests in learning about only those production possibilities that release resources whose uses both yield him utility and are costly for his employer to influence. These can represent decreased as well as increased technical efficiency in the employee's production domain. The employee similarly learns about demands for his outputs only when he directly derives utility from delivering outputs to his internal or external clients or he is directly rewarded for doing so.

Investments directed to the employee's personal replacement cost, especially those involving professional standards and professional societies. When it is not economical for an employer imposing specific responsibility to influence a number of an employee's uses of resources but he does have an idea of the resulting resource diversions, these diversions are limited by the employee's personal replacement cost. The measure of resource diversions might, for example, be based on the value of the excess time it takes the employee to perform a particular function over an amount determined by the employer's "timing" of his job.

When personal replacement cost limits resource diversions, employers estimate these costs and employees attempt to raise them by increasing the uniqueness of their skills. A professional society can provide economies to employers and to employees by establishing professional standards that both represent minimum requirements for employees' performance and "normal" resource diversions approximating personal replacement costs. Professional standards can also require employers to make desirable resources available to employees so they gain more welfare from given amounts of resource diversions.

It can thus be worthwhile both for employees and employers to invest in professional society activities. However, a professional society benefits employees at employers' expense if it can use professional standards as a means of restricting entry of new employees. For example, experience in particular types of subordinate positions might be made a criterion for entry.

While a labor union directly negotiates employees' cash incomes and working conditions, a professional society's direct dealings with an organization concern its members' productivity and are usually not adversarial. The image of involvement with productivity is reinforced by a professional society's task of disciplining employees who do not follow professional standards.

Professional standards have diminished acceptability to employers when they face only modest costs of observing and interpreting applications of employees' skills.

Investments directed to the nearest aggregation of production domains at which overall value responsibility is imposed. Overall value responsibility based on output replacement alternatives is often imposed on a combination of employees under specific responsibility when broader outputs to which these employees' outputs contribute are readily measured and valued. The output replacement limit may be smaller than the sum of the resource diversions allowable individually via specific responsibility to employees within the combination. Thus, individual employees under specific responsibility have the incentive not only to participate in investments that directly increase their individually allowable resource diversions but also increase the diversions allowed at the broader level. Other investments effect the coordination required to keep the combined resource diversions of all employees within the broader limit. Because specific responsibility does not permit employees to benefit as much from a higher allowable limit on resource diversions at the broader level as does overall value responsibility, there will be fewer investments to increase this limit.

This and earlier results enable us to analyze the effects of technological change and Schumpeterian competition on employers' choices of responsibility. We have seen that these forces place incentives on employees to allocate resources to information about how to respond favorably to them and also to adjust suborganization to facilitate flexible responses. These investments benefit employers as well as employees. Employees under specific responsibility devote fewer resources to such investments than if they were under overall value responsibility. Thus, Schumpeterian competition and technological change increase the relative desirability to employers of imposing overall value responsibility.

Summary of basic hypotheses about employees' investment behavior

Investments of individual employees under overall value responsibility. An employee under overall value responsibility directs investments to reducing the costs of producing his outputs, increasing the demands for his outputs, influencing the responsibility imposed on him, and altering suborganization.

i. An employee's cost reducing investments include experimenting with production possibilities in his own production domain and with alternative means of coordinating his actions with those of other employees to deal with spillovers. These investments increase economic efficiency, but the benefits largely accrue to the employee. When there are technological changes that might affect the employee's production domain, the employee devotes resources to learning about them, and these investments benefit employers and internal or external clients as well as the employee.

ii. Investments related to the demands for an employee's outputs include his learning about the preferences or production trade-offs of the internal or external clients using his outputs. These investments also increase efficiency and confer benefits on employers and clients as well as to the employee. An environment of Schumpeterian competition enhances the employee's expected returns to learning about demands for broader outputs to which his own outputs contribute.

iii. An employee's investments to influence the responsibility facing him lead him to obtain information about his employer's options. These include alternative sources of the employee's outputs, the availability of substitutes for these outputs, and the employer's opportunities to switch to specific responsibility. Such investments do not lower the employee's costs of producing his outputs, and when the employee discovers better alternatives for the employer, he does not pass the information on. Thus, these investments do not contribute to economic efficiency.

iv. By using their discretion over relative applications of inputs, employees can invest to alter employers' choices of suborganization. Employees' influences on suborganization can increase or decrease efficiency; increases are most likely in an environment of Schumpeterian competition or technological change.

Investments of individual employees under specific responsibility. An employee under specific responsibility invests in information about his production domain or about demands for his output only insofar as it enables him to make desired uses of resources that are not restricted by his employer. Such investments can lead him to make resource substitutions that increase or decrease efficiency. Employees direct investments to increasing their personal replacement costs when employers measure the diversions that result from resource uses they do not influence. In such cases, professional societies can be objects of investments by both employers and employees when it is costly for employers to observe and interpret applications of employees' skills.

Effects of Schumpeterian competition or technological change on the type of responsibility imposed. Favorable adaptation to Schumpeterian competition and technological change is less costly both for employers and for affected employees when these employees are under overall value responsibility. Thus, the presence of economically desirable investments that can bring about favorable adaptation to these forces increases the likelihood that overall value responsibility will be imposed. Because the affected employees also want to diversify risks, we can expect the same overall value responsibility to be imposed on multiple employees involved with different adaptations to these dynamic forces.

C   The nature of investments to facilitate the coordinated activities of employees

The following discussion analyzes how employees establish means to coordinate their activities and allocate among themselves the resulting benefits and costs. Employees can cooperate voluntarily; alternatively, their coordination can be effected through some employees' possessing authority over others. These cases differ in the nature of the coordination and the incidence of the resulting benefits and costs. I first analyze employees' uses of authority for their own purposes. Subsequently, we consider voluntary coordination and compare the results with the case where authority is used.

Employees' uses of authority for coordination in their own interests

The authority delegated to a managing employee is not necessarily used for the intended purposes. The following discussion first analyzes incentives leading to collaboration between an employee and a managing employee at the expense of the managing employee's employer. Subsequently considered are incentives for a managing employee to allow someone else to exercise the authority he holds over an employee.

Incentives encouraging collaboration between employers and employees. A managing employee's costs and benefits of placing responsibility on employees are usually both lower than they would be for the funding authority; the managing employee's information cost advantages give him lower costs of imposing responsibility, and he ordinarily cannot use reduced diversions of his employees in any way he desires. Because of these differences in costs and returns, a managing employee typically imposes responsibility differently than would the funding authority and may find it in his interest to collaborate with an employee to their mutual benefit.

Although a managing employee under specific responsibility can benefit from collaboration with his employees only when it would increase allowable personal uses of resources that directly yield utility to him, a managing employee under overall value responsibility can more generally benefit from collaboration. Costs of collaboration also differ depending on whether specific or overall value responsibility is imposed on the managing employee. Any employee under specific responsibility treats as costly only those resources used for collaboration whose uses directly affect his utility, whereas an employee under overall value responsibility deriving benefits from resource diversions at the margin values extra quantities of all the resources attributed to him.

As noted in Chapter 5, a managing employee under overall value responsibility can be forced by his employees to collaborate with them if his employees' allowable resource diversions are high enough that they could raise his costs to the point where his employer would replace his output or switch to specific responsibility. The employees' behavior depends on whether they would also suffer income losses.

Incentives for an employer to delegate authority. Consider a managing employee who is permitted to delegate his authority to place responsibility on an employee or can do so without his employer's knowledge. The delegation can be an ad hoc arrangement effective only while a nonrecurring task is performed, or it can be a long-term change in reporting relationships. Job titles, job descriptions, and organization charts can be used. But the delegation can be much less formal, and in extreme cases it can consist merely of the managing employee carrying out recommendations for placing responsibility made by the employee to whom authority is delegated. This employee need not be under the managing employee's authority.

The following paragraphs consider how the type of responsibility imposed on a managing employee affects his reasons for delegating authority. A managing employee voluntarily delegates authority when he personally is better off than he would be if he imposes responsibility himself. If he is under overall value responsibility, the quid pro quo from the employee receiving the authority can include any productive resources or any actions that confer productivity enhancing spillovers; but if the managing employee is under specific responsibility, payment can only be in resources for which he has uses that directly give him utility and are not influenced by his employer.

Employees have many opportunities to coordinate themselves for their own benefit while raising or lowering production costs. These opportunities underlie their willingness to pay for authority. Consider, for example, an employee with an investment option that would yield him a larger return if another employee coordinated his actions with him in a particular way. Offering a bid to this employee's employer for authority over him is an alternative to inducing him to cooperate voluntarily. Both alternatives involve negotiation costs. Obtaining authority requires compensation to the employer, involves the employee's resource diversions, and necessitates the costs of imposing responsibility on him. Voluntary coordination requires negotiation with the other employee, may necessitate verifying his compliance, and often requires some form of payment to him.

The price of authority is a function of the competing uses in which the managing employee holding it can apply it, the incentives facing him, and the presence or absence of competing bidders. Competing cost-saving uses of authority available either to the managing employee or to bidders can raise its supply price for other investments that increase diversion benefits without reducing costs. However, the degree to which cost-saving uses of authority do compete with other uses of authority depends not only on their existence but also on incentives to exploit them, given the responsibility facing those holding authority and those bidding for it.

The use of authority to achieve production and responsibility cost savings by making better uses of information cost advantages is often a major determinant of the price of authority under overall value responsibility.[5] However, a managing employee or an employee bidding for authority who is under specific, as opposed to overall value, responsibility will ordinarily take less account of foregone production or responsibility cost savings when considering other uses of authority that increase these costs while personally benefiting him. Specific responsibility similarly provides a weaker incentive for the managing employee to take account of favorable or unfavorable spillover effects on his own or his other employees' production domains due to the activities that would result from an exchange of authority. Thus, we can conclude that an organization's structure of authority is more likely to be motivated by production and responsibility cost savings when its employees are under overall value responsibility. In contrast, specific responsibility increases the likelihood that the structure of authority reflects opportunities to coordinate employees in ways that increase these costs.

Voluntary coordination of employees

Authority requires managing employees to decide how to coordinate their employees' actions and enforce the decisions via responsibility. Thus, they must have information about each coordinated employee's production domain and often about his preferences too. Whyte (1969, p. 628) summarizes this and other costs of coordination via authority:

It takes time to refer problems up the line and get the attention of higher management officials. When two groups resolve their disputes in this way, they find themselves involved in win–lose competitive transactions . . . The farther up the line a problem is referred, especially in a rapidly changing industry, the less knowledge relevant to the problem is the executive likely to have . . . [An executive] finds himself so harassed with the immediate problems that he is constantly treating symptoms and never has the opportunity of dealing with the underlying problems.

Whyte then raises the question:

Why not settle the problems at the level where they occur? This approach has obvious advantages, and yet what can be done when we find individuals in groups whose activities need to be coordinated expressing conflicting points of view? Which individual or group is to have its way?

The larger the number of voluntarily coordinated employees, the greater the potential economy to these employees from delegating decision making about coordination to a subset of themselves, referred to as *coordinating employees*. One economy results from coordinated employees being able to avoid the time costs of being involved in decision making. Another economy is the possibility of avoiding repeated negotiation. While agreements among subsets of employees would require renegotiation as additional employees are added to the agreement, coordinating employees can initially establish the roles of all coordinated employees. A further benefit is that the fewer the employees involved in discussions about coordination, and the less the communication with the other involved employees, the higher their employers' costs of information about the coordination. Finally, coordinating employees can often avoid costs of employees' understating their own benefits from coordination and overstating the losses to others if they do not participate. The optimal number of coordinating employees is considered later, but note now that there are usually multiple coordinating employees – each with specialized information about some of the production domains involved.

Coordinating employees can be informally selected "leaders" or they can function, for example, as committees, unions, negotiating or grievance teams, and as activists within employees' social groups. These employees invest in three types of information. First, they estimate the net returns to other employees of each employee's participation. Second, they learn about each employee's costs of participation including his alternative opportunities. When employees' benefits from coordination must be taken in kind, preferences of coordinated employees are also of interest. Finally, each coordinating employee learns about his own cost advantage, if any, over other employees in performing his coordination role. Such an advantage depends on the nature of his own production domain and its relationship to other employees', the responsibility facing him, and any relevant advantages of skill, experience, and ability that he may possess.

As a group, coordinating employees involve coordinated employees in such a way as to maximize the capturable gains from coordination after their own costs of the three categories of information. They thus attempt to involve each coordinated employee in such a manner that his contribution to these capturable gains is maximized at a positive value and his marginal return equals the marginal cost of inducing him to participate. Each coordinated employee's inducement to participate must cover his opportunity cost, including the benefits he could receive from other employees' seeking the role of coordinating employees. Some benefits or costs of coordination cannot be distributed in different ways because they accrue directly to individuals. When benefits directly accrue to coordinated employees and costs of capturing them exceed their value to the coordinating employees, coordinated employees' benefits can exceed their opportunity costs of participation.

The number of coordinating employees is determined by the trade-off between the information cost savings that additional coordinating employees can achieve and the necessity of sharing benefits with additional coordinators. Including as "representatives" employees having production domains with similar characteristics to those of some coordinated employees can prevent other coordinating employees from having to obtain the relevant technological information. The amount of benefits that must be shared with the additional coordinating employees depends on these employees' supplies of their coordination efforts, which depend on their alternative opportunities for using time and effort (which are related to the responsibility imposed), and on competition for their coordination roles. When individual coordinating employees have cost advantages over competitors, their own returns can be greater than the amount necessary to induce them to be coordinating employees. Within the group of coordinating employees there is often an incentive to replace those individuals whose competitors can perform their roles more effectively; such replacements can increase the effectiveness of the other coordinating employees.

Coordinating employees are often involved in evaluating how events affect coordinated employees and, accordingly, in coordinating these employees' bargaining positions. Sayles (1958, p. 156) points out that:

Maintaining the same conditions, in a dynamic plant, means sustaining a relative decline in benefits in comparison with those attained by other groups. As in the broader political environment, eternal vigilance is the price of equitable treatment. Even if others were not fighting for increased shares of the economic pie, management is making so many changes in equipment, scheduling, supervision, work methods, and all the rest, that a static position is out of the question.

Coordinating employees' performance of this important role is often a by-product of their roles in achieving cooperative actions in relation to spillovers and shared investments.

We can see from coordinating employees' optimal behavior that information costs and costs of coordination should be incorporated into arguments such as Olson's (1965) that with "the voluntary and independent action of the members of a group . . . the marginal cost of additional units of the collective good must be shared in exactly the same proportion as the additional benefits" (p. 30). However, when there are only a few members in a group, as in many of the cases analyzed by Olson, information and coordination costs may be small enough not to have a significant influence on the results.

By refusing to coordinate his actions with other employees, an employee might be able to cause substantial losses to other participants and thus demand extra benefits for his participation. One defense against such threats is for coordinating employees to control the flow of information to ensure that, while coordinated employees are informed about their own benefits, they lack information about how their participation benefits other employees. Another defense results when there are economies of scale in uses of the coordinating employees' specialized knowledge that lead the same group to coordinate many or all cooperative arrangements among themselves. If an employee threatens to withdraw from one participation, the coordinating employee can in turn exclude him from others. Klein et al. (1978) analyze an analogous case where contracts with independent suppliers are enforced via "seemingly unrelated profitable reciprocal business" (p. 305).

As suggested previously, coordinating employees may not personally be able to capture a large fraction of the benefits of coordination when these benefits directly accrue to the coordinated employees. In such a case, Pfeffer and Salancik (1974) present results that suggest that the budgets of academic departments in one university are influenced by their representations on committees. Here, the coordinated employees have an interest in compensating their "representative" coordinating employees for their opportunity costs. This would explain reduced teaching loads or reduced expectations of research accomplishment for those serving on university committees.

While voluntary coordination can achieve substantial information cost savings, it is not always preferred over authority.[6] In particular cases employees can find it more economical to obtain authority over other employees than to elicit their voluntary coordination. By delegating authority to coordinating employees, managing employees can gain from competition among employees for coordinating roles. (See Section D.) In contrast, managing employees often do not benefit from the results of their employees' voluntary coordination and have little or no direct control over the content of the coordination.

What are often referred to as "liaison" positions can be used with either mode of coordination; liaison personnel can be coordinating employees or they can be employees who assist managing employees' efforts to coordinate via authority.

Summary of basic hypotheses about employees' investments in coordination

Employees can coordinate themselves via authority or voluntarily. They invest to establish and improve these means of coordination.

Coordination via authority. A managing employee will transfer to another employee the authority he holds over one or more of his employees when the responsibility facing him allows him to do so and he would gain thereby. The other employee's quid pro quo depends on his gains from being able to use the authority to coordinate employees, and the managing employee's alternative opportunities to delegate or directly use the authority. Delegating authority can achieve efficiency gains by better utilizing information cost advantages, but authority can also facilitate coordinated actions that increase benefits from resource diversions while decreasing efficiency. The delegation of authority is more likely to be at the expense of efficiency when the managing employees involved in the exchange are under specific responsibility.

Voluntary coordination. The larger the number of employees that benefit from coordinating their actions in a manner not required by responsibility, the more substantial their economies from delegating to coordinating employees the task of specifying each employee's part in the coordination. Coordinating employees use specialized information about spillovers, employees' preferences, and jointly served demands to perform their role, and their own gains are limited to the cost advantages they have in obtaining and utilizing this information. The remaining distributable returns from coordination are allocated among the coordinated employees according to their opportunity costs of participating.

D   A simplified analysis of price and output determination under voluntary coordination and under delegation of authority

This discussion contrasts the effects of voluntary coordination and coordination via authority on the determination of an employee's equilibrium price and output in the presence of spillovers. The analysis will enable us to analyze further the motivation underlying the delegation of discretion to employees. It applies both to the short run and to long-run periods in which investments influence the outcome. However, the discussion does not consider long-run limits on employees' resource diversions, topics dealt with in Chapter 8.

Figure 7.2 illustrates budget and output determination in two separate cases. In the case shown in the left panel, coordination of an employee's actions in relation to spillovers is effected via a voluntary arrangement organized by coordinating employees. In this analysis, the line yz depicts the managing employee's demand for an employee's output while the line fe shows the managing employee's marginal and average variable cost of the employee's output under types of responsibility other than CPOR. Lines gd, hc, and ib all represent the employee's marginal and average variable costs with

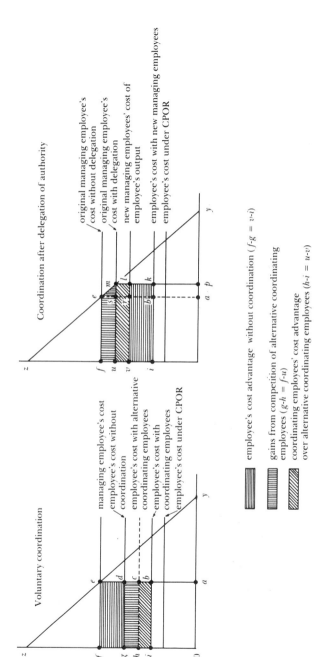

Figure 7.2. Price, budget, and output under voluntary coordination and under a delegation of authority. Marginal and average variable cost is shown.

alternative arrangements for the coordination of spillovers that affect his production domain.

A coordination of employees' actions in relation to spillovers that enhances efficiency could raise a particular employee's costs while they lower combined costs for all employees. For the employee illustrated here coordination reduces costs, a result that may be regarded as the average result for all coordinated employees. Line *gd* represents the employee's marginal and average variable cost in the absence of any coordination other than that provided by the managing employee or required by responsibility. Line *ib* indicates the employee's marginal and average variable cost as a result of coordinating employees' actions. The next higher line, *hc*, shows the employee's marginal and average variable cost if the coordinating employees' closest competitors took over the coordination role. The lowest line represents the employee's marginal and average variable cost under CPOR and shows the most efficient coordination of spillovers among production domains. Of course, the managing employee's variable costs of imposing CPOR are not included in this line.

The employee's equilibrium rate of output is *0a* when CPOR is not imposed. Investments can increase the employee's fixed allowable resource diversions so that he shares in some of the managing employee's potential consumers' surplus (the quantity *fez*). However, the responsibility on the managing employee may limit the portion of this quantity that can benefit him personally. Employees' investments can also influence marginal costs. When employees desire to substitute fixed for variable resource diversions, this lowers marginal costs in the long run. However, the investments with highest returns may increase variable costs; we thus cannot make an a priori prediction of the effects of employees' investments on marginal costs and rates of output.

Coordinating employees can achieve a continuing marginal and average variable cost saving of *g* minus *i*, which exceeds by *h* minus *i* what their competitors could achieve. However, if coordinating employees do not collaborate with the managing employee, the rate of the employee's output does not change. The area *ibdg* equals the decrease in costs, created by coordinating employees, which we shall assume to be capturable by them. To the extent that they and the coordinated employees derive utility from this quantity, it is a welfare gain. They must distribute *hcdg* of these resources to coordinated employees in order to avoid being replaced by competitors, leaving them *ibch*. Note that the managing employee receives none of these benefits and thus they cannot be passed on to the funding authority or the organization's clients.

Now we turn to the case where the managing employee delegates authority to one or more of the coordinating employees and contrast price and output determination under authority and voluntary coordination. In order to focus on the important differences in resource allocation under these alternative modes of organization, I make a number of simplifying assumptions. Although these assumptions are unrealistic, they facilitate understanding of the different effects of the two modes of coordination on price and output. Assume first that coordinating employees to whom authority has been delegated, referred to as new managing employees, continue to achieve the same cost reductions. Actually, the coordinating employees' costs of coordination will ordinarily be different if they are managing employees and must impose responsibility to elicit coordination. For example, the coordinated employees will be less inclined to divulge information to them. A second assumption is that the costs faced by and the allowable diversions of the coordinated employees remain the same under the new managing employees. Because of the new managing employees' information cost advantages over the original managing employee, the coordinated employees' allowable diversions would actually be typically lower. Finally, assume that the original managing employee has no variable costs of imposing responsibility either on the new managing employees or on the coordinated employees.

The right panel of Figure 7.2 depicts resource allocation with coordination by the new managing employees. The assumptions are reflected first in the employee's marginal and average variable cost, $0i$, shown to be equal under the new managing employees to what it was with the coordinating employees. Second, the new managing employees' marginal and average variable cost of the employee's output exceeds the employee's cost ($0v$ exceeds $0i$) by the same amount that the original managing employees' cost exceeds the employee's cost ($0f$ exceeds $0g$) in the absence of coordination. Third, the new managing employees' marginal cost advantage (u minus v) is equal to h minus i, their advantage over their closest competitors in reducing marginal cost as coordinating employees. Note that while these employees' competitors continue to reduce their gains by the same amount, the benefit of the competition now accrues to the original managing employee, not to the coordinated employees. This benefit provides motivation for the original managing employee to delegate authority to the coordinating employees.

Because the marginal and average benefits of competition for the coordination role (g minus h in left panel) now accrue to the original managing employee, his marginal and average variable cost of the employee's output are lower by the same amount (f minus u in the right panel). These lower costs under a delegation of authority to coordinating employees produce the important difference in resource allocation that the equilibrium rate of output increases from $0a$ to $0p$ (assuming that the new managing employees have no demand for this output beyond what they pass on to the old managing employee) and there is a welfare gain of the amount illustrated by *sme* in the right panel plus whatever utility is derived respectively by the coordinated employees and the new managing employees from the increased potential gains from variable allowable diversions *bklr* and *rlms*. In conclusion, a delegation of authority increases equilibrium rates of output, raises the amount of economic welfare within an organization, and alters its distribution.

The simplifying assumptions can be readily altered to reflect realistic magnitudes and the analysis can be readily extended. For example, a new managing employee's relative advantages over prospective competitors could deteriorate as employees refuse to give him information and his stock of information becomes obsolete. This would reduce his cost advantage in future time periods. Alternatively, being a managing employee may open up opportunities for him to coordinate broader areas of economic activity and achieve larger gains.

By reducing their resource diversions below the rate allowed by the responsibility facing them, the coordinated employees can influence the costs faced by different potential coordinating employees. They can similarly affect the original managing employee's returns to delegating authority to a new managing employee. It might seem that coordinated employees would always prefer voluntary coordination. This is not necessarily the case, however. The employees' own negotiation costs have not been considered and may be higher under voluntary coordination. Also, in particular cases individuals' resource diversions allowed by responsibility can be higher under new managing employees.

E   A note on employees' investment behavior and multidivisional suborganization

During the postwar period there has been a tremendous increase in the product diversity and product divisionalization of American corporations.[7] Rumelt (1974, p. 146) has carefully documented this phenomenon and found that:

Seventy per cent of the largest 500 firms fell into the Single or Dominant Business categories of diversification strategy in 1949. By 1969, over half of these firms had either moved to Related or Unrelated Business strategies or had been acquired and had their places in the top 500 taken by more diversified firms. At the same time, the product-division structure, employed by 20 per cent of the large firms in 1949, moved to a position of predominance, being used by 75 percent of the large firms in 1969.

The issue of interest here is, of course, what is the role of employees in these major changes? Chandler's (1962) classic historical study has described these roles, and an economic theory should show why such roles would be in employees' interests.

Our analysis of economic behavior within organizations leads us to seek a definition of multidivisional suborganization that specifically takes separate account of employees' production domains and the responsibility placed on employees. Such a definition might include the following: (1) Top managing employees' production domains encompass the organization's key choices about its product and market strategies, its adaptation to technological change, and perhaps the coordination of employees' actions in relation to some of the spillovers among its divisions. (2) Divisional production domains are largely aligned to production functions for the organization's final outputs. Divisions often, but not necessarily, produce or purchase on the external market many of their own intermediate outputs. In Chandler's words, "Division managers did not depend closely on other units for the sale of their products and their supplies of materials" (p. 311).[8] (3) Overall value responsibility is placed on top managing employees and on each division. Top managing employees are held accountable for the corporation's overall profitability, while each division is usually also under IPOR where returns on alternative deployments of assets constitute the replacement alternative, based on each division's financial results and "comparisons . . . with the results of similar units within the enterprise" (Chandler, 1962, p. 311).

The need for refinement in the analysis of a corporation's multidivisional structure is apparent from this or any similar definition. What specific aggregations of production domains do divisions represent and what alternatives are possible? Specifically, would further divisionalization increase efficiency or benefit stockholders? Would it be preferable to impose responsibility differently within divisions?

For example, would there be gains from placing overall value responsibility on smaller aggregations of divisional employees? Considering the sizes of many corporations' divisions these issues could be very important.

Chandler documented the information cost savings achieved by having separate production domains for planning the organization's overall directions and allocating resources to its divisions. Subsequently, Williamson (1970) provided a theoretical framework for evaluating some of these savings by analyzing information costs as a function of the number of levels in the chain of command and the number of demands on the activities of a single functional department. There exists, however, a wide variety of alternative ways in which the coordination and planning functions of top managing employees could be arranged. For example, different variants on the overall value responsibility placed on top managing employees could influence the degree to which the directions they set for the overall organization are in the interests of stockholders. Also, there are many alternative ways in which top managing employees can place IPOR on divisions as shown by Vancil (1979) and Wrigley (1970). Wrigley points out that restrictions placed by top managing employees on a division's autonomy within the IPOR placed on it depend on the technological interrelationships between the production of the division's outputs and other productive activity within the corporation. To what extent are these restrictions also influenced by the responsibility placed on top managing employees and on divisional employees? Finally, there are alternative specific functional activities that can be performed within the planning and coordinating part of a multidivisional corporation, and this part of the corporation can have alternative suborganizations. Which choices among these alternatives best serve stockholders' interests and economic efficiency?

An analysis of the roles of employees in corporate adoptions of the multidivisional form requires that we disentangle the effects of dynamic external changes, employees' investment behavior, and the resulting division of production functions into production domains and the ways in which responsibility is imposed within the organization. Chandler found that large size (in part a result of diversification) and a dynamic external environment (perhaps a major cause of diversification) led corporations to adopt the multidivisional suborganization. We have seen that technological change and Schumpeterian competition give employees incentives to make investments that align boundaries of production domains to the parts of the organization affected by new products or new technical knowledge. We have also seen that organizations can improve their adaptability to these changes by imposing overall value responsibility on the units whose cooperation is required. However, in order to diversify their risks in such an environment, employees seek to have overall value responsibility imposed at broader aggregations of activity than is in the interests of stockholders.

Each of the corporations analyzed by Chandler is widely owned and the choice to adopt multidivisional suborganization was clearly an investment initiated and dominated by employees. The extent to which this form of organization is also in the interests of stockholders would support the hypotheses that apart from the tendency for excessive diversification, technological change and Schumpeterian competition tend to align the interests of employees and stockholders. Large sizes of divisions also increased the desirability to top managing employees of taking advantage of the information cost economies achievable by placing IPOR on divisions with rate of return criteria for replacement; this aspect of multidivisional organization that is usually in the interests of stockholders became an imperative for many corporations as they grew to immense size. However, stockholders would perhaps benefit from the same variant of IPOR being imposed on a larger number of smaller divisions.

Chandler's documented major role of what are referred to here as coordinating employees in corporate suborganization is of substantial interest. The cooperation of employees with expertise from throughout the corporation was required. Chandler found that knowledgeable employees not having invested substantially in the previous functional organizational form were those willing to make long-term investments in a new form of suborganization and played crucial informal roles in establishing the new multidivisional organizational form.

The employees making the organizational changes created the new responsibility that was placed on top managing employees and divisional managing employees. Chandler emphasizes the value of the multidivisional organizational form in releasing top managing employees from "day-to-day" tasks to play their generalist roles as strategic planners and coordinators. Such generalist roles are often performed by coordinating employees under functional suborganization. In commenting on Alcoa as an organization not accepting multidivisional suborganization, Chandler (1962) states that "informal lines of authority and responsibility have become probably more significant than the formal ones" (p. 340). Presumably, these roles are performed more to the end of profitability in a multidivisional corporation because the top managing employees charged with them are under overall value responsibility based on the organization's overall performance. The tendency of multidivisional organizations to draw important informal roles away from the coordinating employees suggests that it would be useful to analyze how these roles are performed under varying suborganizations and responsibility placed on employees.

F   Employees' investments and external constituencies

We now examine employees' investments that are directed to an organization's external constituencies. These include the influences of employees, particularly in public organizations, over legislative and other demands for their outputs. Employees' investments can also alter governmental regulation of public and private organizations.

Because an upward shift in demand for an organization's outputs raises limits on resource diversions, employees can reap gains from investments that increase demand. We have seen that an upward shift of legislative demand can result from tailoring outputs to the desires of marginal voters in interest groups and lowering information costs for recipients of these outputs and for suppliers to learn about their interests in coordinated voting. Wildavsky (1964, p. 66) describes the behavior of the administrator of an agency with a "large and strategically placed clientele" as follows:

His agency made a point of organizing clientele groups in various localities, priming them to engage in approved projects, serving them well, and encouraging them to inform their Congressmen of their reaction. Informing one's clientele of the full extent of the benefits they receive may increase the intensity with which they support the agency's request.

When communication costs among beneficiaries of an organization's outputs are high, votes based on subsidies can be latent, giving employees investment opportunities to communicate with members of the groups and thereby increase demand. Employees can also ensure that legislators are aware of those groups' benefits. Wildavsky (1964, p. 67) points out that:

The agency can do a lot to ensure that its clientele responds by informing them that contacting Congressmen is necessary and by telling them how to go about it if they do not already know. In fact, the agency may organize the clientele in the first place. The agency may then offer to fulfill the demand it has helped to create. Indeed, Congressmen often urge administrators to make a show of their clientele.

Legislative demand is also increased when information costs to citizens not receiving subsidies are higher, and employees can often raise these costs.

When employees of public organizations experiment with alternative output characteristics and thereby increase votes and demand, the preferences of the relevant interest group's marginal voter determine the characteristics' effects on legislative demand. The more contact an employee has with clients and suppliers in the ordinary course of business, the more he knows about their preferences and the smaller his costs of adjusting output characteristics to their preferences and influencing their votes.[9] There is no necessary connection between the cost of a change in a characteristic of an output and the economic value to the marginal voter of the change. (See Chapter 6.)

Employees of a private corporation can use resource diversions for cost-ineffective marketing efforts to increase market demands, or for cost-ineffective expenditures to coordinate clients to increase legislative demand. This behavior does not necessarily produce a negative relationship between profitability and growth, as is often suggested. (See Chapter 8.)

Because an employee under specific responsibility has less personal interest in the rate of his output in relation to his budget, his returns to increasing demand are lower than for an employee under overall value responsibility. Thus when decentralized employees deal directly with clients and suppliers but are under specific responsibility, the task of increasing demand will be placed at a higher level where overall value responsibility is imposed, even though information costs are higher at this level. In general, when employees having direct contact with clients and suppliers are under specific responsibility, the organization will be less responsive to demands of clients and conditions of supply than when these employees are under overall value responsibility.

Competition among employees in dealing with clients can reduce resource diversions, giving employees an incentive to coordinate their responses to clients' demands. The incentive to compete is greater under overall value than under specific responsibility, and competition thus tends to make employees prefer the former individually and the latter collectively. Competition among employees vis-à-vis clients' demands also tends to make employees collectively prefer coordination via authority to voluntary coordination.

Employees in all types of organizations are more likely to seek legislative regulation when under specific responsibility; by reducing productivity, regulations can be costly to employees under overall value responsibility. Employees under specific responsibility especially desire regulations that prohibit cost-effective applications of specific responsibility or require the employer to permit personal uses of resources from which they derive relatively high utility. Employees under overall value responsibility are prone to seek regulations that increase demand for their outputs or require the employer to allot them inputs yielding relatively high utility.

Employees have advantages over funding authorities in influencing legislative regulations. When employees' outputs or inputs have unique characteristics they ordinarily also have some nonunique characteristics that are common to many employees, observable, and readily subject to regulation. There can thus be a large number of employees in the same and other organizations who would substantially benefit from regulations pertaining to these nonunique characteristics. In contrast, diffuse stockholders of private corporations and numerous small donors to private nonprofit organizations are unlikely to be sufficiently informed to base votes on avoiding such regulations.

One can expect relatively more regulations and other work rules benefiting employees in public organizations. Legislators resist such regulations only when their cost could be spent in another way to obtain an equal election probability. Employees of public organizations have the cost advantage of being able to include negotiations for regulations with budgetary negotiations.

Chapter 9 considers how employees' influences on demand can alter the type of organization that produces their outputs.

G   The funding authority's responses to employees' investment behavior

The funding authority can impose responsibility on employees' investments. However, the returns to this responsibility are reduced by employees' information cost advantages and the coordination costs of the multiple individuals making up the funding authority.

For stockholders of a private corporation or donors to a private nonprofit organization, coordination costs can be very high when more than a few individuals are involved, even when interests are identical. There are additional costs of resolving conflicts in interests, which are likely to be prevalent among a private nonprofit organization's donors. By delegating this coordination task a funding authority creates employees with allowable resource diversions.

Indeed, a legislature can be regarded as performing this coordination task on behalf of citizens, in spite of its being treated here as a funding authority.

As a funding authority, a legislature's valuation of reduced resource diversions in a public organization is limited to its valuation of the votes that result from other spending at the margin; potential benefits to citizens other than these marginal voters do not affect the valuation. The incentives that lead a legislature to make commitments on future legislatures also lead it to place only minimal control over employees' investments.

The higher the costs of information and coordination, the fewer are the investments initiated by the funding authority; at some high levels of these costs, employees dominate most investment projects. Thus, it is not uncommon for employees to have complete discretion over virtually all the investments that occur in an organization.

Funding authorities often attempt to give particular attention to those investments requiring commitments of funds. However, their decisions are usually based on employees' recommendations. Employees can use the released time or reduced workload for discussions about these investments to negotiate coordination that serves their ends.

CHAPTER 8

Equilibrium behavior of public and private organizations in the first long run

In the analysis of the short run it was assumed that current investment behavior has no effect on the same time period's resource allocation. Over longer periods an organization's tangible and intangible capital resources are altered both by employees' investments (analyzed in Chapter 7) and by the funding authority's investments. This and the next chapter analyze price and output determination for public and private organizations during time periods long enough for the investments of employees and the funding authority to influence the outcome.

We have seen that an employee's investments can increase the resource diversions that are allowed by the responsibility facing him. However, an organization's "funding limit" constrains the combined resource diversions of all of its employees, regardless of the amounts allowed by responsibility. Thus, we shall consider the effects of employees' investments within two possibly overlapping time horizons. In the "first long run," employees' investments can have the fullest possible impact on the resource diversions allowed by responsibility within the funding limit. During this time period an organization's funding limit cannot be changed as a result of a merger with another organization or a change in its status as a private corporation, private nonprofit organization, or a public organization. However, because these changes affect funding limits substantially, they are often objects of employees' investments. Such investments are analyzed in the "second long-run" analysis of Chapter 9.

This chapter first considers the funding limit in each type of organization and then analyzes price and output determination in the first long run.

A   Funding limits on employees' resource diversions in each type of organization

An organization's *funding limit* is the response of the revenues that the funding authority makes available to the organization's employees when he faces increases in the costs of disposing the organiza-

210

tion's outputs according to his interests. This constraint can limit total resource diversions in the organization even if the funding authority imposes no responsibility on employees. The funding limit differs for each type of organization and is separately analyzed for each.

The private corporation's funding limit

A private corporation's stockholders are concerned with profits from the sale of this organization's outputs and its funding limit is the response of the external supply of equity capital to the corporation's current profitability. The higher its employees' resource diversions in any time period, the lower the corporation's profits and average rate of return on equity. I assume that stockholders' estimated returns to new investments that they might make are positively related to the existing average rate of return on the corporation's equity.[1] These investments include new equity investments and, when stockholders are well enough informed, reinvestments of the corporation's cash flow. While stockholders usually do not form an estimate of how employees' resource diversions affect their rate of return, the higher that diversions are, the lower these returns and, by assumption, stockholders' estimates of the rate of return to each new investment.

External capital financing normally augments a corporation's growth. This growth can then increase demands for employees' outputs. When an employee has cost advantages over alternative suppliers, he derives increased rent as a result. Hence growth is usually desirable to a corporation's employees. However, corporate growth can result from investments that yield negative as well as positive returns to employees. Thus, it is possible that, within a range, increased stockholder investments in response to lower resource diversions would yield negative returns to employees. However, beyond some point these investments would benefit employees even if only because they maintain the corporation's capability to function.

The funding limit is binding when employees are willing to reduce current total resource diversions to increase stockholders' investments.[2] When there are numerous large investment opportunities benefiting both stockholders and employees, employees are especially willing to control resource diversions if they face relatively low costs of coordinating themselves. Of particular interest is the case where employees expect large shifts in demand resulting from Schumpeterian competition or when they expect technological

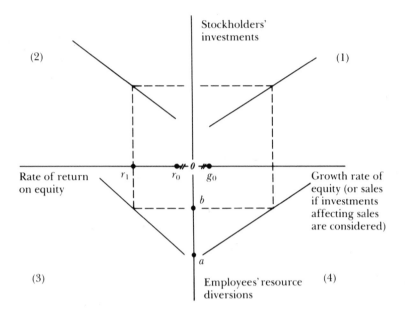

Figure 8.1. Relationship between resource diversions, profitability, and corporate growth.

changes to have significant effects on their production domains. When employees' economic welfare strongly depends on their responses to such changes and the responses that are most desirable for them and for stockholders require financing controlled by stockholders, they have especially strong incentives to limit resource diversions. In situations with fewer investments benefiting both parties or when coordination costs are high, employees' incentives to reduce current diversions below those allowed by responsibility are smaller.

When a private corporation's employees are responsive to its funding limit, there is a positive relationship between the corporation's rate of growth and stockholders' rate of return on its equity. This relationship is derived in Figure 8.1. The first quadrant illustrates a positive relationship between stockholders' investments and the growth rate of the corporation's equity (and sales if we consider investments that increase sales). In the second quadrant, a positive relationship between stockholders' rate of return on the corporation's equity and the rate of stockholders' investments is shown. The third quadrant illustrates the negative relationship between employees' resource diversions and stockholders' rate of return on the corporation's equity capital. At point a current resource diversions equal those allowed by responsibility, and stockholders' rate of return is r_0. When resource diversions are the smaller amount represented by point b, the rate of return increases to r_1. This relationship is a noncapitalized version of Jensen and Meckling's (1976) relationship showing that the value of nonpecuniary employee benefits that are not worthwhile for stockholders to prevent is negatively related to the market value of the corporation's stock.

The relationship in the fourth quadrant, derived from the other three quadrants, illustrates employees' opportunities to select between current resource diversions and corporate growth. If they take all resource diversions allowed by responsibility (the amount $0a$), the corporation's growth rate is g_0. If they reduce diversions below this allowable amount, there is a correspondingly higher growth rate. The selection and enforcement of a rate of resource diversions along this relationship can, for example, be made by top managing employees, coordinating employees, a union, or any combination of these. In cases where employees would not be willing to sacrifice current resource diversions to increase growth or cannot reach or enforce an agreement, diversions will be at the sum allowed by the responsibility individually facing the corporation's employees.

Marris (1971) and other authors suggest that with "managerial motivation" increases in the corporation's growth come at the expense of profitability. For example, in their survey article Marris and Mueller (1980) state "managerialism is a matter of degree, depending on how much utility weight is given to growth per se, relative to the competing claims of stock-market valuation" (p. 41). Solow (1971) shows how cost-ineffective expenditures to increase sales can produce a negative relationship between growth and profitability. We have seen in Chapter 5 that top managing employees under overall value responsibility based on profitability do not necessarily maximize the corporation's gross profits, and they do not have to pass on to stockholders (or profitably reinvest) any profits in excess of the critical amount necessary to avoid replacement of their managerial outputs. When these employees increase sales at the expense of profits (or are forced to by their employees), the foregone profits are within this excess quantity. In general, in order for top managing employees and any other employees under responsibility to increase growth via investments controlled by stockholders, they must reduce their combined resource diversions below those allowed by responsibility. If they do reduce diversions to increase these investments, there is a positive relationship between profitability and corporate growth. In contrast, if there should be no overall value responsibility based on profitability imposed on top managing employees, these employees can choose to face a trade-off between sales and profits passed on to stockholders and, given their objectives, may select an amount of current sales that is at the expense of passed-on profits. However, these employees would thereby decrease stockholders' investments and would thus reduce their corporation's growth. That is, to take this action these employees would have to be unresponsive to the corporation's funding limit.

The private nonprofit organization's funding limit

In the discussions of the funding limits of private nonprofit and public organizations, it is helpful to keep in mind that, by assumption, the funding authority cannot dissolve the organization in the first long run. Thus, during this time period he faces fixed costs, including those of employees' fixed resource diversions and fixed costs of imposing responsibility.

In the following analysis I assume that employees' resource diversions do not consume any of the organization's capital and that this capital is not used to fund any of donors' fixed production and responsibility costs. That is, employees' resource diversions and donors' fixed production and responsibility costs do not reduce the organization's future size. In this case the funding limit on resource diversions in a private nonprofit organization is its incremental donation schedule minus the sum of donors' actual fixed and variable responsibility costs[3] and what would be employees' fixed and variable production costs under CPOR. Regardless of the amount allowed by responsibility, the combined fixed and variable resource diversions of all the organization's employees cannot exceed this amount.

The funding limit can equal zero and it could be temporarily negative after an inward shift of the incremental donation schedule. However, a viable private nonprofit organization's funding limit will normally be a significant positive value, and it will be taken to be positive in the analysis of price and output determination of the first long run. The size of the funding limit in practice strongly depends on the shape and position of the incremental donation schedule, which in turn depends on underlying donors' demand. The availability of substitutes for the organization's output, from the perspective of donors, thus affects its funding limit. For example, alternative means of providing benefits to the organization's clientele and benefits provided to other groups might serve as substitutes in donors' preferences. When there are close substitutes at nearly the same cost, it can be expected that the private nonprofit organization's funding limit is modest. For this reason, the employees of a private nonprofit organization invest to differentiate their outputs. The nature of the funding limit also gives employees entrepreneurial incentives with respect to donor behavior.

Within the limits on their resource diversions, employees in private nonprofit organizations direct the expenditure of returns on the organization's capital away from those benefits desired by donors so as to avoid displacing their current donations. For this reason, in the absence of any effects of tax laws, donors prefer periodic donations rather than one-time donations; they take into account the expected cost of lost control over future expenditures in deciding whether to make donations for the organization's capital. Of course, tax laws (perhaps induced by employees) can create offsetting positive incentives for capital donations. Also, in-kind donations of capital may be useful only for the particular purposes that donors intend.

The public organization's funding limit

The funding limit on resource diversions in a public organization is analyzed under assumptions analogous to those made for a private nonprofit organization. That is, the organization cannot be dissolved in the first long run and the legislature's fixed production and responsibility costs and employees' resource diversions do not deplete any of the public organization's capital. In this case the funding limit in a public organization for which there are no competing suppliers is initially the entire area under the legislature's demand for its output minus the sum of the legislature's actual fixed and variable responsibility costs and what would be employees' fixed and variable production costs under CPOR. The funding limit is assumed to be positive in the analysis of price and output determination in the first long run. (See the discussion of a private nonprofit organization's funding limit.)

Once resource diversions reach this amount, the legislature and the public organization's employees can make exchanges that cause future legislative funding of a public organization and its employees to exceed future legislative demand for the organization's output.

We have seen in Chapter 6 that legislatures have incentives to make commitments on future legislatures at rates that exceed those that would be desired by informed citizens. Among these commitments are exchanges that give employees increased future benefits in return for higher outputs in the present. Such exchanges can be especially attractive to employees when they involve future cash benefits (e.g., pensions or job security in the face of declining demand).

When private organizations offer to supply a public organization's output, the public organization's income can be, for two reasons, more than the amount that these suppliers would charge. First, as noted, earlier exchanges between employees and the legislature subsequently increase the organization's income or directly increase its employees' incomes (e.g., commitments of pensions). Second, for reasons described in Chapter 9, a public organization providing particular combinations of outputs has an advantage over other suppliers in raising citizens' costs of information about benefits to other citizens that they would oppose.

Summary of basic hypotheses about funding limits

The private corporation's funding limit. The higher the rate of employees' resource diversions, the lower the corporation's profits. The funding limit is the response of the external supply of equity capital to the corporation's profitability. By decreasing resource diversions and thus augmenting profitability, employees can attract equity capital and increase growth. The funding limit is binding when employees reduce resource diversions below those allowed by responsibility in order to increase the corporation's growth.

When employees decrease resource diversions in response to the funding limit, there is a positive relationship between a corporation's profitability and its growth.

The private nonprofit organization's funding limit. When resource diversions and donors' fixed costs do not consume the organization's capital, the funding limit for a private nonprofit corporation is its incremental donation schedule minus the sum of donors' actual fixed and variable responsibility costs and what would be employees' fixed and variable production costs under CPOR. The funding limit is binding when the responsibility imposed on employees allows fixed and variable resource diversions in excess of this amount.

The public organization's funding limit. A public organization's funding limit initially equals legislative demand for the organization's output minus the legislature's fixed and variable responsibility costs and what would be employees' fixed and variable production costs under CPOR. Subsequently, the funding limit can increase by the amount of past legislative commitments of economic benefits to the public organization's employees. Whenever the fixed and variable resource diversions allowed by the responsibility facing these employees exceed the funding limit, it is binding.

B   Price, income, and output determination in the first long run

Employees' investments affect the amounts of fixed and variable resource diversions that are allowed by responsibility in the first long run. In order to analyze price, income, and output in this time period, it is necessary first to examine how employees' investments can alter the costs faced by employers. It is then possible to determine the price, income, and output of each type of organization in the first long run.

Effects of investments on fixed and variable costs

Employers' costs of employees' outputs have fixed and variable components in the short run. There continue to be fixed costs in the first long run because of the assumption that the organization cannot be dissolved during this time period. Employees' discretion over input substitutions contributes to employers' fixed costs in the first long run as well as in the short run. Consider an input that in the long run becomes feasible to vary and – in the absence of responsibility costs – would be economically desirable for an employer to have a different quantity of it applied in production. This input will not in fact be varied when it is under the discretion of an employee lacking a desire to change his usage of it and it is not economical for his employer to induce him to do so. Although it is not technically infeasible for the employer to vary such an input, he treats it as fixed nonetheless. An extension of this phenomenon occurs in the first long run when varying an input requires an investment that an employee dominates. Of particular interest in this regard is the influence of an employee under overall value responsibility on such investments. Such an employee deriving utility from resource diversions at the margin wants to gain the largest possible rent on his skills and information cost advantages. Thus, to the extent that he dominates investments he ensures that his production capacity is not replaced (or replicated) in the first long run. An employee on whom specific responsibility has been imposed has similar interests both with respect to his personal replacement cost and any overall value responsibility on a combination of employees that includes him. Employees can further augment employers' fixed costs when they have cost-effective investments available to them that would raise fixed responsibility costs or would increase employers' transition costs of replacing their outputs, switching to specific responsibility, or replacing them personally.

Employees' discretion over resource allocation makes it necessary to augment the traditional analysis of the long-run envelope of cost curves faced by top managing employees or funding authorities. There are alternative input combinations, types and variants of responsibility, and supporting tangible and intangible investments available to employers at any level of the organization. Appropriate choices among these alternatives would minimize these employers' costs for a given rate of the organization's output. (These are actual minimum costs including those of imposing specific or overall value responsibility, not costs under CPOR where responsibility expenses are ignored.) However, when information cost advantages enable the employees of these employers to dominate the relevant choices, the cost-minimizing selections will be made only when they are also in these employees' interests. For example, whenever employees see to it that investments desirable for top managing employees or the funding authority but with negative returns to themselves do not take place, long-run costs are as a result higher and more of these costs are fixed than otherwise. Similarly, investments beneficial to top managing employees or the funding authority can be subsidized by employees also benefiting from them when they would not otherwise occur. Specifically, we have seen that an environment of Schumpeterian competition or technological change can make it worthwhile for employees to help defray the costs of such investments. In such cases, employees' investment behavior reduces top managing employees' or the funding authority's cost of the organization's outputs. In general, employees' investment behavior can change the short-run cost differentials faced by employers and employees and provide a reason aside from entrepreneurship for rising costs in the long run.

Employees' investments that increase variable allowable resource diversions also increase the variable costs that employers face and therefore decrease employees' rates of output in the first long run. But so long as employees' investments that alter allowable fixed diversions do not raise employers' costs enough to exceed the areas under their demand curves for employees' outputs, they do not influence output rates. These costs do affect employees' budgets, however, and their total affects the funding authority's net welfare gain from the organization. For employees, fixed allowable resource diversions have the advantage over variable allowable diversions of being invariant with output so long as they remain within employers' demands and so long as total resource diversions remain within the organization's funding limit. However, in an employee's particular situation, the most attractive investment options may increase allowable limits on variable, not fixed, resource diversions. For this reason, without information about available investment opportunities, one cannot predict a priori the effects of employees' investment behavior on marginal costs faced by employers and thus on rates of output in the first long run.

The figures depicting equilibrium behavior in the first long run show only top managing employees' or the funding authority's marginal costs. Calculations of variable resource diversions and of the welfare effects of excesses of variable costs over those occurring under CPOR would be analogous to those provided in the analysis of the short run in Chapters 5 and 6.

The private corporation's equilibrium behavior in the first long run

The private corporation's equilibrium behavior in the first long run is illustrated in Figure 8.2. Only top managing employees' marginal and average variable cost of the organization's output is shown. (Their employees' variable costs and resource diversions in the first long run can be analyzed in the same manner as in Chapter 5.) The simplifying assumption of constant marginal and average variable costs is maintained. The illustrated demand includes all the effects of employees' investments that impact on the demands for the corporation's output. The analysis determines the organization's total income and the component of its income represented by fixed as well as variable components of costs and diversions.

Price and output are determined under the same assumptions as in the analysis of the short run in Chapter 5 except that the overall value responsibility imposed on top managing employees by large stockholders, directors or takeover threats is now based on the cor-

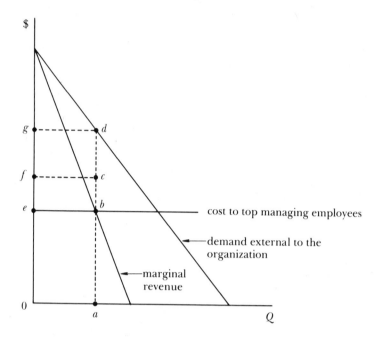

Figure 8.2. Equilibrium behavior of a private corporation in the long run. Marginal and average variable cost is shown.

poration's long-run profitability. One of these assumptions is that top managing employees personally benefit enough at the margin from increases in the corporation's profits beyond those passed on to stockholders to offset their personal costs of taking the managerial actions necessary to achieve these increases. The corporation's equilibrium rate of output $0a$ is determined by the point b of equality between marginal cost to top managing employees and marginal revenue, and its equilibrium price $0g$ is determined by demand at this quantity. The corporation's income is $0adg$, consisting of top managing employees' total variable costs, $0abe$, plus gross profits, $ebdg$. These include profits passed on to stockholders (or demonstrably reinvested profitably), $fcdg$, and the sum $ebcf$ of top managing employees' fixed production and responsibility costs, the fixed diversions of their employees, and all their own resource diversions. (The illustrated breakdown of the quantity $ebdg$ into stockholders' fixed costs and passed-on profits is arbitrary.)

Let us now drop the assumption of Chapter 5 that short-run profitability does not come at the expense of long-run profitability. How do top managing employees respond when at the margin, increased short-run profits can result in lower profits in the long run? For example, top managing employees might achieve short-run profits at the expense of improving products, developing markets, and maintaining equipment. When these employees are under overall value responsibility based on the corporation's profitability, the answer depends on the particular criterion of profitability that is imposed. Directors and large stockholders may be sufficiently informed to impose overall value responsibility based on profitability in the long run. However, when takeover threats limit top managing employees' resource diversions, diffuse stockholders may not know about a conflict between short-run and long-run profits when deciding whether to sell their shares or how to vote them. Profitability might influence the wages of top managing employees via labor market competition (Fama, 1980); potential employers in the same industry would be likely to know about such a trade-off. When top managing employees expect to remain for a long time with their corporation, they have an incentive to inform those imposing responsibility on them about trade-offs between short-run and long-run profits.

When employees are responsive to the funding limit, they deliberately reduce resource diversions below those allowed by responsibility so as to increase stockholders' profits (e.g., reduce fixed diversions within *ebcf* and thereby augment *fcdg*). Note that if they reduce variable resource diversions the analysis becomes more complicated because output, profits, fixed diversions, and variable diversions are interdependent.

To make inferences about employees' responsiveness to the funding limit and the resulting increased profits passed on to stockholders, it is necessary to take account of employees' time preferences, their perceptions of the trade-offs between resource diversions and the corporation's growth, and the costs to them of coordinating themselves to control resource diversions. Whereas the last variable may be measurable, the first two are subjective. However, it may be possible to substitute for the second variable actual relationships between profitability and growth, if one properly controls for the influences of demand and the presence or absence of Schumpeterian competition and technological change. Such controls are necessary also because these dynamic forces directly affect employees' responsiveness to the funding limit. For example, if employees expect to benefit substantially from a change in technology provided that stockholders make

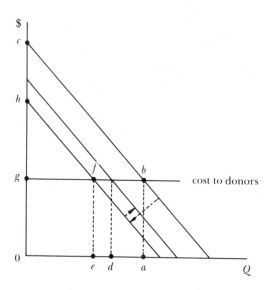

Figure 8.3. Equilibrium behavior of a private nonprofit organization in the first long run.

appropriate investments, they will be more willing to sacrifice re-source diversions to attract investments than if they expect technol-ogy to remain static.

The analysis of the efficiency of the corporation's price and out-put behavior in the first long run is identical to that of Chapter 5.

> *The private nonprofit organization's equilibrium*
> *behavior in the first long run*

Figure 8.3 illustrates price, income, and output determination for the private nonprofit organization in the first long run. To simplify the presentation, donors' demand for the organization's output is omitted; only schedules of the incremental donations that corre-spond to each rate of output are presented. We shall first consider the highest schedule in the figure which represents the realization of all investments desirable for employees that influence donation be-havior. I assume that there are no charges to the organization's clients; an analysis of such charges in the long run would be identical to the short-run analysis of these charges in Chapter 5.

Two cases are considered. In one, the investments that employees find desirable to make bring the rate of resource diversions allowed by responsibility up to the funding limit. For example, with the highest schedule in Figure 8.3, fixed resource diversions are limited by the area *gbc* minus donors' fixed production and responsibility costs. (Note that fixed resource diversions, which are allowed in given quantities by responsibility, are also constrained by the incremental donation schedule through its role in determining the funding limit. Thus, when the funding limit is binding, fixed diversions can vary via this schedule with the rate of output.) In the second case, employees' desirable investments only make the resource diversions allowed by responsibility reach an amount that is less than the funding limit; this leaves some income to the organization that is at the discretion of its donors or the organization's board. In either case, the organization's equilibrium rate of output is 0*a* and its income is 0*abc*.

Consider an exogenously determined inward shift of the incremental donation schedule from the uppermost to the lowest level and assume that all first long-run adjustments take place except any investments that would raise this schedule from the new level. The equilibrium rate of output decreases to 0*e* and the organization's income decreases from 0*abc* to 0*efh*. Variable resource diversions and donors' variable responsibility costs decrease by the cumulative excess of donors' marginal cost over employees' marginal cost under CPOR (not shown) for the change in output. Any decrease in fixed resource diversions depends on whether these diversions were previously constrained by the funding limit. If so, that is, if these diversions plus donors' fixed production and responsibility costs equal the amount *gbc*, employees' actual fixed diversions must decrease enough for this sum to fall to *gfh*. (Recall the assumption that the funding limit is positive in the analysis of the first long run.) Alternatively, if allowable fixed diversions are initially low enough not to be constrained by the funding limit, employees' fixed diversions will decrease by a smaller amount or not at all as a result of the decrease in the incremental donation schedule; in such cases when variable allowable resource diversions are small, employees will experience relatively small decreases in their benefits from resource diversions as a result of an inward shift of the incremental donation schedule.

Now consider the effects of employees' investments to increase the incremental donation schedule. In the case where the allowable limit, that is, the limit on diversions determined by responsibility imposed on employees, equals or exceeds the funding limit at the original schedule, an inward shift of the schedule can significantly reduce employees' resource diversions and the benefits they derive from them. When employees must take these benefits in kind and they derive diminishing marginal utility from them, some investments to increase the schedule that were not previously worthwhile will now become desirable. Consequently, a higher incremental donation schedule will take effect, making smaller the reduction in output that results from the exogenous decrease in the schedule. However, this induced increase in demand is mitigated because the initial decrease in the donation schedule reduces the amounts of resource diversions available for investment. Figure 8.3 illustrates an output decrease to $0d$ (instead of to $0e$) due to induced employees' investments. There are fewer induced investments to increase the incremental donation schedule when resource diversions were not originally constrained by the funding limit, because of employees smaller loss in welfare due to an exogenous inward shift of this schedule.

The public organization's equilibrium behavior in the first long run

The public organization's price, income and output in the first long run are determined in the case where there are no charges to clients for the organization's output. Extension of the analysis to include such charges would be the same as in the short-run analysis of Chapter 6. A separate presentation of employees' variable costs and resource diversions in the first long run would also be the same as in the short-run analysis.

As with the private nonprofit organization, we shall separately consider cases where employees' investments succeed in making the amount of resource diversions allowed by responsibility reach the funding limit during the first long run, and where this amount remains below the funding limit. The highest solid-lined demand in Figure 8.4 is taken to be an initial legislative demand based on current voter behavior to which the legislature and the organization's employees are fully adjusted in the first long run. It is assumed that commitments of past legislatures do not contribute to this demand. Let there be an exogenous change in voter behavior that inwardly shifts legislative demand to the lowest shown in the figure. The middle demand represents the increase from the lowest demand brought about by employees' investments that are induced by the inward shift of demand.

The organization's equilibrium rate of output is originally $0b$. At

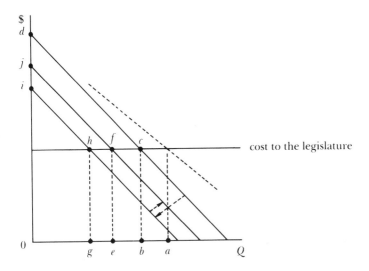

Figure 8.4. Equilibrium behavior of a public organization in the first long run.

this output, its income is 0*bcd* when the combined resource diversions allowed by the responsibility facing its employees equals or exceeds the funding limit. However, the organization's income is less than 0*bcd* by the amount that total resource diversions allowed by responsibility are less than the funding limit. Without any induced investments to increase demand, the drop in demand would lead the organization's rate of output to fall to 0*g* and its income to decrease to a maximum of 0*ghi*. If before demand drops responsibility allows an amount of resource diversions that is less than the funding limit, and thus the organization's original income is less than 0*bcd*, the reduction in its income after the drop in demand is smaller than if responsibility permitted resource diversions to equal or exceed the funding limit. If the resource diversions allowed by responsibility remain below the new funding limit after the inward shift of demand, the organization's income will fall only by the decrease in the legislature's variable costs. Thus, changes in the first long run in a public organization's income in response to changes in demand are strongly influenced by the amount of diversions allowed by responsibility imposed within the organization in relation to its funding limit.

Subsequently, induced investments by employees offset some of the decrease in legislative demand. The new demand schedule would reduce employees' resource diversions. If employees derive decreasing marginal utility from in-kind benefits from these diversions, some investments to increase legislative demand that were formerly undesirable will now become worthwhile. However, there will be fewer induced investments to increase demand when resource diversions were not originally constrained by the funding limit. The resulting increase in legislative demand is illustrated by the middle solid-lined demand in Figure 8.4, which brings about increases in the rate of output to $0e$ and raises the organization's income to a maximum of $0efj$. As pointed out in the case of the private nonprofit organization, the reduced amount of resource diversions available for investment after the initial decrease in demand mitigates the subsequent induced increase in demand.

These points can be illustrated somewhat differently with an example of a new legislative demand that leads a legislature to establish a new public organization.[4] Initially, the amount of resource diversions allowed by the responsibility facing the new organization's employees could be relatively low. Over time, however, employees' investments increase this amount, producing regular increases in the organization's income even with a constant demand for its output. Subsequently, if the legislature's demand shifts inward, the resulting decrease in the public organization's income depends on two factors. The first is the amount of resource diversions allowed by responsibility in relation to the funding limit. If this amount did not reach the original funding limit and in fact remains below the new funding limit, the organization's income will decrease only by the change in the legislature's variable costs over the decreased output quantity. However, if employees' investments were able to make this amount equal or exceed the original funding limit, the decrease in demand brings about a much larger decrease in the organization's income. The second factor is the degree to which induced employees' investments offset the decrease in legislative demand.

The dependence of a public organization's income on current voting behavior based on its output is diminished when legislative demand is determined in part by past legislative commitments. We have seen in Chapter 6 that past commitments of future economic benefits to voters, along with past commitments of increased future benefits to employees in exchange for reduced diversions, can result in a component of legislative spending that is independent of current voting behavior. The commitments to a given organization's employees are often met in the form of an increased demand for the organization's output for two reasons: (1) direct benefits such as pensions may be equal for all public organizations, due in part to employees' voting; and (2) there may be some voter support for increased output. The influence of past commitments is included within the dashed demand line in Figure 8.4 that increases the public organization's output from $0b$ to $0a$ and raises its funding limit. As a result of past legislative commitments, changes in current voting behavior based on its output have smaller proportional influences on a public organization's income.

It is interesting to contrast the present analysis with Niskanen's (1971) seminal analysis. His model is based on the assumption that the public organization ("bureau" in his terminology) is able to charge the legislature for its output on an "all or nothing" basis. The bureau's output and income are determined by the point on demand at which all of the legislature's consumers' surplus is exhausted. Given Niskanen's specification of demand and cost functions, the equilibrium at relatively low positions of legislative demand is at a rate of output where the legislature's marginal value of output remains positive, but marginal cost exceeds this positive value. At higher positions of demand, the equilibrium occurs where this marginal value equals zero. (Niskanen specifies only one "minimum" cost function.)

In contrast, the legislature is hypothesized to have continuous control over the rate of the public organization's output in the present analysis; provided that the organization's employees receive at each rate of output the lesser of the combined resource diversions allowed by the responsibility individually facing them and those permitted by the funding limit, the legislature may select whatever output it desires. Specifically, a rate of output at which marginal cost to the legislature exceeds legislative demand represents a disequilibrium setting in force actions that reduce output. (See Chapter 6, Section C.) Niskanen subsequently modified his analysis in a 1975 article to incorporate a legislature's uses of "control devices" (discussed by Breton and Wintrobe, 1975). Such devices are like applications of specific responsibility, but – instead of reducing the legislature's cost of the organization's output – they directly reduce output below that of the zero consumers' surplus solution. Depending on the cost effectiveness of such devices, the rate of output can remain where the legislature's marginal cost exceeds demand.

The present analysis requires taking account of differences in variable costs faced by the legislature and by employees in the analysis of economic efficiency; whereas the legislature's marginal cost equals demand in equilibrium, the employees' marginal cost is less than demand. (See Chapters 5 and 6.) The analysis of economic efficiency also requires comparison of employees' costs under the responsibility imposed on them with those that would occur under CPOR. In his 1975 modification, Niskanen specifies a "maximum budget that would be approved by the government review group" (p. 619), and the difference between this budget and "minimum" cost determines the public organization's "discretionary budget." Because the resource diversions allowed by responsibility are not always equal to or greater than the funding limit, such a maximum budget should be definable for each possible rate of output based on the fixed and variable costs that the legislature faces at that output.

We have also seen that it is necessary to take account of possible divergences between legislative and citizens' demand in order to evaluate economic efficiency when any organization supplies legislative demand.

Summary of basic hypotheses about price, income, and output determination in the first long run

Effects of investments on fixed and variable costs. Employees' dominance over investments required for input substitutions alters the short-run differences in costs faced by employers and employees, and provides a reason aside from entrepreneurship for increasing costs in the long run.

Although employees not expecting demands for their outputs to increase have a preference for equal amounts of fixed over variable allowable resource diversions, their most attractive investment opportunities may yield increases in allowable variable diversions. Thus without information about the nature of employees' investment opportunities one cannot predict the effects of employees' investment behavior on employers' marginal costs of employees' outputs, and hence the equilibrium rates of these outputs.

The private corporation's price, income, and output. Equilibrium price, income, and output are determined in the same manner in the first long run as in the short run. In particular, the equality of marginal revenue and top managing employees' marginal cost determines the corporation's equilibrium rate of output. This marginal cost includes the variable resource diversions of those reporting to top managing employees, which could be less than those allowed by responsibility if these employees should reduce them in response to the funding limit. The analysis of the long run determines the total of employees' resource diversions, including fixed diversions charged against gross profits. This total can be less than the amount allowed by responsibility when employees reduce diversions in order to attract equity capital for the corporation's growth.

The private nonprofit organization's price, income, and output. The analysis of the first long run determines the total of employees' resource diversions, including the fixed quantities charged against total donations. This total is the lesser of the amounts allowed by responsibility and the funding limit. The rates of the organization's income and output are determined in the same manner as in the analysis of the short run.

Employees have an entrepreneurial interest in making investments to increase donations. These investments include those that are induced by exogenous decreases in donations and thus tend to stabilize the organization's income.

The public organization's price, income, and output. The total resource diversions allowed by the responsibility facing a public organization's employees are determined in the first long run. When this total equals or exceeds the funding limit, the organization's income equals the area under legislative demand for its output up to the organization's equilibrium rate of output, plus the present expense of past legislative commitments of benefits to the organization's employees. To the extent that resource diversions allowed by responsibility sum to less than the funding limit, the organization's income is smaller. The rate of the organization's output and any price charged for it are determined as in the analysis of the short run.

Employees' investments are directed both to increasing the resource diversions allowed by responsibility when these are below the funding limit and to raising legislative demand. When resource diversions are constrained by the funding limit, employees make investments that tend to stabilize both legislative demand and the organization's income.

CHAPTER 9

The demand and supply of nonmarket resource allocation

This chapter analyzes economic behavior in the second long run, a time period long enough for organizations to merge or change their status, for instance, from private to public or profit to nonprofit. If a merger or change in status increases the amount of economic activity occurring within organizations, the smaller the allocative role of market incentives relative to that of incentives within organizations. If these changes are accompanied by an increase in legislative demand, this additional intervention between citizens' demand and the organization's employees further reduces the allocative role of market incentives.

A change in an organization's status or its merger with another organization is an investment that can be initiated by employees as well as by the funding authority, but the funding authority can exercise the right to approve before one of these changes may take place. The investments that can alter an organization's status in various ways or merge it constitute the supply of these changes. There would be a change in the funding authority's returns from the organization as a result of these investments taking place. Employees' separate investments that influence the funding authority's expectations about these returns are their demands for mergers or changes in organizations' status. Demand affects supply when employees can sufficiently influence the funding authority's expected returns to a merger or change in the organization's status to alter his choice whether to permit it to take place.

The demands of an organization's employees for a merger or a different status for the organization are motivated by possibilities for increased income, including unrealized potential for benefits from resource diversions. We have seen that in the first long run the sum of the resource diversions allowed by the responsibility imposed on its employees can exceed an organization's funding limit on diversions. When there is another type of organization with a larger funding limit, the unrealized potential for resource diversions may be large enough to call forth employees' investments to influence choices to merge or change the organization's status. For example, a

230

potential merger partner's funding limit may exceed the resource diversions allowed by the responsibility facing its employees. Another example is that with the same demand for final outputs, the funding limit can be larger in a public organization than in a private corporation supplying them.

In the second long run, laws and attitudes in the broader society affect the outcome. In particular, laws may prohibit some mergers or changes in status that would be the objects of employees' investments.[1] Similarly, social attitudes can directly affect the outcome when they translate into voter responses to legislative influence over mergers or changes in an organization's status.

The following changes in organizations are considered separately: mergers and acquisitions of private corporations; mergers of public organizations; the transfer of production from private corporations to public organizations and vice versa; and the analogous transfer of production between private nonprofit and public organizations. The focus is on the role of employees' investment behavior in each of these changes. The final section considers the relevance of the present theory of economic behavior within organizations to the broader topic of comparative evaluation of alternative economic systems.

A   Mergers and acquisitions of private corporations

Stockholders favor mergers or acquisitions that enhance market power or reduce costs (e.g., internalize technological externalities, enable scale economies in uses of indivisible inputs) to the extent that the benefits accrue to them. However, within the lesser of the amounts of resource diversions that are allowed by responsibility and the funding limit, both of which can be changed by a merger or acquisition, employees reap the benefits from any economies achieved by combining organizations. The roles of stockholders not actively involved in management are usually limited to approving employees' proposals for mergers or acquisitions, and stockholders often delegate even this role to directors.

Mergers or acquisitions can benefit employees by raising funding limits through enhancing the supply of equity capital; increasing the resource diversions that are allowed by responsibility; and providing employees with more diversification or with access to additional resources for personal use so they can increase their welfare without necessarily increasing resource diversions. Whenever corporate employees currently sacrifice resource diversions to raise profitability and thus attract equity capital, they are likely to be interested also in acquisitions or mergers that have the effect of increasing profitability or equity capital. Increases in market power can achieve this end, as can merger or acquisition partners that are more profitable or would reduce costs. Provided that such combinations do not make responsibility more effective in limiting diversions at the same time that they increase the funding limit, employees can benefit.

The resource diversions allowed by responsibility can rise as a result of a merger or acquisition. For example, the additional coordination may increase demands for some employees' outputs and thereby raise their personal or output replacement costs. Indeed, employees may be able to use their information cost advantages to ensure that merged or acquired units are combined in such a way as to create larger demands for their coordination capabilities. Mergers or acquisitions can increase an employee's utility from a given amount of resource diversions by increasing opportunities to exchange resources used for in-kind benefits and by broadening the diversification of risks. Regarding risk, stockholders can (ignoring tax considerations) readily diversify stockholdings, but an employee's own investments in the corporation cannot so easily be diversified – a merger or acquisition or corporate expansion may, however, help achieve this goal.[2]

An environment of new product introductions and technological change makes mergers and acquisitions more desirable to employees. Employees involved with introducing new products or adopting new production techniques are particularly interested in diversification because they can reap only limited gains from successful decisions. They thus attempt to broaden participation in losses from unsuccessful decisions by encouraging employers to impose overall value responsibility on aggregations of activity that include employees involved with other outputs or production techniques. (See Chapter 7.) Depending on employees' choices along the trade-off between reduced accountability for losses and increased flexibility of adaptation to these dynamic changes, additional merger or acquisition partners can present attractive opportunities for diversifying risks. This benefit is reinforced when the merger or acquisition also increases the supply of external financing; increased external capital investments are especially desirable to those adapting to new products or technological change because of the attendant capital requirements.

Mueller (1969) has analyzed reasons for conglomerate mergers that include diversification of employees' risks and increased combined growth from acquiring relatively fast-growing companies. We can consider an additional reason for conglomerates. By imposing

IPOR with rate-of-return criteria on each company, a conglomerate's top managing employees may either be able to impose a lower funding limit on resource diversions in each company than would occur if each were independent or to more effectively impose responsibility on each company's employees. An important issue is, of course, the amount of the resulting increased profits that a conglomerate's top managing employees must pass along to stockholders or profitably reinvest on their behalf.

From the foregoing it can be seen that employees can benefit from particular mergers and acquisitions that increase or reduce profitability, or enhance or decrease economic efficiency. For example, a merger or acquisition can bring about net welfare losses due to higher allowable resource diversions and the usually attendant incentives for inefficient resource allocation, or it can enhance efficiency by achieving cost-reducing economies. Although employees benefit from mergers and acquisitions that facilitate favorable adaptations to Schumpeterian competition or technological change, these dynamic forces exacerbate the tendency for employees' returns to diversification to exceed those of stockholders.

We now consider how employees can elicit the approval of stockholders for merger or acquisition proposals. Steiner (1975) comprehensively analyzes the likelihood of a merger or acquisition taking place under alternative combinations of approval of each corporation's stockholders and its employees. The likelihood is lower if the stockholders of a corporation to be acquired or merged are opposed because they must receive a higher price or amount of stock in the combined company. Opposition of an acquiring corporation's stockholders reduces the likelihood by decreasing the price or amount of stock to be offered. The opposition of employees in either corporation reduces the likelihood to the extent that they can lower their own stockholders' expected returns to the combination. Consider the possibility, however, that the employees in one corporation would benefit substantially from a combination and that the employees of another corporation stand to lose. If the potentially losing employees can sufficiently reduce their stockholders' expected returns to effect their disapproval, the potentially gaining employees have an incentive to offer the other employees compensating arrangements related to suborganization, working conditions, and job security. In such circumstances, employees' costs of making and enforcing such agreements can be a major determinant of whether a merger or acquisition occurs.[3]

A shareholder's consent for an acquisition or merger depends on the price he must receive for his stock to tender it or his estimate of the value of the stock he owns after the combination.[4] Thus, employees' influence depends on whether they can affect stockholders' estimates of returns on their equity. By controlling resource diversions, employees can affect stockholders' estimates of profitability without a merger or acquisition. Employees can use their information cost advantages to learn about profitable opportunities of which stockholders are unaware. By controlling this information, or information about how to take advantage of these opportunities, employees can influence stockholders' estimates of what profitability would be with and without a merger or acquisition. Employees can also communicate their own interests in future growth to stockholders, and their plans can imply a willingness to decrease resource diversions in order to increase profitability. This may help explain why relatively large corporations often pay premium prices to acquire faster growing companies. Usually the acquired company is too small to enhance significantly the growth of the larger one. But the acquisition can convey to stockholders that the employees of the larger corporation are interested in growth and will make the necessary sacrifices of resource diversions to increase overall growth.

In conclusion, employees can obtain approval for as well as benefit from particular acquisitions and mergers that would decrease, as well as increase, stockholders' welfare and social welfare. The foregoing arguments also apply to employees' influence to prevent socially desirable or undesirable mergers or acquisitions that would reduce their own welfare. Thus, it is not possible to predict whether the influence of employees on acquisitions or mergers is generally harmful or beneficial.

B   A legislature's choice of type of organization to produce a subsidized good or service and determination of the size of each public organization

So far it has been taken as given that legislatures establish public organizations. However, it is possible to analyze a legislature's choice to have a public organization produce subsidized goods and services in terms of its competitive advantage over other types of organizations in yielding votes to legislators. In the following discussion we first consider a legislature's choice of a type of organization to produce a subsidized good or service; we then consider the size of each public organization.

*A legislature's choice of a type of organization to
produce a subsidized good or service*

An organization's competitive advantage in producing a subsidized good or service need not derive from a cost advantage. We have seen in Chapter 6 that a legislator can lose votes by including in his utility-maximizing platform economic benefits for one voter group at the expense of another. However, the higher the information costs faced by the voters not desiring a benefit, the smaller the vote loss.

A public organization has competitive advantages over private organizations in raising costs of information about the separate costs of each group's benefits. When the multiple benefits are not fully jointly produced, competing private organizations would analyze the separate costs of each even if requested to make a single bid for all benefits. The legislature might conceivably require each bidder to keep his cost analysis secret, but this would be costly to enforce and the requirement itself could alienate voters. Secrecy may, in fact, be infeasible because an individual legislator has an incentive to publicize information about the costs of subsidies that do not benefit his constituents.

In contrast, if a public organization is the exclusive provider of a combination of legislatively funded benefits to constituents, information about the separately identifiable cost of each can be very costly or unobtainable to legislators and citizens.[5] By adjusting each output benefiting a constituency and observing the funding responses, a public organization's employees need not themselves possess accurate information about the separate costs of each. Thus vote losses can be avoided by having the competing groups' economic benefits provided by a single public organization without separate appropriations for each benefit.

A public organization's competitive vote advantage in providing subsidies to multiple constituencies makes a legislature willing to pay it more than a private organization for the same goods and services. That is, enhanced costs of information faced by those preferring that subsidies not be provided make the legislature's demand higher when the goods and services involved are supplied by a public rather than a private organization. (See the discussion of Figure 6.3.) However, the amount by which demand is higher is limited by the fact that the legislature has the option to use private suppliers and spend the premium to provide additional vote-yielding economic benefits. Thus, the premium will not exceed the amount that could be spent to offset the decreases in election probabilities that a public organization prevents.

A public organization has another competitive advantage when a private organization requires a large risk premium to make the necessary investment to supply legislative demand. This occurs when the invested capital and skills of employees involved in the production of an output demanded only by a legislature lack alternative uses. A legislature can avoid making current cash outlays for risk premiums by assuming this risk. It can do this by funding these investments within a public organization or by providing private organizations with long-term contracts or guarantees against losses. The latter action has the advantage of employing private savings for the investment itself, whereas the former has the advantages of raising citizens' costs of information about possible future losses and of avoiding premiums required to prevent supply interruptions (Klein et al., 1978). Either action is an example of a legislature making commitments on future legislatures. (See Chapter 6.) When the former advantage is more important to a legislature, a public organization has another allowable cost premium over private suppliers equal to the amount at which the legislature is indifferent to these two means of dealing with risk.

Determinants of the equilibrium size of each public organization

Any beneficiary of legislative spending faces varying costs of information about different gains that other citizens receive from legislative spending. These costs depend on the similarity of the goods or services received by others, and on the amounts of contact that beneficiaries have with each other, for example, as competitors, being in similar occupations, or sharing common ideologies. When costs of information about benefits to others are low, legislators face especially large vote losses in response to any group's gains. However, the same groups facing low costs of information about each other's benefits could often potentially gain from cooperating because of economies from sharing information about common interests in coordinated voting, lobbying resources, and campaign fund raising resources. In situations like this, a single public organization providing benefits to several such groups is attractive to a legislature. When citizens perceive that increases in the organization's total appropriation will raise their own benefits, they are in effect forced to support the benefits received by others in order to support their own. The organization's internal budgeting and suborganization can be such as to raise costs of information about each group's benefits; when the mix of benefits it provides is thus not well known to the groups, they give less weight to the benefits of others when supporting the organization's total appropriation. Legislators may also find it in their interest to require each public organization to provide some outputs that benefit a large portion of the public, whether or not public goods, in order to prevent losses of votes from those who do not gain from any of the benefits provided to the competing groups.

However, when citizens seeking diverse benefits share lobbying and other resources, there is still conflict over the relative support to seek for particular subsidies. Thus citizens basing votes on particular benefits have a continuing interest in evaluating whether they would be better off with a separate agency or a separate appropriation for their own benefits. For a given group, economies from sharing lobbying resources and its gains from competing groups' higher costs of information about its benefits can be offset by the loss of benefits due to it having to support benefits received by others. In this case, the group is better off with a separate agency. Such a group of citizens currently sharing a public organization may thus seek a separately funded organization to provide only their own subsidies or attempt to ensure that their part of a public organization has a separate appropriation. The larger their numbers, and the more effectively the group coordinates its voting and fundraising, the more likely that a legislature will approve a separate organization or appropriation.

Against this background, it is possible to analyze the influence that employees of public organizations have on the combinations of outputs produced by these organizations and to consider employees' demands for mergers of public organizations. When employees can themselves determine the separate costs of individual items in a combination of benefits, their information cost advantages usually enable them to control the availability of this information to others. In such cases, when there is a proposal to have an output provided by another organization, employees can affect the choice by appropriately influencing the cost estimates on which the decision is based. For example, costs attributable to other outputs can be attributed to the output in question, or vice versa.

A relatively small public organization standing alone may find that the sum of the resource diversions allowed by the responsibility imposed on its employees is smaller than its funding limit. Such a situation might result from a lack of employees' investment opportunities for creating complexity of its operations. Merger with such an organization is desirable to employees in a larger public organization for which the sum of employees' resource diversions allowed by responsibility exceeds its funding limit. In general, when the resource diversions allowed by responsibility in a public organization sum to an amount greater than its funding limit, its employees can benefit from taking on additional outputs having high demands in relation to employees' costs of production. Resource diversions can temporarily "subsidize" a new output if necessary, and a legislature benefits from avoiding start-up costs for a new organization. The incentives for legislators to make commitments on future legislatures enhance employees' returns to providing the legislature with temporary savings. Any subsequent desires of the legislature or voters to have another organization provide the output can be inhibited by control over cost information and by forcing the legislature to incur high transition costs.

The employees in the relatively smaller organization may fear that they will personally not gain from their unused funding limit and may lose resource diversions allowed by responsibility if some of their tasks are taken over by employees in the other organization. If these employees can influence the outcome, the employees in the larger organization may, as in the case of mergers of private corporations, elicit their support by offering them opportunities for benefits from resource diversions (e.g., promotion for the same tasks, favorable work rules, improved offices, etc.) in the expanded organization. The employees in both public organizations would face costs of negotiating and enforcing agreements among themselves.

When employees of public organizations find it in their interest to produce multiple outputs in order to take advantage of unused funding limits, they tend to reinforce legislators' desires for the separately identifiable benefit to each constituent to be ambiguous. Thus, the interests of employees and legislators, along with citizens' economies from sharing lobbying and other resources, all help determine the combinations of economic benefits that are provided by the same public organization.

C   Public capital financing of private corporations

The votes underlying legislative capital financing of private corporations result from the rents that employees, customers, and suppliers derive from these organizations. Legislative capital financing can be desirable to employees in firms that have become unattractive to private investors. It may not be possible to raise profitability enough so the firm can attract the private capital needed to grow with its markets, or even to continue to function; in other cases, it may be necessary for employees to decrease resource diversions substantially in order to achieve a desirable degree of profitability. Without adequate private financing, the long-run supplies of the corporation's outputs will fall. The lost rents to specialized suppliers and customers can lead these individuals also to base votes on legislative financing. Because of coordination and information costs, votes for legislative financing may be latent. An exogenous decrease in demand could trigger these votes by reducing profitability enough to threaten employees' jobs and specialized suppliers' and clients' rents.

The incentive to base votes on public financing is greater the more unattractive an industry to private investors, the higher the entry costs for new firms, and the more specialized the skills of employees and the demands of customers. Nonetheless, if the number of individuals receiving or seeking rents is large enough and their votes are readily coordinated, it can be worthwhile for citizens to base their votes on legislative financing for an industry such as agriculture with low entry costs and a ready supply of private financing. However, if such an industry remains attractive to investors, its beneficiaries seek subsidies rather than production in a public organization.

A legislature's choice whether to subsidize an industry's producers in an industry that has become unattractive to private investors or to arrange for a public organization to produce their outputs is influenced by financing issues and costs of information to citizens who may be opposed to the arrangement. Expenditures to purchase corporate securities are highly visible; the costs of information about such expenditures to citizens not benefiting from them are low. Also, the price of such purchases can be high and requires current taxes or borrowing. Alternatively, the legislature can make use of private savings by providing guarantees or subsidies to private investors. Legislative guarantees are also less visible and are another example of how a legislature can impose commitments on future legislatures. Subsidies have the advantage of being readily concealed. In societies where stockholders are a small percentage of the population, a legislature's appropriating corporate assets at prices below what stockholders would voluntarily accept is always a possibility. In some cases where stockholding is widespread, a particular corporation's stockholders may not be able to influence a large number of votes; if the corporation's assets are dissimilar to assets used in other industries, as, for example, in the case of railroads, stockholders of other corporations may not strongly oppose an appropriation of them.

Employees can find it in their interest to take actions that discourage legislative funding. In order to respond favorably to new products introduced by competitors and to new production techniques that affect their production domains, employees need capital financing that is sensitive to the profitability of new products and techniques rather than to votes. To attract such financing from private investors, employees find it less worthwhile to use resources to coordinate voting than to learn about profitable products and production techniques and to reduce resource diversions in order to raise profitability.

D   Public financing of private nonprofit organizations

An important influence on the supply behavior of a private nonprofit organization's employees is whether or not legislative demand tends to displace private donations. For example, when future streams of legislative and private funding are equally certain, these employees are willing to accept increased legislative funding that would fully displace private donations, only when it would cover all fixed as well as variable costs that are paid by private donors. Thus, the employees of private nonprofit organizations search for opportunities to increase legislative demand in ways that retain private donations. The key to holding both private and public funding is differentiation among outputs and clienteles. To this end, a private nonprofit organization's employees are most likely to seek legislative support for relatively uniform benefits to large numbers of individuals. More individualized benefits or benefits to client groups in amounts that vary independently of the groups' political influence are most likely to be funded by private donors. The less politically popular the clients, the greater the financing role of private donors and the less information is made available to other citizens and to legislatures about these benefits. Different clients' benefits can be combined within broadly comprehensive budgets, facilitating the provision of selective information to particular parties.

As a private nonprofit organization increases its supply to legislative demands, three factors affect the likelihood of a change in its status to that of a public organization. If a large part of the organization's income is private donations on behalf of politically unpopular

clients, a change in status to a public organization is especially unlikely. The second factor derives from the gains to legislators from
making commitments obligating future legislatures. If employees expect a large portion of their donations to decline (e.g., because of an
impending demographic change that will reduce numbers of potential clients) and do not expect offsetting increases in other donations,
they prefer legislative funding when it is committed for the future.
The third factor is donors' willingness to transfer ownership of the
organization's capital resources to the government. If donors believe
these resources could not be placed in uses other than those they
desire and if commitments for future public support accompany the
transfer, it may be permitted with only token compensation.

It is possible to contrast the possibilities of public ownership of
private corporations and private nonprofit organizations. Whereas
the owners of private corporations seek compensation for their assets, this is not necessarily so and is often not the case for private
nonprofit organizations. Thus the supply of public ownership is
higher for private nonprofit organizations than for private corporations. In contrast, on the demand side, public ownership can create a
more substantial increase in the funding limit for employees of private corporations. However, technological change or Schumpeterian
competition makes employees in private corporations give weight to
profit-oriented rather than vote-responsive capital financing. Employees of private nonprofit organizations give weight to the flexibility to cater to both legislative and donor financing.

**E   Summary of basic hypotheses about employees'
economic behavior in the second long run**

Mergers and acquisitions of private corporations

The effects of mergers and acquisitions on employees' welfare include changes in the resource diversions allowed by responsibility
and the corporation's funding limit. Employees can affect stockholders' expected returns to mergers or acquisitions because of their
control over current corporate profitability and their information
cost advantages in evaluating combinations with other corporations.
Because employees can benefit from and influence both socially desirable and socially undesirable mergers and acquisitions, it is not
possible to predict whether their influence is generally harmful or
beneficial.

*A legislature's choice of type of organization to produce
a subsidized good or service*

Competitive advantages of public organizations. Public organizations have
a competitive advantage over private organizations in raising costs of
information about different groups' benefits from legislative spending. These organizations frequently also have a competitive advantage in facilitating a legislature's gaining current votes for its members by making commitments on future legislatures.

The influence of employees on the sizes of public organizations. By controlling a legislature's costs of adding outputs to existing public organizations, employees can influence legislative choices whether to
establish new organizations. Similarly, employees can use their control over costs to influence a legislature's choices whether to merge
public organizations, and they are motivated to do so in part by the
presence of organizations with unused funding limits.

Public capital financing of private corporations

Employees can influence legislative capital financing of private corporations under particular circumstances. These include cases where
employees', customers', and suppliers' rents are substantial, where
the industry is not attractive to private investors, and where information and coordination costs are modest. Legislatures are inhibited by
the visibility and costs of compensating stockholders and thus are
most likely to use financing arrangements such as subsidies and guarantees that involve commitments on future legislatures.

Public financing of private nonprofit organizations

Employees devote resources to differentiating the roles of legislative
and private donor financing. As a result, legislative financing of
private nonprofit organizations tends to be concentrated on relatively similar benefits to large numbers of individuals. More differentiated benefits and those provided to politically unpopular clients
are most likely to be financed by donors.

The likelihood of a private nonprofit organization becoming a
public organization depends on the fraction of its income from private donations on behalf of clients lacking political support and its
employees' expectations of donors' continuing support. Donors are

often willing to transfer a private nonprofit organization's assets to the government with only token compensation.

F   Comparative economic systems

This section very briefly describes the potential applicability of the economic theory presented in this book to the comparative evaluation of economic systems. Economic systems often differ in the type of organization that supplies a given output. The theory provides separate and comparable hypotheses about the price and output behavior and effects on economic efficiency of private corporations, private nonprofit organizations, and public organizations, in both short-run and long-run contexts.

However, this discussion is concerned with the broader issue of whether such an economic theory could contribute to evaluation of alternative interventions in economic systems that are based on governmental authority. This issue could be analyzed in a "third" long run in which the coalitions that can alter governing institutions undergo changes. It should be possible to provide, for example, an analysis of the economic incentives that form coalitions such as those that caused the social changes documented in Moore's (1966) classic study.[6] Individuals can be regarded as deriving rents from living in a society, and coalitions of individuals can in a variety of ways give governments varying degrees of authority to extract these rents. Thus a government has authority over individuals and groups of citizens that is analogous to the authority of employers over employees, even though with varying effectiveness citizens can act as a government's funding authority. Rather than develop this point here, the present discussion takes as given the coalitions that shape governing institutions and sketches the relevance of the theory presented in this book to the evaluation of the resulting governmental authority within a society's economic system.

Three aspects of governmental authority give relevance to this theory. One is the distinction between those who make decisions and those who, it might be said, "carry them out." A person who "carries out" a decision is one who holds discretion over resource substitutions within one or more relevant production functions. The decisions can alter market prices, directly pertain to priorities about availabilities of inputs or outputs, or they can establish restrictions or priorities on actual choices of resource substitutions. That a decision is made does not, of course, necessarily imply that the decision maker's desired uses of resources are accomplished. The second issue is the extent to which (if at all) decisions are, in this sense, carried out. This issue relates, of course, to the responsibility imposed on those who hold discretion over the relevant portions of production functions. The third issue is the responsibility imposed on the planners and decision makers themselves. A "planner" is one who presents information to decision makers. A planner may also be a decision maker; even if he is not, he nonetheless often influences decisions via the selective provision of information.

The responsibility placed on planners, decision makers, and those whose economic actions are the subject of planning has behavioral implications that can be analyzed and empirically investigated. Aside from the direct effects of responsibility on resource allocation, responsibility also creates incentives, roughly comparable to those in an organization, for governmental authorities and citizens to devote resources to obtaining information. These incentives should be an important part of the evaluation of an economic system because the resulting expenditures on information can be substantial. The following discussion develops these points.

For present purposes, a *primary decision maker* holds discretion over resource substitutions within one or more production functions. A *secondary decision maker* makes decisions which, if carried out, are acted upon by primary decision makers. A primary decision maker can be influenced by multiple secondary decision makers. In organizations, employees are primary decision makers whereas managing employees are both primary and secondary decision makers. Organizations' funding authorities and clienteles are secondary decision makers.

Responsibility can be imposed on secondary as well as primary decision makers. At one extreme one could imagine a perfectly competitive economic system (with CPOR within organizations whose intermediate outputs are priced at marginal cost) where CPOR in combination with market competition would govern primary decision makers (individual employees contributing to the production of each output) and market competition would govern secondary decision makers (consumers of each output and producers when they are market purchasers of intermediate outputs). However, the present discussion is concerned with alternative economic systems where some governmental secondary decision makers who are not themselves users of the outputs affected by their decisions attempt to alter resource allocation from that occurring in a market to achieve some social welfare goal. This goal can be to achieve Kaldor-Hicks efficiency gains (taking into account where necessary differences between legislative demands and underlying citizens' demands), or it can be based on a given social welfare function. The cases where these secondary decision makers possess legal authority to impose alternative types and variants of responsibility on primary decision makers can be separately considered. Also, the behavioral effects of alternative responsibility imposed on governmental secondary decision makers can be systematically analyzed.

Whatever responsibility is imposed by governmental secondary decision makers, primary decision makers have other responsibility imposed on them via their roles as employees or via the market if they are independent agents. Analysis of the behavioral effects of any responsibility imposed by governmental secondary decision makers must take account of how this responsibility interrelates with the other responsibility. Regarding the responsibility placed on governmental secondary decision makers, it might, for example, be intentionally designed to restrict these decision makers to exacting less than a citizen's rent from living in a society. However, the difficulty of such a task is most apparent from the experience of totalitarian states where such restrictions often either do not exist or are not enforced and where migration costs are frequently made very high. The behavioral effects and costs of responsibility imposed on and by governmental secondary decision makers should be an important part of the evaluation of alternative economic systems.

When authority to impose responsibility does not accompany governmental secondary decision making, primary decision makers may in their own interests coordinate themselves to follow the decisions. For example, governmental secondary decisions may facilitate collusion or coordinated voting.

The resource diversions of governmental planners and secondary decision makers are relevant to the evaluation of an economic system. Planners' most important resource diversions most likely result from the selective provision of information. Their own ideologies can guide the information they do and do not provide to secondary decision makers; thereby planners influence policy according to their ideologies. Even in a dictatorship where a single enforceable social welfare function for society is theoretically possible, the actual detailed specification of such a function would be left to planners and their resource diversions would be defined into it. Planners' diversions are limited by secondary decision makers' options to obtain information from other sources. However, this option is effective only when competing planners have diverse ideologies. The analysis of planners' resource diversions should be incorporated into the evaluation of economic systems.

The analysis of governmental secondary decision makers' resource diversions vis-à-vis the public must take account of their allowable diversions vis-à-vis the demands for their outputs that face them, and the differences between these demands and citizens' demands for these outputs. For example, we have already considered the differences in legislative and citizens' demands that result from information costs, voting on platforms of benefits, and a legislature's capability to provide nonpublic goods and public goods that benefit small groups of citizens. The allowable diversions of governmental secondary decision makers depend on constraints on the authority they have to appropriate resources from citizens and constraints on the benefits they must pass on to citizens. Note that while planners' resource diversions would influence the detailed definitions of theoretical social welfare functions, the allowable diversions of each secondary decision maker can contribute to achievement in his own personal social welfare function.

An economic system's demands for information include those for the information useful in imposing responsibility as well as those for information that is useful in making resource allocation choices. The writings of Hayek ([1940] 1965), von Mises ([1951] 1965), and Lange ([1938] 1965) are largely applicable to both categories of information, although they focus on the latter.[7] In regard to the former category, if CPOR is an economic system's sole type of responsibility and is costlessly imposed by secondary decision makers, and if there are no externalities, an economic system can be informationally decentralized according to Hurwicz's definitions. However, when it is costly to impose CPOR or if any other type of responsibility is imposed, there are very substantial demands by secondary decision makers for information about other citizens' production functions and preferences, both for imposing responsibility and for making resource allocation choices. Primary decision makers under types of responsibility other than CPOR would have substantial demands for information about the production functions and preferences of others.

The state's authority to extract rents from primary decision makers does not necessarily derive from its owning the property with which they work. For example, governmental actions behaviorally comparable to output replacement can result from governmental secondary decision makers' switching procurement policies when they have monopsony power. Similarly, antitrust policies, regulatory policies, adjustments of tariffs or other international trade relationships,[8] and domestic trade restrictions can all create incentives comparable to those of overall value responsibility when primary decision makers perceive that particular deviations of their own actions from those desired by governmental secondary decision makers would trigger switches in these policies. Competition among citizens for governmental benefits can make it economical for secondary decision makers to impose overall value responsibility when information on replacement costs emerges from competitive bidding. Totalitarian systems often use threats of very costly specific responsibility if overall productivity does not reach prescribed levels,[9] and such threats are not unheard of in democratic societies. Tax audits, antitrust suits, and enforcement of regulations can have the effects of specific responsibility.

Extension of the theory presented in this book to the comparative analysis of economic systems should result in improvement of its hypotheses about economic behavior within organizations.

CHAPTER 10

A brief summary and proposed directions for further work

This book's purpose has been to extend economic analysis to the behavior of an organization's individual employees. We have seen that, as a result, hypotheses can be derived about an organization's internal resource allocation and its supply behavior for short-run and long-run periods. Given an organization's production functions and employees' information cost advantages, it is possible to analyze the extent of employees' discretion over resource allocation and the types of constraints employers place on employees. The degree to which employees can use resources delegated to them to pursue their personal goals can be determined, and the responsiveness of the organization's internal economy to employees' welfare as well as to external economic forces can be established. Within this internal economy the range of derivable hypotheses about supplies, demands, costs, and investment behavior is approximately comparable to the range of existing hypotheses about these variables when organizations are taken as the smallest unit of analysis.

In the short run, where the effects of current investments are not considered, hypotheses about resource allocation have been derived for the cases where overall value and specific responsibility are imposed. We found that when an employee under overall value responsibility derives utility at the margin from personal uses of any of the resources delegated and attributed to him, he infers his employer's marginal value of each of these resources and, given his information about production possibilities, he allocates resources efficiently within his production domain according to these values. Because efficiency gains accrue to him, the employee obtains information about more efficient production possibilities whenever his marginal utility of the enhanced personal benefits exceeds the marginal utility of inputs applied to obtain information. There are inefficiencies under overall value responsibility. These include inadequate incentives for employees to coordinate their actions in relation to spillovers so as to achieve efficiency and employees' discount of benefits from resource diversions taken in kind below the cash values of the resources involved to employers. Further, when an employee supplies all of his output to his employer, the employer's marginal cost of obtaining this output from another source or through specific responsibility, not the employee's own marginal production cost, equals the employer's marginal value of output in equilibrium.

Specific responsibility retains and ordinarily adds to the effects of these sources of inefficiency and also provides incentives for inefficient resource allocation within an employee's production domain. An employer's choice in imposing specific responsibility on his employee's use of a particular resource determines the implicit price that guides this usage. Because this price depends to a significant degree on the cost of imposing specific responsibility, it inaccurately reflects the employer's marginal valuation of the resource. Changes in external market prices of the resources delegated to employees do not change the cost of imposing specific responsibility on their uses. Thus, a marginal analysis of economic choices under this type of responsibility can explain a tendency for some organizations' resource substitutions to be insensitive to changes in market prices, as was found, for example, by Lester (1946).

The demand of an employee under specific responsibility for information about production possibilities within his production domain is confined to his discovery of uses of resources that both yield him utility and are not worthwhile for his employer to discourage. Such possibilities can, indeed, represent less efficient resource allocation within the employee's production domain. Contrary to what one might expect, an employer with an information cost disadvantage has the incentive to learn about some of the production possibilities of an employee's production domain as he makes choices among alternative applications of specific responsibility.

A managing employee's marginal cost of his employee's outputs (or contributions to outputs) includes the employee's marginal allowable resource diversions and the employer's marginal responsibility cost as well as minimum marginal production cost. The costs faced by top managing employees – those who report directly to the funding authority – include the allowable resource diversions of the employees who report to them directly, the resource diversions that these employees must allow their employees, and their responsibility costs. Marginal allowable resource diversions and responsibility costs enter into the decision making about desired rates of employees' outputs by managing employees at each level of the organization; increases in these amounts, as well as in minimum production costs, result in reduced desired rates of employees' outputs.

We have assumed that the responsibility imposed on a corporation's top managing employees holds them accountable for the corporation's profitability. When these employees find it worthwhile at the margin to take the needed managerial actions to increase profits beyond those they are required to pass on to stockholders (or demonstrably reinvest profitably in the firm) and thus raise diversion benefits for themselves, the equilibrium rate of a corporation's output is determined by the equality of marginal revenue and top managing employees' marginal cost. This marginal cost includes the marginal allowable resource diversions of the employees who report directly or indirectly to top managing employees and marginal responsibility costs. Corporate employees' resource diversions in the form of cost-ineffective expenditures to increase sales do not reduce profitability below what it would be if they were to use their allowable resource diversions in other ways.

A private nonprofit organization's equilibrium output rate is determined by the equality of donors' marginal cost and the marginal response of donations to the rate of the organization's output, that is, the organization's incremental donation schedule, which lies below donors' demands. The equilibrium rate of output for a public organization is established by the equality of legislative demand and the legislature's marginal cost. We have seen that the demand of a legislature for the goods and services that it provides to constituents can be derived from an economic analysis of a legislature as an organization.

The analysis of efficiency of any organization's equilibrium rate of output depends on resource allocation within the organization as well as any monopoly power the organization might possess vis-à-vis its external constituencies. In particular, it is necessary to take account of (1) the degree to which employers' marginal costs exceed those of their employees; (2) the extent to which the incentives created by responsibility lead employees to make choices about resources that result in inefficiency; and (3) the amount by which employees discount below cash value the benefits from resource diversions that they receive in kind. When an organization supplies part or all of its output in response to legislative demand, efficiency further depends on the relationship between legislative demand and citizens' demands for the goods and services involved.

The endogenous investments of employees and funding authorities affect an organization's long-run resource allocation. These include the intangible investments employees make that alter the division of the organization's production functions into production domains, influence employers' choices in imposing responsibility, and create the mechanisms by which employees coordinate themselves in their mutual interests. Employees coordinate their actions for the following purposes: to alter suborganization and the responsibility placed on them in ways that benefit them; to deal advantageously with spillovers among their production domains; to adapt in their interests to Schumpeterian competition and technological change; and to maintain resource diversions within the constraints jointly facing them.

Particular coordinations of employees' actions are effected either through specialized employees who broker voluntary coordination agreements or through responsibility. By delegating the authority to impose responsibility to a coordinating employee in a situation where coordination achieves production economies, a managing employee gains the benefits from competition among potential coordinating employees. Without this delegation, the coordinated employees would benefit from the competition. In cases where coordination increases employees' allowable resource diversions while raising production costs, an employer might personally benefit from delegating authority that is used for this purpose. However, uses of authority that achieve production economies can compete at the margin; the more valuable those uses to a managing employee, the less he delegates for other purposes. A managing employee under overall value responsibility attaches more value to available uses of authority that result in production economies than does a managing employee under specific responsibility.

Although investments can increase allowable resource diversions by reducing the cost effectiveness of responsibility, the combined resource diversions of an organization's employees are also constrained by the organization's funding limit. For a private corporation, this constraint is the response of the external supply of equity capital to the corporation's profitability. When employees control their combined resource diversions in order to attract equity capital, there is a positive relationship between the corporation's rate of growth and the rate of return on its equity. The funding limits for private nonprofit and public organizations are respectively the areas under incremental donation schedules or legislative demand curves, minus fixed and variable responsibility costs and employees' fixed and variable minimum production costs. Any inward shift of the incremental donation schedule or legislative demand thus usually decreases employees' benefits from resource diversions. To the extent that these benefits must be taken in kind and employees derive diminishing marginal utility from them, some investments to increase donations or legislative demand that were not previously worthwhile will become desirable. Em-

ployees' investments therefore tend to stabilize the incremental donation schedule or legislative demand.

An increase in legislative demand for an output of a public organization will initially raise its income while making it possible for new
investments that enhance the resource diversions allowed by responsibility to be realized. As a result of these investments, there will be
further increases in the organization's income while it supplies the
same amount of the output. If legislative demand should subsequently fall, the amount of the decrease in the organization's income
depends on whether these investments have enabled the combined
resource diversions of the organization's employees to reach the
higher funding limit. If not, a drop in legislative demand will produce a relatively small decline in the organization's income.

Employees' investments can also influence whether organizations
merge or change their status, such as from private to public, or
profit to nonprofit. Thus employees, as well as funding authorities
and laws and attitudes in a society, can affect the composition of
organizations and the portion of society's resource allocation that
occurs within organizations. Employees can influence mergers or
acquisitions of private corporations because they have control over
the corporation's current profitability, and they often possess cost
advantages in evaluating stockholders' costs and benefits of combining with other corporations. By controlling a legislature's costs and
benefits of adding to existing organizations, employees can influence
legislative choices whether to establish new public organizations. In
some cases employees can encourage legislatures to provide capital
or loan guarantees for private corporations and obtain public financing or takeovers of private nonprofit organizations.

Further work remains to be done on the analysis. It also appears
likely that it would be worthwhile to extend the analysis to provide a
positive theory of economic planning and comparative economic systems. Equally important are extensions for normative analysis and the
need for hypothesis testing. The following paragraphs briefly touch
on some possible contributions of the positive theory to normative
analysis and on some likely data requirements for empirical work.

A   Some issues on possible contributions of positive theory to normative analysis

Extensions of the positive theory can facilitate the evaluation of normative proposals in three ways. First, a positive theory points out
possibilities that may not otherwise come to attention. For example,

we have seen many possibilities for increasing efficiency by altering responsibility or by establishing arrangements in which employees receive cash for reduced resource diversions. Other examples are reversing many of the effects of employees' investments on suborganization; using overall value responsibility to increase responsiveness within the organization to external economic forces, and to elicit creative and other efforts when employees find them disagreeable; using suborganization as another means to enhance the influence on employees of economic forces determined outside the organization; establishing correct prices of all economically important inputs and outputs when overall value responsibility is imposed; and making suborganization and responsibility encourage competition between employees. Such possibilities can form the basis for normative proposals. We have also seen that an organization's internal efficiency can be increased by the presence of an environment of Schumpeterian competition and by the existence of rapid technological change affecting the production functions for its outputs. Policies that nurture such environments can thus contribute to efficiency within organizations.

The second contribution of positive theory is in the evaluation of the potential cost effectiveness of proposed policies. The most important element in this evaluation is prediction of policies' behavioral effects. Prediction depends not only on the incentives introduced by a new policy but also on how these incentives relate to existing incentives. Consequently, an understanding of existing incentives and their behavioral effects is required.

Finally, positive theory can assist in the evaluation of the implementability of normative proposals. Although there is widespread interest in new management techniques for organizations, decisions about whether to adopt them are not determined by anticipated effects on economic efficiency alone. Individuals within an organization's constituencies, such as its employees or clients, would base support for a managerial change on their perceptions of effects of the change on their own welfare regardless of the effects on efficiency. Thus a management technique that receives support from a constituency may not increase efficiency and, indeed, may decrease it. For instance, if employees under overall value responsibility make investments leading employers to impose specific responsibility instead, efficiency will decrease. As another example, consider a public organization producing an output for which legislative demand exceeds citizens' demand. If recipients of the output could reduce the legislature's cost of the output by providing information that makes it less expensive to impose responsibility on the organization's employees, the resulting increase in output would be at the expense of efficiency. A positive theory permits the predictions about behavior necessary to evaluate the effects on efficiency of proposals made by an organization's employees or clientele. Such a theory also makes it possible to evaluate the incidence of a proposal's costs and benefits among those who can influence whether it will be implemented.

B   Some possible data requirements for hypothesis testing

The specification of models and estimation procedures for testing the hypotheses presented in this book constitute the tasks of numerous separate investigations. It is possible to characterize these hypotheses in two categories that are useful for considering the likely requirements for data to test them. In one category are hypotheses about the responses of employees' uses of resources or supplies of outputs to incentives generated within the organization. In the other category are hypotheses about the organization's resource uses or supplies of its outputs in response to external incentives. In order to test either category of hypothesis, it is necessary to obtain sample observations over which there is variation in the incentives that are hypothesized to influence employees' uses of resources and their supplies of outputs.

Newly created data would be required to test most of the hypotheses in the first category. We have seen that it is typical for organizations not to maintain in their files measures of many of the economically important characteristics of employees' inputs and outputs. Also, organizations do not usually measure or otherwise explicitly characterize how employers place incentives on employees. An added problem is that interpretation of employees' uses of resources may require information about their production domains.

Consider the following somewhat artificial distinction between two types of newly created data. "Engineering" data are generated by the researcher through his direct observation and measurement. For instance, he might measure inputs, outputs, or production possibilities by spending time, perhaps even working, in an organization. "Experimental" data result from employers' deliberately devoting resources to altering divisions of production functions into production domains or altering employers' choices in imposing responsibility according to a research design. Of course, both types of newly created data would be costly, and experimental data would usually be more costly than engineering data.

In a cross-sectional analysis, comparable data on different employees' responses to varying incentives are required for hypothesis testing. Uniqueness of an organization's intermediate and final outputs can make employees' responses to incentives sufficiently atypical that comparison with responsiveness of any other employees would be inappropriate. In such cases, when time series analysis would not be possible, it would be necessary to obtain experimental data. However, we have seen in Chapter 2 that uniqueness of outputs does not necessarily present serious comparability problems; the particular types of uniqueness determine whether this occurs. It may be that many hypotheses could be tested with engineering data by confining hypothesis testing to situations where there is comparability in particular respects. For example, it should be possible to test hypotheses about the effects of alternative applications of specific responsibility on the uses of a fairly broad category of resources by employees producing a range of different outputs.

In contrast, data maintained by organizations as a by-product of ordinary productive activities should suffice for testing most of the second category of hypotheses. Such data include those used for budgeting, accounting, financing, scheduling, delivery, etc., and those reported as required by government or trade associations. When organizations produce diverse outputs, cross-sectional comparisons should nonetheless be possible for testing the hypotheses pertaining to funding limits. Hypotheses about supplies of unique outputs are perhaps testable with time series data. Of course, it can be costly to obtain data in organizations' files.

Table 10.1 provides an overview of possible data requirements for hypothesis testing and is intended only to be suggestive. It seems reasonable to conclude, based on the foregoing discussion, that it would be costly to test many of the theory's hypotheses. Perhaps the resulting contribution to normative analysis would justify some of these costs.

Table 10.1. *Likely types of data needed to test hypotheses*

	Available data	Engi- neering	Experi- mental
Divisions of production functions into production domains; inferences about production possibilities and uniqueness of what is known about production possibilities		X	X
Employees' information cost advantages		X	
Employers' choices in imposing responsibility		X	
Allowable resource diversions		X	
Short-run economic behavior under overall value responsibility and specific responsibility			
Employees' demands for information about production domains and preferences		X	
Implicit prices that guide resource uses		X	X
Employees' total incomes from the organization		X	
Derived input demands		X	X
Efficiency		X	X
Coordination of employees' actions in relation to spillovers		X	X
Short-run response of an employee to managing employee's demand	X	X	
Short-run response of private corporations to demand	X		
Short-run response of nonprofit organizations to incremental donations	X		
Legislative demand as a function of price	X		
Short-run response of public organizations to legislative demand	X		
Employees' investment behavior		X	X
Effects of coordinating employees on resource allocation		X	X
Funding limits for each type of organization	X		
Resource allocation in the first long run			
Effects of employees' investments on fixed and variable costs	X		
The private corporation's price, income, and output	X		
The private nonprofit organization's price, income and output	X		
The public organization's price, income, and output	X		
Resource allocation in the second long run			
Mergers and acquisitions of private corporations		X	
A legislature's choices of type of organization to produce a good or service it demands	X		
Public capital financing of private corporations	X		
Public capital financing of private non-profit organizations	X		

Notes

1 Introduction

1 The interesting concept of organizational "slack" representing the resources necessary to elicit the cooperation of employees to achieve the organization's goals somewhat resembles the concept of an employee's allowable resource diversions. However, the amount of resource diversions that must be allowed to elicit a given amount of an employee's output can be determined by the costs and effectiveness of imposing resource responsibility on him.

2 A theory that contains elements of both the Baumol and Niskanen theories is in Migué and Belangér (1974).

3 Stiglitz (1975) has addressed the issue of authority as a limitation of the Alchian and Demsetz theory. His analysis of conditions leading to authority in organizations is compatible with the analysis of authority in the present theory.

4 Klein et al. refer to this amount as a quasi rent because "even if there were free and open competition for entry to the market, the specialization of the installed asset to a particular user (or more accurately the high costs of making it available to others) creates a quasi rent, but no 'monopoly' rent" (p. 299). Here, the term rent refers both to the Klein et al. case of quasi rent and to monopoly rent where, for example, information costs restrict competition. There are often mixtures of these two cases in organizations. Klein et al. treat rent as an increased asset value rather than a component of a single period's income. For an employee the increased asset value is his present value of his expected streams of cash and (cash-equivalent) in-kind incomes from the organization over the minimum present value income stream that he would accept.

5 Much of this work was directly or indirectly inspired by Lange's (1938) proposals on "trial and error" pricing in the absence of information about preferences and production functions. Stiglitz (1975) has explored how information costs can influence a firm's choices among alternative authority relationships among employees with corresponding implications for incentives. Mirrlees (1976) has analyzed optimal incentive schemes and related authority relationships when employers possess imperfect information about employees' abilities. Marschak's (1976) analysis of optimal incentives explores a bargaining process between an "organizer" and employees and the determination of optimal incentives for both. There are many other important theoretical contributions to the analysis of incentives. Empirical work on the behavioral effects of incentives (which may

257

not be intended) that are implicit in instructions to employees includes that of Blau (1963) and Cohen (1965). Practical issues in establishing a formal "incentive" system along with empirical evidence on the behavioral effects of such systems are described in a publication of the International Labour Office (1951).

2 Definitions and determinants of employees' discretion over an organization's resources and production

1 Schumpeter (1954, pp. 1026–53) provides what is perhaps the most thoughtful general discussion of production functions.

2 An organization's activities could represent selections of inputs and outputs from less than entire production functions as, for example, when a producer outside the organization controls an input that affects one or more of the organization's outputs. Our concern, however, is only with those selections of inputs and outputs that occur within an organization.

3 Chapter 15 in Lerner (1944) is a valuable discussion of indivisibilities. I do not deal with entrepreneurship of an organization's owners as an indivisible resource because owners are not assumed to be actively involved in management. However, employees may analogously be indivisible with respect to their own production domains.

4 If the entrepreneur can start another firm or invest capital to be managed by others, such actions compete with adding to the firm's outputs as means of diversifying risk of his capital. However, it is usually harder (due to nonportable in-kind income) for employees to make investments independently of the organization to diversify their risks regarding investments in their jobs. (See Chapter 7, Section B.) Thus, employees often have larger diversification gains from adding to the organization's outputs.

5 Rosen (1981) has specified production functions with time input for direct supervision of each employee and "the effects of skills that are independent of time inherent in a command system and which apply equally to all workers who are controlled by [a] particular person" (p. 7). The supervisor's time with individual employees reduces this time available for activities that enhance all workers' productivities, thus offsetting this source of increasing returns to supervision.

6 Lawrence and colleagues' (1976) use of the term *task certainty* encompasses not only what is referred to here as external design but also the employer's imposition of specific responsibility. They find that "one problem with the concept of task certainty is that it is very broad and often difficult to apply to a specific task within a subsystem" (p. 213).

7 Differences among organizations in what is known about a production function can result, of course, from differences in factor prices facing them, an assumption that is not made in this discussion. The analysis in later chapters implies that there can be diverse marginal valuations by

different employees of resources having given marginal values to the funding authority.

8 The possible entry of new firms with suborganization that achieves lower costs forces existing firms to adopt the new suborganization.

3 Employees' resource diversions and the imposition of resource responsibility

1 This analysis is not concerned with the effects of incentives on the degree of an employee's commitment to his employer's welfare, a topic dealt with by Leibenstein (1976). Also not dealt with here are inspiration or widely adhered to higher level goals such as in a crisis or a war.

2 In any time period the minimum cash income that an employee will accept varies not only with the non-pecuniary income from his job but also with his present valuation of any options that remaining in the job provide for future employment within or outside the organization. As one example, an employee will often accept less cash income because of the benefits he expects from on-the-job training. As another example, an employee's current job could give the option to hold a future job in which his income would not be taxed to his compensated opportunity cost. This prospective benefit could make him willing to accept a smaller cash income in the present. I assume that when an employer taxes an employee's cash income to his compensated opportunity cost, that both parties expect this practice to continue in the future.

3 Veblen used the term *sabotage* to refer primarily to "manoeuvres of delay, obstruction, friction, and defeat, whether employed by the workmen to enforce their claims, or by the employers to defeat their employees, or by competitive business concerns to get the better of their business rivals or to secure their own advantage" (1921, p. 3). Although the term *resource diversion* encompasses such a definition of employees' sabotage, diversions usually result from employees' continuing modes of operation rather than temporary periods of conflict or negotiation, and can reflect employees' production of undemanded outputs.

4 A complementary discussion of information costs as a source of authority in organizations is provided by Stiglitz (1975). Lindblom (1977) discusses economic roles of authority.

5 I am ignoring possible positive income effects on the employee's supply behavior that could make it worthwhile for an employer to allow an employee's income to exceed his compensated opportunity cost. The analysis of CPOR could readily be extended to include such cases. There is also a variant of CPOR in which the employer pays all employees performing completely identical tasks within the organization the compensated opportunity cost of the marginal employee within this group.

6 Another case adding complexity to the analysis is interdependence of demands for employees' inputs or outputs (see Hirshleifer, 1956, 1957)

which imposes additional information costs for CPOR. There can be interdependence of demands arising from within the organization as well as outside it; internal purchasers can regard different intermediate outputs as substitutes, and the situation where inputs applied within one production domain affect productivity in other production domains can also make demands for intermediate outputs interdependent.

7 Jensen and Meckling (1976) make an analogous point regarding an owner-entrepreneur's optimal trade-off between wealth and consumption of nonpecuniary benefits.

8 The conditions of CPOR, including employees' incomes being adjusted to compensated opportunity costs, must hold in order for Hirshleifer's (1956, 1957) rules for interdivisional charges within a firm to achieve the highest possible level of the firm's net income.

9 Lucas (1979) analyzes the choice originally posed by Alfred Marshall between allotting a worker a share of his output and hiring him as an employee. In the former case the worker receives part of the residual return to capital (land rent in his model) and thus has incentives similar to ownership; in the latter case the employer has what Lucas refers to as "monitoring costs." Hurwicz and Shapiro (1978) analyze alternative formulas for assigning to a worker a share of his output. They find that a 50–50 split maximizes the owner's return in a broad class of cases. All types of responsibility, including CPOR, are alternatives to assigning ownership to employees.

Another apparent shortcut to CPOR is use of the recently developed incentive schemes that would lead employees to reveal information about their production possibilities so that employers can receive benefits of CPOR without bearing costs of imposing it. In Groves' (1973) well-known scheme, employees' bonuses depend on forecast output (or profits) of other employees plus their own output (or profits). In another well-known mechanism described by Weitzman (1976), bonuses depend on employees' choices of output targets and their accuracy in meeting these targets. These incentive systems can elicit information about an employee's production possibilities in the restrictive case where it is not personally costly for him to supply more output to his employer, that is, he derives no utility from resource diversions at the margin. Specifically, these two schemes respectively can provide incentive for employees to yield accurate information about their production possibilities when employers' decisions about input allocations do and do not depend on this information (see Loeb and Magat, 1978; Conn, 1979). However, in the case where employees derive disutility from effort in supplying outputs to employers, Miller and Murrell (1981) prove that there is no incentive scheme that simultaneously leads employees to provide accurate information and results in maximization of the employer's objectives, without the employer having to obtain independent information about employees' production domains and preferences.

The proof can be straightforwardly extended to the general case where employees derive utility from resource diversions at the margin. The authors also show that this result holds when bonuses are treated as costs faced by employers.

10 An employee's personal replacement cost cannot exceed his output replacement cost if he lacks an information cost advantage in a production domain other than his own (e.g., because he has no experience with other production domains). However, if the employee has skills productive in other production domains, his personal replacement cost can exceed his output replacement cost. Both an employee's personal replacement cost and output replacement cost are affected by his experience and specific skills.

11 In principle the employer can imprecisely measure prices, uses of resources, and compensated opportunity costs so that there is a level of resource diversions lower than the output replacement cost or specific responsibility trigger cost limit of IPOR. I do not consider this continuum of intermediate possibilities which offers in some situations the potential of responsibility constraints allowing smaller resource diversions than does overall value responsibility or specific responsibility, at less than prohibitive cost to employers. Hurwicz's (1979) paper explores how information held by an employer can enable him to design incentives that improve his welfare along such a continuum. Many directions for future research are suggested in this paper.

12 The amount that the independent supplier can charge is his total output replacement cost at the point where the buyer's demanded quantity of the output equals the supplier's marginal output replacement cost. Any attempt by the purchaser to pay less than this amount would lead to a diminution of supply until total output replacement cost for that output is reduced to the lower payment; here, the buyer would be worse off by the excess of his demand over marginal output replacement cost for the reduced quantity. (See Chapters 4 and 5.)

13 This assumption is compatible with analyses of employment contracts that are incomplete due to employers' lack of information about employees' individual abilities and efforts. See, for example, Miyazaki (1977) and Rothschild and Stiglitz (1976). Prescott and Visscher (1980) analyze how a firm's choice of its growth rate is interrelated with the costs and effectiveness of devoting time and resources to screening workers for assigned tasks.

14 Harris and Raviv (1978), Holmström (1979), Shavell (1979), and Ross (1973) have analyzed how different attitudes towards risk, as well as employees' information cost advantages, and their disutility of effort, affect the design of Pareto optimal contracts between employer and employee. In these analyses the consideration of social welfare is restricted to the welfare of the "principal" and the "agent," although that of others often changes. Choices of constraints can reduce employers'

costs of employees' outputs throughout the organization which increases the welfare of the organization's clientele and its funding authority. Although these welfare gains are often larger than enough to compensate employees for their losses, such compensation usually does not take place, resulting in Kaldor-Hicks efficiency gains. Once responsibility constraints are in place, however, there can be exchanges between employers and employees that achieve Pareto efficiency gains. For example, the restriction of in-kind benefits from resource diversions opens up opportunities for exchanges where the employee reduces diversions in return for the employer permitting access to resources that yield the employee more utility. But the costs of making such agreements and ensuring that they are honored can inhibit them. Other possibilities for Pareto efficiency gains require employees to disclose information about production possibilities that might occur only when collective bargaining or other concerted enforcement by other employees is assured. In regard to Pareto optimal agreements between employer and employee based on their preferences toward risk, another issue arises in addition to costs of effecting and enforcing agreements. Many short-term risks that are clearly not attributable to the current period performance of either party, for example, those related to market demands, technological changes outside the organization, and the state of nature, may be most efficiently diversified by being absorbed over broad categories of employees or even at the level of the entire organization when there are multiple, independent risks for different parts of the organization.

15 For example, the cost of monitoring or measurement for specific responsibility and the cost of determining output replacement cost for overall value responsibility often vary with suborganization. In selecting among alternative suborganizations, employers take these costs into account. (See Chapter 7.)

16 This section has benefited much from suggestions made by Thomas P. Chester.

17 Excellent discussions of stochastic dominance are provided in a book edited by Whitmore and Findlay (1978); see especially the chapter by Fishburn and Vickson therein. The proofs in Hanoch and Levy (1969) are particularly relevant to the present discussion.

18 This is first-degree stochastic dominance, which is taken as the employer's criterion. Under higher degree stochastic dominance, a preferred CDF can be above another for some values of cash benefits.

19 If the employee's activities influence productivity elsewhere within the organization, this spillover can be treated by his employer as a separate output, and the employer might impose a different type of responsibility vis-à-vis this output.

20 Imposing specific responsibility can facilitate the employer's attribution to employees of the inputs they use.

4 Short-run resource allocation under fixed budgets

1 If the employer's best alternative is to obtain a substitute for Q_1 or Q_2, he would for each quantity of Q_1 or Q_2 select an amount of the substitute such that his combined cost of it and of any adjustments of resource uses to be equally well off using it is minimized. The curve *ef* would then have a counterpart where for each amount of Q_1 or Q_2 that the employee might supply there is an equivalent quantity of the substitute that the employer could obtain as his best alternative. The employer's costs of adjusting resource uses for each unit of the substitute would be subtracted from the sum of resources underlying this curve.

2 These terms of Buchanan and Stubblebine (1962) are applied to internal technological spillovers as follows. Consider two employees who apply inputs within separate production domains. A spillover is inframarginal or marginal depending on whether the application of inputs within one production domain affects productivity within the other inframarginally or at the margin. Potentially relevant, as opposed to irrelevant, spillovers occur when an employee would be willing to devote some resources to influence the other's behavior. A spillover is Pareto relevant when the two employees could reach an agreement about it that makes one better off without making the other worse off. In addition to payoffs to other employees, resources allocated to information and negotiation are included within employees' costs of coordinating spillovers.

3 Davis and Whinston (1962) distinguish between separable and nonseparable externalities among firms' cost functions where the output of one firm enters the cost function for another. The distinction between separable and nonseparable spillovers in the present analysis is based on production functions. A separable spillover is present when the output of one production domain affects the output of another additively, and thus does not affect the marginal productivity of any of its inputs. A nonseparable spillover is present when the output of one production domain affects the marginal productivity of one or more inputs applied within another. When spillovers directly result from variation in inputs within a production domain, they are analogously placed in separable and nonseparable categories.

4 This is one reason for employers to issue directives with instructions instead of using price incentives such as those of a Davis–Whinston scheme to deal with spillovers. However, price incentives can be designed to deal with inframarginal spillovers by basing prices in part on measures of the joint productivity of the two employees.

   Employees can coordinate their actions in relation to spillovers in a manner that effectively merges their production domains. (See Chapter 7.)

5 If the employees were to report to different managing employees and CPOR were imposed throughout the organization, the prices would be

somewhat different. Managing employees would be required to establish prices that in turn would lead their employees to coordinate actions in such a manner as to maximize the net income of the nearest employer to whom the managing employees commonly report, directly or indirectly.

Hurwicz (1969) demonstrates an alternative to the Davis–Whinston scheme that could be used to coordinate employees' actions in relation to Pareto relevant spillovers. This mechanism could have lower information costs and would not require the employer to be involved in communication among employees. However, the employer would have to obtain detailed information about preferences and production domains under this scheme – as he would under the Davis–Whinston scheme – to ensure that the employees maximize their net incomes.

6 Following Radner (1961) one could evaluate an organization's "information structure" by specifying the information that each employee obtains, corresponding to different values of the organization's production functions, the demands for the organization's outputs and the supplies of its inputs, and the responsibility imposed within it. The organization's information structure would thus be behaviorally determined by the incentives individually facing employees in these situations. Changes in the type and variant of responsibility placed on each employee cause each employee's and the funding authority's net incomes to vary, often in opposite directions, while also influencing employee's choices in obtaining information. It is interesting to consider the optimization problem, where one specifies the value of the information structure in terms of its contribution to the funding authority's net income. In this problem, one could determine the choices of imposed resource responsibility that maximize the expected value of the funding authority's net income and then examine the content of the corresponding information structure. The costs of imposing CPOR would usually prevent this type of responsibility from achieving the maximum. Because of spillovers and the incentives inherent in resource responsibility constraints, the optimal information structure would include specific communications among employees about each other's production domains and preferences.

5 Short-run resource allocation in response to demand

1 When the employer imposes overall value responsibility based on output replacement cost, it is possible that at each rate of the employee's output the employer's total variable cost (his variable responsibility costs plus the variable component of the employer's cost of acquiring the output or an amount of a substitute and adjusting resource uses so as to be equally well off with it) is lower than the employee's total variable cost of his output. If so, the employer's fixed costs sufficiently exceed the employee's to make his combined fixed and variable costs at the expected level of demand exceed the employee's total fixed and variable costs. Thus, a large enough increase in the employer's demand would result in the employee's output

being replaced. Such a situation might occur, for example, when employees are working with obsolete equipment. In contrast, the employer's fixed costs can be lower than his employee's. In this case, it is expected that the employer's demand will remain high enough that the employee's lower variable costs are offsetting.

2 An employer's transition cost to replace an employee's output can vary with his demand for this output; demand affects his opportunity cost of any interruption in availability of the employee's output during the transition period of replacing it or switching to specific responsibility.

3 When some of the employee's inputs are not attributed to him, the equilibrium rate of his output is higher except when he is under overall value responsibility based on output replacement and these inputs are attributed to alternative suppliers. In extreme cases, unattributed inputs can make the employer's known cost of the employee's output lower than what his true cost (excluding responsibility costs) would be under CPOR.

4 While the prices that maximize profits depend on demand, the top managing employees held accountable for profits need not have information about demand or think consciously about it, as pointed out by Machlup in his (1946, 1947) criticism of questionnaire evidence such as that of Hall and Hitch (1939); they can achieve profit goals by experimenting with prices and rates of output.

5 See Table 2, p. 400, of Leibenstein (1966).

6 As noted in this chapter and analyzed in Chapter 7, the more decentralized the discretion over choices about rates of the organization's intermediate and final outputs, the larger the rates of these outputs when benefits from resource diversions increase with them; some of the managerial improvements noted by Leibenstein (1966) could have made decision making more decentralized.

7 Weisbrod (1977) analyzes conditions under which a public good would not be governmentally provided. He emphasizes the median voter model, but his analysis straightforwardly applies to the marginal interest-group voter model of Chapter 6. This section has very much benefited from Weisbrod's work.

8 Weisbrod's (1980) paper develops a measure of the publicness of private nonprofit organizations' outputs.

9 This discussion does not take account of tax incentives on the donor or the intertemporal considerations that lead him to make donations for the organization's capital.

6 Legislative demand and short-run price and output of the public organization

1 Riker and Ordeshook (1973) point out that formal proofs are lacking in many cases. In these cases, conjectures based on formal proofs for closely related cases are made. Hinich (1977) also shows that when votes

are probabilistically a function of voter preferences there is no median voter equilibrium.

2 In Riker and Ordeshook's words, "It is easily verified now that a successful coalition-of-minorities strategy exists whenever an equilibrium under majority rule fails to exist. First, recall the correspondence between equilibrium spatial strategies and the core of an n-person game. Specifically, if an equilibrium strategy exists, the corresponding n-person game has a core; and if an equilibrium strategy does not exist, the game has no core. Second, if a game does not have a core, a majority coalition of players (citizens) cannot be found that is stable against all other coalitions. Hence, if an equilibrium spatial strategy does not exist, a candidate can propose or advocate some package of policies (i.e., an imputation) that forms a coalition of citizens that defeats (dominates) the imputation of his opponent's coalition" (p. 344).

3 However, such benefits can be provided in the absence of information costs when distributions of voters' most preferred policies are multimodal and some citizens abstain from voting because of distance of candidates' positions from their own most preferred ones. See Mueller (1976, p. 409) and the references he mentions on this point.

4 Tullock (1967, chap. 10) proposes a proportional representation system that is not dependent on districts. Under this system, a legislator's votes within the legislature are weighted by the number of votes he receives as a candidate. The behavior of such a legislature differs substantially from one with geographic representation and equal votes for legislators. In Tullock's words, "The voting on each individual measure would come as close to a national referendum as any representative body can achieve" (p. 145). Existing proportional representation legislatures may be regarded on a continuum from a district representation legislature analyzed in this chapter to Tullock's proposal.

5 A candidate's vote plurality comes at the expense of his benefits from resource diversions, and thus his tendency to minimize his plurality has a certain resemblance to Riker's (1962) analysis where the winners in a zero sum game under majority rule are better off the larger the minority. In the analysis presented here, when a candidate prefers at the margin incremental resource diversions to an increase in his election probability, he reduces his commitments of benefits to constituents. Fiorina (1974) posits that a candidate is a "maintainer" through seeking a given probability of election. "Maintaining" behavior is consistent with a candidate's adhering to a given acceptable probability of election and letting his expected resource diversions vary accordingly, i.e., inversely with his opponent's attractiveness to voters.

6 The prospect of promised benefits not being provided can lead voters to specify alternative outcomes that can result from support of a given candidate and attach probabilities to them. This refinement is discussed in Chapter 3 of Riker and Ordeshook (1973).

7 Under certain conditions, no single combination of issues receives a larger vote than any other and endlessly repeated voting or "cycling" can result. (A good discussion of cycling is provided in Chapters 2 and 3 of Tullock, 1967). Coordinating legislators not only economize on negotiation and information costs but also prevent cycling.

8 For example, this proposition suggests that the U.S. Senate tends to distribute economic benefits equally among states, while the U.S. House of Representatives tends to distribute economic benefits among states proportionally to their populations. When individual legislators include in their utility maximizing platforms benefits from the same public goods in other legislators' platforms or include public or private goods subject to economies of scale in production, coordinating legislators have an incentive to take advantage of these choices as economies to the legislature as a whole. Because such benefits do not influence the value of individual legislators' votes, they do not affect the distribution among legislators of influence over legislative spending.

9 Different types of taxes differentially affect voter groups and individual legislators' constituencies. The legislature's choices among alternative types of taxes, deficits, debt accrual, and "off-budget" financing can be analyzed in the same manner as its spending choices.

10 Economists have provided estimates of legislative demand functions that are derived from the "median voter model." However, these studies (see, for example, the pioneering studies of Bergstrom and Goodman, 1973; Borcherding and Deacon, 1972) do not provide empirical tests of the median voter model against any competing hypothesis about legislative behavior. The variables entered into estimating equations intended to reflect the preferences of the median voter are in fact aggregative proxies for socioeconomic characteristics such as per capita income, which could pertain to many voters or voter categories. In contrast, the economic costs and benefits of legislative outcomes to marginal interest group voters are, in principle, observable. The separate behavior of legislatures demanding outputs, on the one hand, and of the organizations providing them, on the other, should be specified in a structural model. The behavior of organizations is addressed theoretically in Borcherding and Deacon, where it is in effect hypothesized that public organizations provide outputs at marginal cost under CPOR.

11 When benefits from resource diversions contribute to a legislator's marginal utility from goods or services demanded by the legislature, the ratios of marginal election probabilities to price need not be equal. Thus the explanation of how election probabilities influence legislative demand is made somewhat awkward. However, in this case, the influence of election probabilities on legislative demand is essentially unchanged; legislators have the same interest in allocating the benefits they provide to constituents according to their effects on election probabilities.

12 Citizens' vote responses can lead a legislature to spend part of the addi-

tional funds that result from a lower price of a good or service on providing resources to citizens that they regard as substitutes for this good or service. As a result, there could be a large enough decrease in votes based on the good or service with the lower price that the legislature actually demands a smaller quantity of it, providing an analogy of the Giffen paradox. An example might be a lower cost of providing inner city urban housing leading to larger subsidies for freeways and other urban transportation that shift citizens' housing demands (and vote responses to subsidies) to the suburbs.

13 A legislature can provide future benefits with current funding, such as when it provides currently financed capital facilities. This is especially likely to occur when suppliers of legislatively financed capital goods (e.g. building trades) form voting blocs.

14 In the present analysis, the size of government and the effects of legislative spending and taxation on aggregate income distributions are determined by (1) the cumulative effects of the optimal choices of marginal voters in interest groups with respect to their own directly received gains from the legislature; (2) equilibrium behavior of individual legislators and the legislature as a whole; (3) the behavior of the organizations supplying legislative demands; and (4) the constraints on legislative spending mentioned below. An alternative approach in which the size of government and its aggregate effect on the income distribution are the results of direct choices about these variables is provided by Meltzer and Richard (1981).

15 This discussion is simplified by assuming that votes based on employees' and external suppliers' rents affect only the legislature's demand for the organization's output. This can occur, for example, when employees and suppliers achieve economies by joining lobbying forces with the recipients of the organization's output. In contrast, if employees and suppliers also act independently (as assumed in the long-run analysis), they may receive additional funding for the organization or directly for themselves beyond the legislature's minimum cost of eliciting its desired rate of the public organization's output. In this case the amount of the additional funding is limited to an amount that is competitive with other vote yielding legislative expenditures.

7 Employees' investment behavior and implications for suborganization

1 The effect of one investment on another's returns could be accounted for by showing the return for multiple investments taken together. There can be jointness between employer- and employee-initiated investments, as well as between different investments of either party.

2 Without this assumption it would be necessary to show a separate minimum return for each investment.

3 The minimum return is a necessary but not a sufficient condition for an investment to take place. Sufficient conditions depend on the size of the budget for investments and sizes of investments when these vary. Alternative criteria such as benefit-cost ratios or differences between benefits and costs can produce inconsistent rankings of investment projects. However, if he has an estimate of each investment's present value costs and benefits to him, an employee with a given set of feasible projects and a given investment budget can select the particular combination of investments that maximizes his own expected cash-equivalent net income.

4 One might expect that employees exert substantial influence on employers' cost-benefit calculations of technology adoptions when production domains are internally designed. An important empirical study of determinants of costs of technology transfers is provided by Teece (1977). The costs considered are measured corporate expenses of particular technology transfers, including the costs of analyzing concepts underlying new technology, the engineering and research and development (R&D) costs, and the costs of training personnel. Employees should be able to affect these costs within the limits imposed by responsibility on the amounts and potential uses of their resource diversions. Teece estimated the influences of seven variables on transfer cost as a fraction of total project cost. A dummy variable controlling for whether there were no previous applications of the same technology by the transferer could control for the absence of external design, and a variable for the number of other firms utilizing a similar technology perhaps reflects the presence of external design. Another two variables, age of the technology and manufacturing experience of the firm, might act as crude proxies for external design. Other variables include the ratio of research and development to sales for the recipient firm, the size of the recipient firm measured by sales, and the per-capita gross national product (GNP) of the country of the recipient.

The author had only 26 observations on firms in three industry categories adopting new techniques. The sign of the estimated coefficients of the two variables interpreted to control for external design and of the two variables that might proxy for external design support the proposition that external design reduces transfer costs. In most cases these coefficients are statistically significant at the 0.10 level for a one-tailed test (see equations in Teece, 1977, Table 3, p. 252). According to the theory presented here, the most important omitted variable is a measure of the benefit or loss to employees who are directly affected by the adopted technology; this variable would control for their behavior in reducing or enhancing the transfer costs. The more externally designed the project, however, the smaller this influence. The insignificant or ambivalent results in Teece's equations for a firm's size or R&D budget are also of interest; perhaps these variables are not as important as external versus internal design and employees' benefits or losses. Future research on technology transfer should analyze these transfers as part of general resource substitution behavior within organizations and take account of when substitutions are and are not dominated by employees.

5 Stiglitz (1975) provides cases where the delegation of authority results in lower production costs because information cost advantages are more effectively utilized.

6 The analysis can be extended to the case where multiple employees voluntarily cooperate to obtain authority over themselves as a means of coordinating their actions.

7 The discussion in Section E has greatly benefited from Caves's (1980) excellent survey article.

8 Multidivisional suborganization is consistent with some amount of what has been termed "matrix" organization (see Davis and Lawrence, 1977) in which separate divisions produce intermediate outputs for other divisions. In the most common case under multidivisional suborganization, the central office provides information to the divisions.

9 By encouraging clients to influence legislative demand, employees make the "voice" option suggested by Hirschman (1970) more frequently exercised. An evaluation of the economic desirability of this option in comparison with that of the "exit" option should take into account: (1) the relationship between the resulting increases in legislative demand and the citizens' demand for the goods and services involved; and (2) the appropriateness of the types of supplying organizations under these two options (see Chapter 9), and the resource diversions within them.

8 Equilibrium behavior of public and private organizations in the first long run

1 The particular form of this relationship depends on the composition of the corporation's invested capital, its new investment opportunities, and stockholders' information costs.

2 Employees' responsiveness to the funding limit can be a function of the history of the demand for the corporation's output. For example, there may be an upward shift of demand and a subsequent unanticipated shift back to its original level. If investments are mistakenly made in response to the temporary higher demand, employees' desires for investment will remain lower than if demand had never increased until the new investments are depreciated.

3 Managing employees' responsibility costs can be allocated between resource diversions and the funding authority's responsibility costs, depending on the interests the responsibility serves.

4 A legislature's choice whether to establish a new public organization or place an additional demand on an existing public or private organization is analyzed in Chapter 9.

9 The demand and supply of nonmarket resource allocation

1 Goldberg (1974) suggests that these laws may be endogenous. For example, employees of organizations might base their votes on obtaining laws that do not prevent or even facilitate mergers that benefit them. See also Coase (1974) on Goldberg's article.

2 Mueller (1969), Steiner (1975), and others make the identical point.

3 Data on profitability before and after a combination, such as those used by Gort and Hogarty (1970), have limited value in explaining the motivation for the combination because they do not show employees' costs and benefits.

4 Steiner analyzes the separate components of these stock values.

5 In their evaluation of the U.S. Government's experience with Planning-Programming-Budgeting Systems, Merewitz and Sosnick (1971) describe the difficulties in using object-of-expenditure data to infer programmatic costs and explain the tasks required to measure the latter costs when individual outputs of public organizations are not separately funded.

6 The analytical contributions of Brennan and Buchanan (1980) and Frohlich et al. (1971) are important steps in the direction of such a theory.

7 These writings are interpreted by Hurwicz (1960a) within a precise definition of informational decentralization.

8 Krueger's (1974) classic article provides evidence on the behavioral effects of international trade restrictions.

9 Schweitzer (1977) provides an example: "Selection of the pricing *formula* was an act of public power in which the technical details came from tax accountants and efficiency engineers, but the power of price fixing was a prerogative of the leader's agents, while ultimate power of implementation rested with the *Gestapo*" (p. 103).

References

Alchian, Armen A., and Demsetz, Harold. 1972. "Production, Information Costs, and Economic Organization," *American Economic Review*, 62(December): 777–95.

Allardt, Erik, and Rokkan, Stein, eds. 1970. *Mass Politics: Studies in Political Sociology*. New York: Free Press.

Arrow, Kenneth J. 1975. "Vertical Integration and Communication," *Bell Journal of Economics*, 6(Spring): 173–83.

Arrow, Kenneth J., Karlin, S., and Suppes, P., eds. 1960. *Mathematical Methods in the Social Sciences, 1959*. Stanford, Cal.: Stanford University Press.

Baumol, William J. 1959. *Business Behavior, Value and Growth*. New York: Macmillan.

Baumol, William J., and Fabian, Tibor. 1964. "Decomposition, Pricing for Decentralization and External Economies," *Management Science*, 11 (September): 1–32.

Berg, Ivar. 1963. "Some Unlikely Sources of Initiative and Creativity," in *Individualism and Big Business*, ed. Leonard R. Sayles, pp. 35–46. New York: Wiley.

Bergstrom, Theodore C., and Goodman, Robert P. 1973. "Private Demands for Public Goods," *American Economic Review*, 63(June): 280–96.

Berliner, Joseph S. 1957. *Factory and Manager in the USSR*. Cambridge, Mass.: Harvard University Press.

Blau, Peter M. 1963. *The Dynamics of Bureaucracy: A Study of Interpersonal Relations in Two Government Agencies*. Chicago: University of Chicago Press, 2nd ed.

Blauner, Robert. 1964. *Alienation and Freedom: The Factory Worker and His Industry*. Chicago: University of Chicago Press.

Borcherding, Thomas E., and Deacon, Robert T. 1972. "The Demand for the Services of Non-Federal Governments," *American Economic Review*, 62(December): 891–901.

Bornstein, Morris, ed. 1965. *Comparative Economic Systems: Models and Cases*. Homewood, Ill.: Irwin.

Bower, Joseph L. 1970. *Managing the Resource Allocation Process: A Study of Corporate Planning and Investment*. Boston: Division of Research, Graduate School of Business Administration, Harvard University.

Brennan, Geoffrey, and Buchanan, James M. 1980. *The Power To Tax: Ana-*

lytical Foundations of a Fiscal Constitution. Cambridge: Cambridge University Press.

Breton, Albert, and Wintrobe, Ronald. 1975. "The Equilibrium Size of a Budget-maximizing Bureau: A Note on Niskanen's Theory of Bureaucracy," *Journal of Political Economy*, 83(February): 195–207.

Buchanan, James M., and Stubblebine, William Craig. 1962. "Externality," *Economica*, 29(November): 371–84.

Burns, Tom, and Stalker, G.M. 1961. *The Management of Innovation*. London: Tavistock.

Caves, Richard E. 1980. "Corporate Strategy and Structure," *Journal of Economic Literature*, 18(March): 64–92.

Chandler, Alfred D., Jr. 1962. *Strategy and Structure: Chapters in the History of the Industrial Enterprise*. Cambridge, Mass.: MIT Press.

Clarkson, Kenneth W., and Martin, Donald L., eds. 1980. *The Economics of Nonproprietary Organizations*. Greenwich, Conn.: JAI Press.

Clausen, Aage. 1973. *How Congressmen Decide: A Policy Focus*. New York: St. Martin's Press.

Coase, Ronald H. 1937. "The Nature of the Firm," *Economica* [N.S.], 4(November): 386–405.

1974. "The Choice of the Institutional Framework: A Comment," *Journal of Law and Economics*, 17(October): 493–6.

Cohen, Harry. 1965. *The Demonics of Bureaucracy, Problems of Change in a Government Agency*. Ames, Iowa: The Iowa State University Press.

Conn, David. 1979. "A Comparison of Alternative Incentive Structures for Centrally Planned Economic Systems," *Journal of Comparative Economics*, 3(September): 261–76.

Cyert, Richard M., and March, James G. 1963. *A Behavioral Theory of the Firm*. Englewood Cliffs, N.J.: Prentice Hall.

Dantzig, George B. 1963. *Linear Programming and Extensions*. Princeton: Princeton University Press.

Dantzig, George B., and Wolfe, Philip. 1960. "Decomposition Principle for Linear Programs," *Operations Research*, 8(January– February): 101–11.

Davis, Otto A., and Whinston, Andrew. 1962. "Externalities, Welfare, and the Theory of Games," *Journal of Political Economy*, 70(June): 241–62.

1966. "On Externalities, Information and the Government-Assisted Invisible Hand," *Economica*, 33(August): 303–18.

Davis, Stanley M., and Lawrence, Paul R. 1977. *Matrix*. Reading: Addison-Wesley.

Downs, Anthony. 1957. *An Economic Theory of Democracy*. New York: Harper & Row.

1967. *Inside Bureaucracy*. Boston: Little, Brown.

Drucker, Peter F. 1974. *Management: Tasks, Responsibilities, Practices*. New York: Harper & Row.

Fama, Eugene F. 1980. "Agency Problems and the Theory of the Firm," *Journal of Political Economy*, 88(April): 288–307.

Farney, Dennis. 1979. "House Panel Chairmen, Their Powers Reduced, Use Guile, Persuasion," *Wall Street Journal*, May 3, Eastern Ed., p. 1, col. 1.

Fiorina, Morris P. 1974. *Representatives, Roll Calls, and Constituencies*. Lexington, Mass.: D. C. Heath.

Fishburn, Peter C., and Vickson, Raymond G. 1978. "Theoretical Foundations of Stochastic Dominance," in *Stochastic Dominance: An Approach to Decision-Making Under Risk*, ed. G. A. Whitmore and M. Chapman Findlay, pp. 39–113. Lexington, Mass.: D. C. Heath.

Frohlich, Norman, Oppenheimer, Joe A., and Young, Oran R. 1971. *Political Leadership and Collective Goods*. Princeton: Princeton University Press.

Garson, Barbara. 1979. "Women's Work: Some Lousy Offices to Work In, and One Good One," in *Life in Organizations: Workplaces As People Experience Them*, ed. Rosabeth Moss Kanter and Barry A. Stein, pp. 225–39. New York: Basic Books.

Goldberg, Victor P. 1974. "Institutional Change and the Quasi-Invisible Hand," *Journal of Law and Economics*, 17(October): 461– 92.

Gort, Michael, and Hogarty, Thomas. 1970. "New Evidence on Mergers," *Journal of Law and Economics*, 13(April): 167–84.

Gouldner, Alvin. 1954. *Patterns of Industrial Bureaucracy*. Glencoe, Illinois: Free Press.

Gross, Bertram M. 1964. *Organizations and Their Managing*. New York: Free Press.

Grossman, Gregory, ed. 1960. *Value and Plan: Economic Calculation and Organization in Eastern Europe*. Berkeley: University of California Press.

Groves, Theodore. 1973. "Incentives in Teams," *Econometrica*, 41(July): 617–31.

Hall, Robert L., and Hitch, Charles J. 1939. "Price Theory and Business Behavior," *Oxford Economic Papers*, 2(May): 12–45.

Hanoch, G., and Levy, H. 1969. "The Efficiency Analysis of Choices Involving Risk," *Review of Economic Studies*, 36(July): 335–46.

Harris, Milton, and Raviv, Artur. 1978. "Some Results on Incentive Contracts with Applications to Education and Employment, Health Insurance, and Law Enforcement," *American Economic Review*, 68(March): 20–30.

Hayek, Friedrich A. 1965 [1940]. "Socialist Calculation: The Competitive 'Solution,' " in *Comparative Economic Systems: Models and Cases*, ed. Morris Bornstein, pp. 95–115. Homewood, Ill.: Irwin.

Hinich, Melvin J. 1977. "Equilibrium in Spatial Voting: The Median Voter Result Is an Artifact," *Journal of Economic Theory*, 16(December): 208–19.

Hirschman, Albert O. 1970. *Exit, Voice, and Loyalty: Responses to Decline in Firms, Organizations, and States*. Cambridge, Mass.: Harvard University Press.

Hirshleifer, Jack. 1956. "On the Economics of Transfer Pricing," *Journal of Business*, 29(July): 172–84.

1957. "Economics of the Divisionalized Firm," *Journal of Business*, 30(April): 96–108.

Holmström, Bengt. 1979. "Moral Hazard and Observability," *Bell Journal of Economics*, 10(Spring): 74–91.

Hurwicz, Leonid. 1960a. "Conditions for Economic Efficiency of Centralized and Decentralized Structures," in *Value and Plan: Economic Calculation and Organization in Eastern Europe*, ed. Gregory Grossman, pp. 162–83. Berkeley: University of California Press.

1960b. "Optimality and Informational Efficiency in Resource Allocation Processes," in *Mathematical Methods in the Social Sciences, 1959*, ed. Kenneth J. Arrow, S. Karlin, and P. Suppes, pp. 3–15. Stanford, Cal.: Stanford University Press.

1969. "Centralization and Decentralization in Economic Systems: On the Concept and Possibility of Informational Decentralization," *American Economic Review*, 59(May): 513–24.

1972. "On Informationally Decentralized Systems," in *Decision and Organization*, ed. C.B. McGuire and Roy Radner, pp. 297–336. New York: Elsevier North-Holland.

1979. "On the Interaction Between Information and Incentives in Organizations," in *Communication and Control in Society*, ed. K. Krippendorff, pp. 123–47. New York: Gordon and Breach Science Publishers.

Hurwicz, Leonid, and Shapiro, Leonard. 1978. "Incentive Structures Maximizing Residual Gain Under Incomplete Information," *Bell Journal of Economics*, 9(Spring): 180–91.

International Labour Office. 1951. *Payment by Results*. International Labour Office Studies and Reports, New Series, No. 27.

Jackson, John E. 1967. "Some Indirect Evidences of Constituency Pressures on Senators," *Public Policy*, 16(Spring): 253–70.

1971. "Statistical Models of Senate Roll Call Voting," *American Political Science Review*, 65(June): 451–70.

Jensen, Michael C., and Meckling, William H. 1976. "Theory of the Firm: Managerial Behavior, Agency Costs and Ownership Structure," *Journal of Financial Economics*, 3(October): 305–60.

Kanter, Rosabeth Moss, and Stein, Barry A., eds. 1979. *Life in Organizations: Workplaces As People Experience Them*. New York: Basic Books.

Keefe, William J., and Ogul, Morris S. 1968. *The American Legislative Process: Congress and the States*. Englewood Cliffs, N.J.: Prentice Hall, 2nd ed.

Kessel, John. 1964. "The Washington Congressional Delegation," *Midwest Journal of Political Science*, 8(February): 1–21.

Klein, Benjamin, Crawford, Robert G., and Alchian, Armen A. 1978. "Vertical Integration, Appropriable Rents, and the Competitive Contracting Process," *Journal of Law and Economics*, 21(October): 297–326.

Krippendorff, K., ed. 1979. *Communication and Control in Society*. New York: Gordon and Breach Science Publishers.

Krueger, Anne O. 1974. "The Political Economy of the Rent-Seeking Society," *American Economic Review*, 64(June): 291–303.

Lange, Oskar. 1965 [1938]. "On the Economic Theory of Socialism," in *On the Economic Theory of Socialism*, ed. Benjamin E. Lippincott, pp. 57–129. New York: McGraw-Hill.

Lawrence, Paul R., Barnes, Louis B., and Lorsch, Jay W. 1976. *Organizational Behavior and Administration: Cases and Readings*. Homewood, Ill.: Irwin, 3rd ed.

Lawrence, Paul R., and Lorsch, Jay W. 1967. *Organization and Environment: Managing Differentiation and Integration*. Boston: Division of Research, Graduate School of Business Administration, Harvard University.

Leibenstein, Harvey. 1966. "Allocative Efficiency vs. 'X-Efficiency,' " *American Economic Review*, 56 (June): 392–415.

    1975. "Aspects of the X-Efficiency Theory of the Firm," *Bell Journal of Economics*, 6(Autumn): 580–606.

    1976. *Beyond Economic Man: A New Foundation for Microeconomics*. Cambridge, Mass.: Harvard University Press.

    1979. "A Branch of Economics is Missing: Micro-Micro Theory," *Journal of Economic Literature*, 17(June): 477–502.

Lerner, Abba P. 1944. *The Economics of Control: Principles of Welfare Economics*. New York: Macmillan.

Lester, Richard A. 1946. "Shortcomings of Marginal Analysis for Wage Employment Problems," *American Economic Review*, 36(March): 63–82.

Lindblom, Charles E. 1977. *Politics and Markets: The World's Political-Economic Systems*. New York: Basic Books.

Lippincott, Benjamin E., ed. 1965 [1938]. *On the Economic Theory of Socialism*. New York: McGraw-Hill.

Loeb, Martin, and Magat, Wesley A. 1978. "Success Indicators in the Soviet Union: The Problem of Incentives and Efficient Allocations," *American Economic Review*, 68(March): 173–81.

Lorsch, Jay W. 1965. *Product Innovation and Organization*. New York: Macmillan.

Lorsch, Jay W., and Allen, Stephen A., III. 1973. *Managing Diversity and Interdependence: An Organizational Study of Multidivisional Firms*. Boston: Division of Research, Graduate School of Business Administration, Harvard University.

Lucas, Robert E.B. 1979. "Sharing, Monitoring, and Incentives: Marshallian Misallocation Reassessed," *Journal of Political Economy*, 87(June): 501–21.

McGuire, C.B., and Radner, Roy, eds. 1972. *Decision and Organization*. New York: Elsevier North-Holland.

Machlup, Fritz. 1946. "Marginal Analysis and Empirical Research," *American Economic Review*, 36(September): 519–54.

    1947. "Rejoinder to an Antimarginalist," *American Economic Review*, 37(March): 148–54.

MacRae, Duncan, Jr. 1952. "The Relation Between Roll Call Votes and Constituencies in the Massachusetts House of Representatives," *American Political Science Review*, 46(December): 1046–55. 1958. *Dimensions of Congressional Voting, A Statistical Study of the House of Representatives in the Eighty-first Congress*. Berkeley: University of California Press.

Marris, Robin. 1964. *The Economic Theory of Managerial Capitalism*. London: Macmillan.

1971. "An Introduction to Theories of Corporate Growth," in *The Corporate Economy: Growth, Competition and Innovative Potential*, ed. Robin Marris and Adrian Wood, pp. 1–36. Cambridge, Mass.: Harvard University Press.

Marris, Robin, and Mueller, Dennis C. 1980. "The Corporation, Competition, and the Invisible Hand," *Journal of Economic Literature*, 18(March): 32–63.

Marris, Robin, and Wood, Adrian, eds. 1971. *The Corporate Economy: Growth, Competition and Innovative Potential*. Cambridge, Mass.: Harvard University Press.

Marschak, Jacob. 1976. *Optimal Incentives in an Organization*. Working Paper No. 256, Los Angeles: Western Management Science Institute, University of California, October.

Marshall, Alfred. 1920. *Principles of Economics*. New York: Macmillan, 8th ed.

Meltzer, Allan H., and Richard, Scott F. 1981. "A Rational Theory of the Size of Government," *Journal of Political Economy*, 89(October): 914–27.

Merewitz, Leonard, and Sosnick, Stephen H. 1971. *The Budget's New Clothes: A Critique of Planning-Programming-Budgeting and Benefit-Cost Analysis*. Chicago: Markham Publishing Co.

Migué, Jean-Luc, and Bélanger, Gérard. 1974. "Toward a General Theory of Managerial Discretion," *Public Choice*, 17(Spring): 27–43.

Miller, Jeffrey, and Murrell, Peter. 1981. "Limitations on the Use of Information–Revealing Incentive Schemes in Economic Organizations," *Journal of Comparative Economics*, 5(September): 251–71.

Miller, Warren E. 1970. "Majority Rule and the Representative System of Government," in *Mass Politics: Studies in Political Sociology*, ed. Erik Allardt and Stein Rokkan, pp. 284–311. New York: Free Press.

Miller, Warren E., and Stokes, Donald E. 1969 [1963]. "Constituency Influence in Congress," in *New Perspectives on the House of Representatives*, ed. Robert L. Peabody and Nelson W. Polsby, pp. 31–53. Chicago: Rand McNally.

Mirrlees, James A. 1976. "The Optimal Structure of Incentives and Authority within an Organization," *Bell Journal of Economics*, 7(Spring): 105–31.

Miyazaki, Hajime. 1977. "The Rat Race and Internal Labor Markets," *Bell Journal of Economics*, 8(Autumn): 394–417.

Moore, Barrington, Jr. 1966. *Social Origins of Dictatorship and Democracy: Lord and Peasant in the Making of the Modern World*. Boston: Beacon Press.

Mueller, Dennis C. 1969. "A Theory of Conglomerate Mergers," *Quarterly Journal of Economics*, 83(November): 643–59.

   1976. "Public Choice: A Survey," *Journal of Economic Literature*, 14(June): 395–433.

   1979. *Public Choice*. Cambridge: Cambridge University Press.

Neyman, Jerzy, ed. 1961. *Proceedings of the Fourth Berkeley Symposium on Mathematical Statistics and Probability*, Vol. 1: *Contributions to the Theory of Statistics*. Berkeley: University of California Press.

Niskanen, William A. 1971. *Bureaucracy and Representative Government*. Chicago: Aldine.

   1975. "Bureaucrats and Politicians," *Journal of Law and Economics*, 18(December): 617–43.

Olson, Mancur. 1965. *The Logic of Collective Action: Public Goods and the Theory of Groups*. Cambridge, Mass.: Harvard University Press.

Peabody, Robert L., and Polsby, Nelson W., eds. 1969. *New Perspectives on the House of Representatives*. Chicago: Rand McNally, 2nd ed.

Peltzman, Sam. 1976. "Toward a More General Theory of Regulation," *Journal of Law and Economics*, 19(August): 211–40.

Penrose, Edith. 1955. "Research on the Business Firm: Limits to the Growth and Size of Firms," *American Economic Review*, 45(May): 531–43.

   1959. *The Theory of the Growth of the Firm*. New York: Wiley.

Pfeffer, Jeffrey, and Salancik, Gerald R. 1974. "Organizational Decision Making As a Political Process: The Case of a University Budget," *Administrative Science Quarterly*, 19(June): 135–51.

Porter, Lyman W., and Lawler, Edward E., III. 1968. *Managerial Attitudes and Performance*. Homewood, Ill.: Irwin.

Prescott, Edward C., and Visscher, Michael. 1980. "Organization Capital," *Journal of Political Economy*, 88(June): 446–61.

Radner, Roy. 1961. "The Evaluation of Information in Organizations," in *Proceedings of the Fourth Berkeley Symposium on Mathematical Statistics and Probability*, Vol. 1, ed. Jerzy Neyman, pp. 491–530. Berkeley: University of California Press.

   1972. "Teams," in *Decision and Organization*, ed. C.B. McGuire and Roy Radner, pp. 189–215. New York: Elsevier North-Holland.

Riker, William H. 1962. *The Theory of Political Coalitions*. New Haven, Conn.: Yale University Press.

Riker, William H., and Ordeshook, Peter C. 1973. *An Introduction to Positive Political Theory*. Englewood Cliffs, N.J.: Prentice-Hall.

Rosen, Sherwin. 1981. "Output, Income and Rank in Hierarchical Firms," in *Working Papers in Economics*, E-81-10, The Hoover Institution, Stanford University, August.

Ross, Stephen A. 1973. "The Economic Theory of Agency: The Principal's Problem," *American Economic Review*, 63(May): 134–9.

Rothschild, Michael, and Stiglitz, Joseph E. 1976. "Equilibrium in Competitive Insurance Markets: An Essay on the Economics of Imperfect Information," *Quarterly Journal of Economics*, 90(November): 629–49.

Rumelt, Richard P. 1974. *Strategy, Structure, and Economic Performance*. Boston: Division of Research, Graduate School of Business Administration, Harvard University.

Sayles, Leonard. 1958. *Behavior of Industrial Work Groups: Prediction and Control*. New York: Wiley.

   1963, ed. *Individualism and Big Business*. New York: McGraw-Hill.

Sayles, Leonard, and Strauss, George. 1966. *Human Behavior in Organizations*. Englewood Cliffs, N.J.: Prentice-Hall.

Schumpeter, Joseph A. 1950. *Capitalism, Socialism and Democracy*, 3rd. ed. New York: Harper & Row.

   1954. *History of Economic Analysis*. New York: Oxford University Press.

Schweitzer, Arthur. 1977. "Plans and Markets: Nazi Style," *Kyklos*, 30: 88–115.

Shavell, Steven. 1979. "Risk Sharing and Incentives in the Principal and Agent Relationship," *Bell Journal of Economics*, 10(Spring): 55–73.

Simis, Konstantin. 1981. "Russia's Underground Millionaires," *Fortune*, June 29, pp. 36–42, 47, 50.

Simon, Herbert A. 1961. *Administrative Behavior: A Study of Decision-Making Processes in Administrative Organization*. New York: Macmillan.

Solow, Robert M. 1971. "Some Implications of Alternative Criteria for the Firm," in *The Corporate Economy: Growth, Competition and Innovative Potential*, ed. Robin Marris and Adrian Wood, pp. 318–42. Cambridge, Mass.: Harvard University Press.

Steiner, Peter O. 1975. *Mergers: Motives, Effects, Policies*. Ann Arbor: University of Michigan Press.

Stigler, George J. 1947. "Professor Lester and the Marginalists," *American Economic Review*, 37(March): 154–7.

   1971. "The Theory of Economic Regulation," *Bell Journal of Economics and Management Science*, 2(Spring): 3–21.

Stiglitz, Joseph E. 1975. "Incentives, Risk, and Information: Notes Towards a Theory of Hierarchy," *Bell Journal of Economics*, 6(Autumn): 552–79.

Stokes, Donald E., and Miller, Warren E. 1962. "Party Government and the Saliency of Congress," *Public Opinion Quarterly*, 26(Winter): 531–46.

Teece, David J. 1977. "Technology Transfer by Multinational Firms: The Resource Cost of Transferring Technological Know-how," *Economic Journal*, 87(June): 242–61.

Thompson, James D. 1967. *Organizations in Action: Social Science Bases of Administrative Theory*. New York: McGraw-Hill.

Tullock, Gordon. 1965. *The Politics of Bureaucracy*. Washington: Public Affairs Press.

   1967. *Toward a Mathematics of Politics*. Ann Arbor: University of Michigan Press.

Turner, Julius. 1951. *Party and Constituency: Pressures on Congress*. Baltimore: Johns Hopkins University.

Vancil, Richard F. 1979. *Decentralization: Managerial Ambiguity by Design*. New York: Dow Jones–Irwin.

Veblen, Thorstein. 1921. *The Engineers and the Price System*. New York: B. W. Huebsch, Inc.

von Mises, Ludwig. 1965 [1951]. "Economic Calculation in Socialism," in *Comparative Economic Systems: Models and Cases*, ed. Morris Bornstein, pp. 79–85. Homewood, Ill.: Irwin.

Weingast, Barry R., Shepsle, Kenneth A., and Johnson, Christopher. 1981. "The Political Economy of Benefits and Costs: A Neoclassical Approach to Distributive Politics," *Journal of Political Economy*, 89(August): 642–63.

Weisbrod, Burton. 1977. *The Voluntary Nonprofit Sector: An Economic Analysis*. Lexington, Mass.: D. C. Heath.

1980. "Private Goods, Collective Goods: The Role of the Nonprofit Sector," in *The Economics of Nonproprietary Organizations*, ed. Kenneth W. Clarkson and Donald L. Martin, pp. 139–70. Greenwich, Conn.: JAI Press.

Weitzman, Martin L. 1976. "The New Soviet Incentive Model," *Bell Journal of Economics*, 7(Spring): 251–257.

Whitmore, G.A., and Findlay, M. Chapman, eds. 1978. *Stochastic Dominance: An Approach to Decision-Making Under Risk*. Lexington, Mass.: D.C. Heath and Co.

Whyte, William F. 1969. *Organizational Behavior: Theory and Application*. Homewood, Ill.: Irwin.

Wildavsky, Aaron. 1964. *The Politics of the Budgetary Process*. Boston, Mass.: Little, Brown.

Williamson, Oliver E. 1964. *The Economics of Discretionary Behavior: Managerial Objectives in a Theory of the Firm*. Englewood Cliffs, N.J.: Prentice-Hall.

1970. *Corporate Control and Business Behavior: An Inquiry into the Effects of Organization Form on Enterprise Behavior*. Englewood Cliffs, N.J.: Prentice-Hall.

1975. *Markets and Hierarchies: Analysis and Antitrust Implications: A Study in the Economics of Internal Organization*. New York: Free Press.

1979. "Transaction-Cost Economics: The Governance of Contractual Relations," *Journal of Law and Economics*, 22(October): 233–61.

Williamson, Oliver E., and Wachter, Michael L., and Harris, Jeffrey E. 1975. "Understanding the Employment Relation: The Analysis of Idiosyncratic Exchange," *Bell Journal of Economics*, 6(Spring): 250–78.

Winter, Sidney G., Jr. 1964. "Economic 'Natural Selection' and the Theory of the Firm," *Yale Economic Essays*, 4(Spring): 225–72.

Woodward, Joan. 1965. *Industrial Organization: Theory and Practice*. New York: Oxford University Press (2nd ed., 1980).

Wrigley, Leonard. 1970. *Divisional Autonomy and Diversification*. Unpublished D. B. A. thesis, Harvard Business School.

Core definitions

Complete pricing overall responsibility (CPOR) CPOR is a set of prices on the employee's resources and a tax on his income which lead the employee to maximize the achievement of his employer's objectives.

Employee An employee applies inputs within the production functions for an organization's outputs and usually has discretion over choices about these applications. He either lacks a residual interest in the organization's overall performance, or has an interest that is small in relation to his salary and any other monetary or nonmonetary income he receives from the organization.

Employer An employer is either the funding authority or a managing employee. This term is used when the analysis applies to the behavior of either.

Funding authority An organization's funding authority is the individual or group holding authority to restrict the availability of revenues to the organization's employees, and to impose resource responsibility on them. The funding authority of a private corporation is its owners, whereas donors constitute the funding authority of a private nonprofit organization. A legislature is the funding authority of a public organization, and in turn a legislature's funding authority consists of those citizens who are eligible to vote.

Funding limit The funding limit is the response of the resources that the funding authority makes available to employees when he faces increases in the costs of disposing the organization's outputs according to his interests. A private corporation's stockholders are concerned with profits from the sale of this organization's outputs; the corporation's funding limit is the response of the external supply of equity capital to the corporation's profitability. The funding limit of a private nonprofit organization is determined in part by the response of donations to its outputs, while legislative demand helps establish a public organization's funding limit.

Incomplete pricing overall responsibility (IPOR) IPOR is a type of overall value responsibility that is imposed when some, but not all, inputs and outputs are given cash prices and an accounting profit is attributed to the employee's production domain.

281

Managing employee A managing employee has the authority (derived from the funding authority) to impose resource responsibility on other employees, and his production domain includes this managerial task. The term managing employee is used instead of the frequently used term manager to emphasize that he is an employee as well as a manager and the analysis of constrained employee resource diversion behavior always applies to him.

Nonpricing overall responsibility (NPOR) Under the NPOR variant of overall value responsibility, there are not necessarily any cash prices for the employee's inputs or outputs and there is no accounting profit attributed to his production domain.

Overall value responsibility (OVR) Overall value responsibility holds the employee accountable for the estimated value of his contribution via his production domain in relation to the estimated value of the inputs delegated to him. If the value of this contribution falls below a critical value, the employer either decides to obtain this contribution or a substitute under a different supply arrangement or he switches to imposing specific responsibility on the employee. (See also IPOR and NPOR definitions.)

Production domain An employee's production domain is the one or more production functions, or the subset of them, within which he holds discretion over his choices about applications of inputs. A production domain is *internally designed* if information about it held within the organization is originated by the employee having discretion over it. A production domain is *externally designed* if the organization's information about it originates with someone else.

Resource diversions An employee's resource diversions (or *diversions*, for short) constitute the cash equivalent cost to his employer as a result of his uses of resources in ways other than those that would maximize the employer's welfare.

Resource responsibility Resource responsibility (or responsibility, for short) is a costly constraint that is deliberately imposed on an employee by the funding authority or a managing employee. Imposing responsibility constraints requires authority, derived from that of the funding authority, to extract or augment employees' rents from working in the organization. There are alternative types of responsibility constraints, all of which have in common that they connect employees' actions, or results of their actions, with the monetary or nonmonetary incomes they receive from the organization. If an employee were under a completely specified contract, resource responsibility would constrain the degree to which he can avoid performing some of his contractual obligations. However, employers usually do not find such contracts economical, and resource responsibility also limits employers' costs of employees' outputs when employment contracts are incomplete. (See also CPOR, IPOR, NPOR, OVR, and SR definitions.)

Specific responsibility (SR) Specific responsibility influences the employee's particular uses of individual resources and does not hold him accountable for the value of his contribution via his production domain in relation to the value of the inputs delegated to him. The alternative means to influence the employee's resource uses can be direct (e.g., rewards or penalties) or indirect (e.g., enforcing regular work hours to reduce the employee's alternative uses of his time). The employer selects among these according to cost effectiveness in particular situations and often does not find it worthwhile to influence some of the employee's uses of resources.

Index

aggregation of goals, 11–12

Alchian, Armen A., 12–13, 14, 19–20, 45, 49, 54–5, 185, 197, 236, 257n4

alienation, 27

Allen, Stephen A., 102, 104–5, 183, 187

allowable limit, *see* resource diversions

antitrust, 246, 247

applications of specific responsibility: categories of, 80; complements or substitutes for resource uses, 85–6; defined, 56–7; prices attached to resource uses, 83–5; work rules, 85

appropriations committees, 151

Arrow, Kenneth J., 14

attributed inputs, *see under* budget, employee's

authority: employer's choices to delegate, 192–4; governmental, 243–7; legislature's, to tax, 162–3; limits on employer's authority, 41; often absent when spillovers occur, 101; price of, 193; in relation to resource responsibility, 5, 13, 40–1; structure of, motivated by cost savings vs. other purposes, 193–4; vs. voluntary coordination, effects on resource allocation, 198–202

backward bending legislative demand, 159

Barnes, Louis B., 25

Baumol, William J., 12, 14, 44, 126, 131, 257n2

Belangér, Gerard, 257n2

Berg, Ivar, 30

Bergstrom, Theodore C., 267n10

Berliner, Joseph S., 51, 76, 77, 85, 86–7

Blau, Peter M., 31, 257–8n5

Blauner, Robert, 22, 27, 98

bonuses, *see* cash exchanged for increased output

Borcherding, Thomas E., 267n10

bounded rationality, 11

Bower, Joseph L., 54, 176, 178

Brennan, Geoffrey, 153, 271n6

Breton, Albert, 227

Buchanan, James M., 153, 263n2, 271n6

budget, employee's: additional inputs not attributed to employee, 58, 76, 118, 185, 265n3; defined, 58; equilibrium determination, 121–2; in-kind vs. cash, 58, 69; nature of inputs delegated to employee, 58; underpriced, or overpriced, inputs, 76; unspent balance, 77

budget, organization's, *see* income, private nonprofit organization's; income, public organization's

Burns, Tom, 183

campaign contributions at expense of votes, 148

candidate, legislative: advantages, or disadvantages, of incumbency, 145, 149; commitments to constituents, 149–50; maximizes utility, not election probability, 145–6; risk averse, 146, 150; trade-off between resource diversions and election probability, 146

cash exchanged for increased output, 74–6, 85,

cash salaries, determination under OVR and SR, 59–61

cash vs. in-kind income, *see under* income, employee's

Caves, Richard E., 270n7

Chandler, Alfred D., Jr., 183, 202–6

Clausen, Aage, 141

Coase, Ronald H., 20, 271n1

Cohen, Harry, 257–8n5

collaboration, between managing employees and their employees, 191–2

committee, *see* coordinating employees; coordinating legislators

committee chairmen, declining influence, 153

comparative economic systems, 108, 243–7

compensated opportunity cost: definition, 35; information required to determine, 45–6; role in imposition of CPOR, 42–4

competition, employees': can affect output replacement cost, 47; over coordination role, 200–2; in dealing with clients, 207

complements, as an application of specific responsibility, 85–6

complete pricing overall responsibility (CPOR): defined, 6, 42–3, 281; employee's information demands, 44, 103–4, 109; employer's information requirements, 43–6

conglomerate mergers, 232–3

Conn, David, 260n9

constant marginal cost assumption, 117

constant returns to scale production function estimates, 117

contract, employment, compared with resource responsibility, 5

contract, enforcement costs leading to production in an organization, 19–20, 54–5

284

coordinating employees: economic roles, 194–7, 198; in multidivisional firm, 205

coordinating legislators, defined, 151

coordination in employees' interests (see also coordinating employees): via authority, 191–4, 197–8; to force a managing employee to pursue his employees's ends, 131, 192; in relation to funding limit, 211–12, 221–2; in relation to nearest level at which OVR is imposed, 189; voluntary, 194–7, 198; voluntary vs. via authority, effects on resource allocation, 198–202

coordination in relation to internal technological spillovers: under CPOR, 103–4; employees' choices, when under OVR or SR, 105–7, 107–8; employer's choices, when imposing overall value or specific responsibility, 104–5, 107

costs, of comparing production possibilities, 28–9

costs of employee's output: under CPOR, 35–6, 42–3; CPOR compared to OVR and SR, 113–17; faced by employee and employer, compared, 69–73, 94–5, 113–17, 120–1; fixed and variable components, 115–16, 217–19, 228; increases in the long run, 218; OVR and SR, compared, 94–5

costs of imposing resource responsibility: CPOR, 43–7; effects of costly information on employer's choice between OVR and SR, 63–6; fixed and variable components, 61–2; managing employee's personal costs, 118–19; OVR, 49–50, 62, 65; SR, 65, 84–6, 90–1

costs of organization's output, see output determination, equilibrium

CPOR, see complete pricing overall responsibility

Crawford, Robert G., 14, 19–20, 54–5, 197, 236, 257n4

cycling, 267n7

Cyert, Richard M., 11, 129

Dantzig, George B., 14, 44

data bases, limited usefulness, 31

Davis, Otto A., 15, 103, 106–7, 263n3, 263n4, 263–4n5

Davis, Stanley M., 270n8

Davis-Whinston scheme: applied under CPOR, 103–4, 263n4, 263–4n5; applied under OVR, 106–7, 263n4

Deacon, Robert T., 267n10

decentralization (see also delegation of authority; suborganization): effects on employees' influence on and responsiveness to external demands, 207; and employees' preferred resource responsibility, 207; informational, 108, 246; of pricing decisions, 123–4

decomposition method, 44

deficit, legislative, 147

delegation of authority (see also decentralization; suborganization), 192–4, 201–2

demands: of beneficiaries, private nonprofit organization, 135–7; of clients, private nonprofit organization, 137–9; of clients, public organization, 170–2; for corporation's output, problematical, 129; of donors, compared to incremental donation schedule, 135–7; for information, see information demands; for inputs, organization's, 96–7; for mergers, changes in organization's status, 230–1; for resource uses, employee's, 81–3; legislature's, see legislative demand; managing employee's, for employee's outputs, 117–20, 124–5; top managing employees', for corporation's output, 130, 133–4; uncertainty about (see also Schumpeterian competition), 182; unrevealed by employer, 181

Demsetz, Harold, 12–13, 45, 49, 185

diversions, see resource diversions

dominated investments, defined, 177

donors, as funding authority, 135–7, 139, 222–4, 240–1

Downs, Anthony, 38, 142, 150, 164

Drucker, Peter F., 30–1

effectual reorganization, defined, 184

efficiency: employee's response to managing employee's demand, 122, 125–6; Kaldor-Hicks vs. Pareto, 132, 163, 169, 262n14; of organization's output rate, 250; private corporation, 132, 134; private nonprofit organization, 136–7, 139; public organization, 167–9, 172; vote trades, 153, 154

efficiency in employee's production domain: CPOR, 35–6, 42–4; effects of in-kind vs. cash income, 44, 73, 79–80; OVR, 72–3, 79–80, 94–5, 248–9; SR, 94–7, 100, 249

election probability, legislator's: composition of and number of votes, 148; trade-off with expected resource diversions, 146, 266n5

employee, defined, 281

employer, defined in relation to managing employee and funding authority, 6, 41, 281

employment decisions, sensitivity to wage rates, 97

engineering data, 254–6

envelope, long-run costs, 218

experience, see internal design; investments of employees

experience, market value of (see also cash salaries, determination), 32–3

experimental data, 254–6

external design: conditions leading to, 25–6; defined, 25; effects of market competition, 33; in spite of employee's information cost disadvantage, 57, 93

Fabian, Tibor, 15, 44

Fama, Eugene F., 127, 128, 221

Farney, Dennis, 153

Findlay, M. Chapman, 262n17

Fiorina, Morris P., 141, 266n5

first long run, defined, 8, 210

Mirrlees, James A., 257n5
Miyazaki, Hajime, 261n13
Moore, Barrington, Jr., 243
Mueller, Dennis C., 126, 127, 142, 213, 232, 266n3, 271n2
multidivisional suborganization, 202–6
Murrell, Peter, 260n9

Niskanen, William A., 12, 227–8, 257n2
new companies, started by employees, 186
new product introduction, *see* Schumpeterian competition
noneconomic issues, effects on electoral outcomes, 150
nonmaximizing behavior, 94
nonpricing overall responsibility (NPOR), defined, 55–6, 282
normative analysis, contributions of positive theory, 252–4
NPOR, *see* nonpricing overall responsibility

object output, defined, 170
Ogul, Morris S., 152
Olson, Mancur, 196
Ordeshook, Peter C., 142, 143, 265n1, 266n2, 266n6
output determination, equilibrium: employee's, 121–2; private corporation, 129–31, 133–4, 219–22, 228–9, 250; private nonprofit organization, 135–9, 222–4, 229; public organization, 165–7, 170–2, 224–8, 229; voluntary coordination and coordination by authority, compared, 198–202
output, increased, exchanged for cash, 74–6, 85
output of an employee, defined, 23
output replacement cost: contrasted with personal replacement cost, 48; defined, 48–9; employee's demand for information, 110–11; employee's influence over, 182; employer's demand for information, 49–50, 111–12
overall value productivity, defined, 39
overall value productivity measures: costs affect employer's choices in imposing responsibility, 62; uses for making inferences about resource diversions, 39–40
overall value responsibility (OVR): broadly imposed for risk diversification, 186, 205, 232; defined, 6, 47–56, 282; efficiency in employee's production domain, 72–3, 79–80, 94–5; employee's, or employer's, information demands, *see under* information demands; imposed on a combination of employees under SR, 57, 67, 189, 207; imposed together with SR, 66–7; output replacement limit, *see* output replacement cost; potential switch to SR, 48, 50, 71; resource allocation contrasted with that under SR, 94–7; resource allocation under, 69–77
OVR, *see* overall value responsibility
owner-entrepreneur, 3, 20–1

ownership interest, as an alternative to imposing responsibility, 46

Pareto efficiency vs. Kaldor-Hicks efficiency, *see* efficiency
Pareto relevant spillovers, 103, 263n2
parties political, roles of, 154–5
Peltzman, Sam, 144
penalties, *see* rewards and penalties
Penrose, Edith, 174
pensions, public employees', 227
perfect competition model, 31
personal replacement cost: contrasted with output replacement cost, 48, 86–7, 261n10; defined, 48, 86–7; increased by investments, 188, 190; indispensable employee, 86–7
Pfeffer, Jeffrey, 197
planner, definition, 244; resource diversions, 245
planning-programming-budgeting systems, 271n5
platform, *see* candidate's commitments to constituents; legislative spending
potentially relevant spillovers, 102, 105–6, 263n2
power, as a nonpecuniary benefit, 37, 73
Prescott, Edward C., 32, 261n13
price and output determination, *see* output determination, equilibrium
prices (*see also* implicit prices, incentives, pricing of outputs): effects of external market prices on resource uses, 96–7; under CPOR, 35, 42–5
pricing of outputs: delegation of pricing decisions, 123–4; employee's, 122–4; private corporation's, 129–31; private nonprofit organization's, 137–9; public organization's, 170–2
primary decision maker, defined, 244
private corporation: funding limit, 127, 211–14, 216, 221–2; growth, 211–14; mergers and acquisitions, 231–4; multidivisional suborganization, 202–6; price and output determination, 129–31, 133–4, 219–22, 228–9, 250; public capital financing, 238–40, 242; sales, at expense of profitability, 126–7, 131, 213–14; stockholders as funding authority, 127–8, 133, 211–14; top managing employees, 126–9, 203–4, 219–21, 233
private nonprofit organization: donors, 135–7, 139, 222–4, 240–1; funding limit, 214–15, 216, 222–4; output determination, 133–4, 135–9, 222–4, 229; pricing of outputs, 137–9; public financing, 240–1, 242–3
production domain (*see also* external design; internal design; production functions): comparability, 28–33; defined, 4, 22, 282
production functions (*see also* production domain): definition, 16–17; effects of technological change, 24; encompassed by an organization, 17–21; information about production possibilities is often costly, 17

288

professional society, 188, 190
professional standards, 188
profit center (*see also* incomplete pricing overall
  responsibility), 52
profits: critical amount passed on to stockholders, 128, 131, 213; and private corporation's growth, 211–14; short-run at the
  expense of long-run profits, 220–1
promotion, opportunities, effects on resource
  diversions, 180
public organizations: competitive advantage in
  avoiding risk premiums, 236; competitive
  advantage in raising information costs,
  235–6; equilibrium size, 236–8; funding
  limit, 215–16, 217, 224–7, 237–8; legislature, as funding authority, 165–7, 172,
  215–16; mergers, 238; output determination, 165–7, 170–2, 224–8, 229; pricing of outputs, 170–2

Radner, Roy, 14, 264n6
rationally ignorant voter, 150, 164
Raviv, Artur, 13, 261n14
regulations: affected interest groups influence
  legislation, 144; employees' influence
  over those enacted, 208; as example of
  governmentally imposed responsibility,
  246, 247
rent, quasi vs. monopoly, 257n4
reorganization (*see also* suborganization): effectual, defined, 184; as means of replacing
  employee's output, 47, 128
representative firm, 33
resource diversions: of coordinating legislators, 152; and corporate growth, 211–
  14; defined, 4, 36–9, 282; defined into
  social welfare functions, 245; effects of
  promotion opportunities, 180; equilibrium determination, *see* output determination, equilibrium; fixed and variable
  components, 116; of governmental planners, 245; of governmental secondary
  decision makers, 246
resource diversions, allowable limit: coordinating legislators', 152; increased by employees' investments, 182, 184–5, 187–9,
  189–90, 217–19; under OVR, 49; under
  SR, 94
resource responsibility (*see also* complete pricing
  overall responsibility; incomplete pricing
  overall responsibility; nonpricing overall
  responsibility; overall value responsibility;
  specific responsibility): defined, relation
  to authority and employment contracts, 5,
  40–1; 282–3; effects of Schumpeterian
  competition and technological change,
  186, 189, 190–1; employees affect employer's choices, 182–3, 184–5, 190; employer's choice biased in favor of SR, 63–
  7; faced by a legislature, 163; from multiple sources, placed on primary decision
  makers, 245; influences on employer's
  choice, 61–3; OVR and SR imposed together, 66–7; placed on, or by, secondary
  decision makers, 244–7; placed on private

corporation's top managing employees,
  127–8; types of, 41
responsibility, *see* resource responsibility
rewards and penalties (*see also* specific responsibility): employer's choice between, 84;
  employer's measurement costs, 84; in-
  kind vs. cash, 84–5
Richard, Scott F., 268n14
Riker, William H, 142, 143, 265n1, 266n2,
  266n5, 266n6
risk diversification, employees' gains exceed
  funding authority's, 186, 205, 232, 233,
  258n4
Rosen, Sherwin, 258n5
Ross, Stephen A., 13, 261n14
Rothschild, Michael, 261n13
Rumelt, Richard P., 203
Russian economy, 51, 76
Russian factories, 38

sabotage, 259n3
Salancik, Gerald R., 197
salaries, *see* cash salaries
sales, at the expense of profitability, 126–7,
  131, 213–14
Sayles, Leonard, 30, 51, 101, 196
schedule of incremental donations, 135–9,
  222–4
Schumpeter, Joseph A., 186, 258n1
Schumpeterian competition: defined, 186; effects on mergers and acquisitions, 232,
  233; effects on relative attractiveness of
  public, private financing, 240; effects on
  resource diversions and employees' investments, 218, 221–2; effects on resource responsibility, 186, 189, 190–1;
  effects on suborganization, 186, 204–5;
  and multidivisional firm, 204–5
Schweitzer, Arthur, 271n9
second long run, defined, 8–9, 230
secondary decision maker, defined, 244
selective rationality, 93
separable vs. nonseparable spillovers, 102, 106,
  263n3
Shapiro, Leonard, 260n9
Shavell, Steven, 13, 261n14
short run, defined, 7, 68
short-run profits, *see* profits
Simis, Konstantin, 38
Simon, Herbert A., 11, 129
slack, organizational, 257n1
social welfare function, 245, 246
Solow, Robert M., 213
Sosnick, Stephen H., 271n5
Soviet economy, 51, 76
Soviet manager, 77
span of control, 24
specific responsibility (*see also* applications of
  specific responsibility; rewards and penalties): complements, substitutes, work
  rules, as applications of, 85–6; defined, 6,
  56–7, 80–1, 283; difficulty of eliciting
  thought or creativity, 57; employee derives less utility from resource diversions,
  97; employer's, or employee's, informa-

specific responsibility (*cont.*)
tion demands, *see* information demands; employer's optimal choices, 87–92; imposed together with OVR, 66–7; inefficiency in employee's production domain, 94–7, 100, 249; jointly determined with delegation of inputs and number of employees hired, 91–2; organization's input demands relatively insensitive to external market prices, 96–7; potential switch to under OVR, 48, 50, 71; resource allocation behavior under and contrast with that under OVR, 94–7
spillovers, *see* internal technological spillovers
SR, *see* specific responsibility
Stalker, G. M., 183
Steiner, Peter O., 233–4, 271n2, 271n4
Stigler, George J., 9, 97, 144
Stiglitz, Joseph E., 257n3,5, 259n4, 261n13, 270n5
stochastic dominance, 64
stockholders: approval of mergers and acquisitions, 233–4; as funding authority, 127–8, 133, 211–14; involvement in management, 127–8; supply of equity capital, 211–14
Stokes, Donald E., 142
Strauss, George, 51, 101
Stubblebine, William Craig, 263n2
suborganization (*see also* decentralization; delegation of authority): effects of conscious planning vs. market competition, 33; effects of employees' investments, 183–7; effects of Schumpeterian competition, 186–7, 204–5; interrelated with choices in imposing resource responsibility, 184–5; as means to raise competing constituents' information costs, 237
substantive committees, 151
substitutes, as application of SR, 85–6
supply: employee's in response to managing employee's demand, 121–2, 125; employee's, OVR, 72, 79; employee's, SR, 92, 99–100; of labor to the organization, 59–61; organization's, *see* output determination, equilibrium

takeover threats, as resource responsibility on corporate top managing employees, 49, 127, 221
taxes: affected by interest groups, 267n9; can exceed benefits from legislature, 163; desired level related to vote trading efficiency, 154; underlie opposition to legislative spending, 147
technological change: adaptation to as a managerial intermediate output, 17–18; and multidivisional firm, 204–5; related to production functions, 24

technological change, effects on: demands for information, 181; employees' investments, 180–1, 186–7, 189; mergers and acquisitions, 232, 233; relative attractiveness of private, or public, financing, 240; resource diversions, 218, 221–2; resource responsibility, 189; suborganization, 186, 204–5
technology adoptions, 269–70n4
Teece, David J., 269–70n4
Thompson, James D., 101–2
timing of tasks, 40, 84, 188
top managing employees, corporate, 126–9, 203–6, 213, 219–22, 233, 250
Tullock, Gordon, 102, 142, 266n4, 267n7
Turner, Julius, 141

uncertainty, effects (*see also* Schumpeterian competition; technological change): on employer's expenditures on information, 63–6; on responsibility imposed, 62
union, *see* labor union
unique production possibilities, 27–9
U.S. Congress, 151, 153
U.S. House of Representatives, 267n8
U.S. Senate, 267n8

Vancil, Richard F., 53, 58, 204
variable costs, *see* costs of employee's output; costs of imposing resource responsibility
Veblen, Thorstein, 259n3
Vickson, Raymond G., 262n17
Visscher, Michael, 32, 261n13
voice vs. exit option, effect on legislative demand, 270n9
von Mises, Ludwig, 246
vote, choices whether to, 146–7
voters, categories of citizens, 147

wasted resouces: defined, 83; under SR, 90, 97
Weingast, Barry R., 144
Weisbrod, Burton, 265n7, 265n8
Weitzman, Martin L., 260n9
welfare, analysis of, *see* efficiency
Whinston, Andrew, 15, 103, 106–7, 263n3, 263n4, 263–4n5
Whitmore, G. A., 262n17
Whyte, William F., 194
Wildavsky, Aaron, 151–2, 167, 206
Williamson, Oliver E., 14, 19, 24, 204
Winter, Sidney G., Jr., 129
Wintrobe, Ronald, 227
Wolfe, Philip, 14, 44
Woodward, Joan, 25, 33, 125, 183, 187
work rules, as an application of SR, 85–6
Wrigley, Leonard, 204

X-efficiency, 15, 132–3